SANDMAN MYSTERY THEATRE

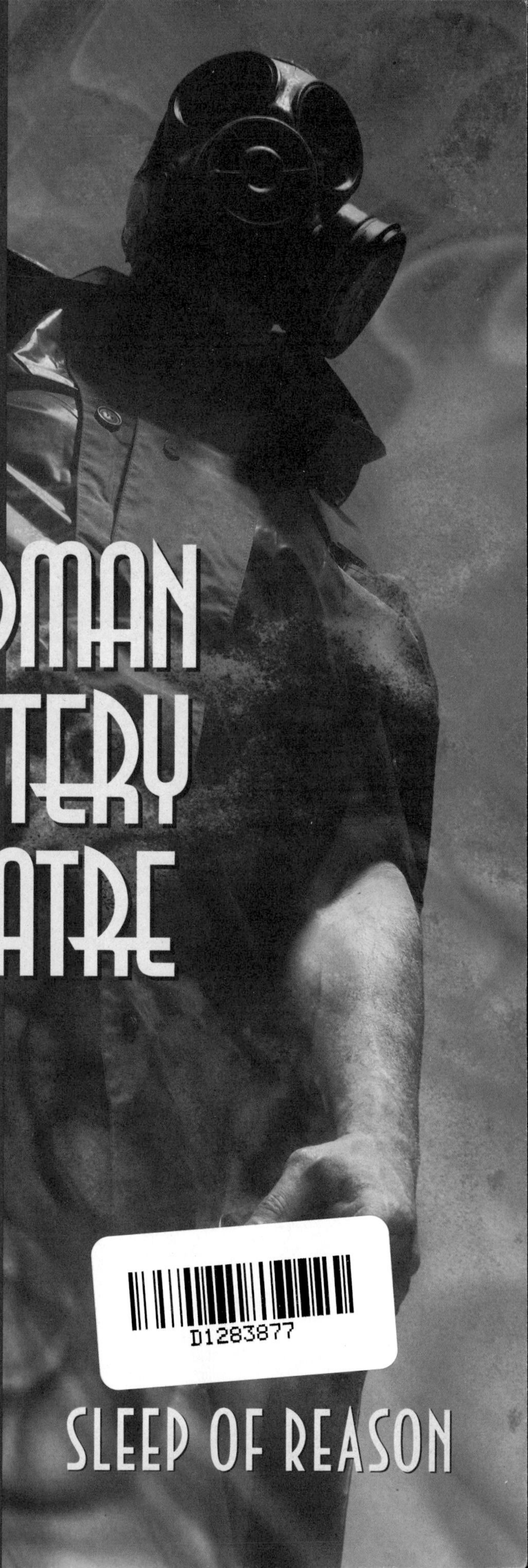

SLEEP OF REASON

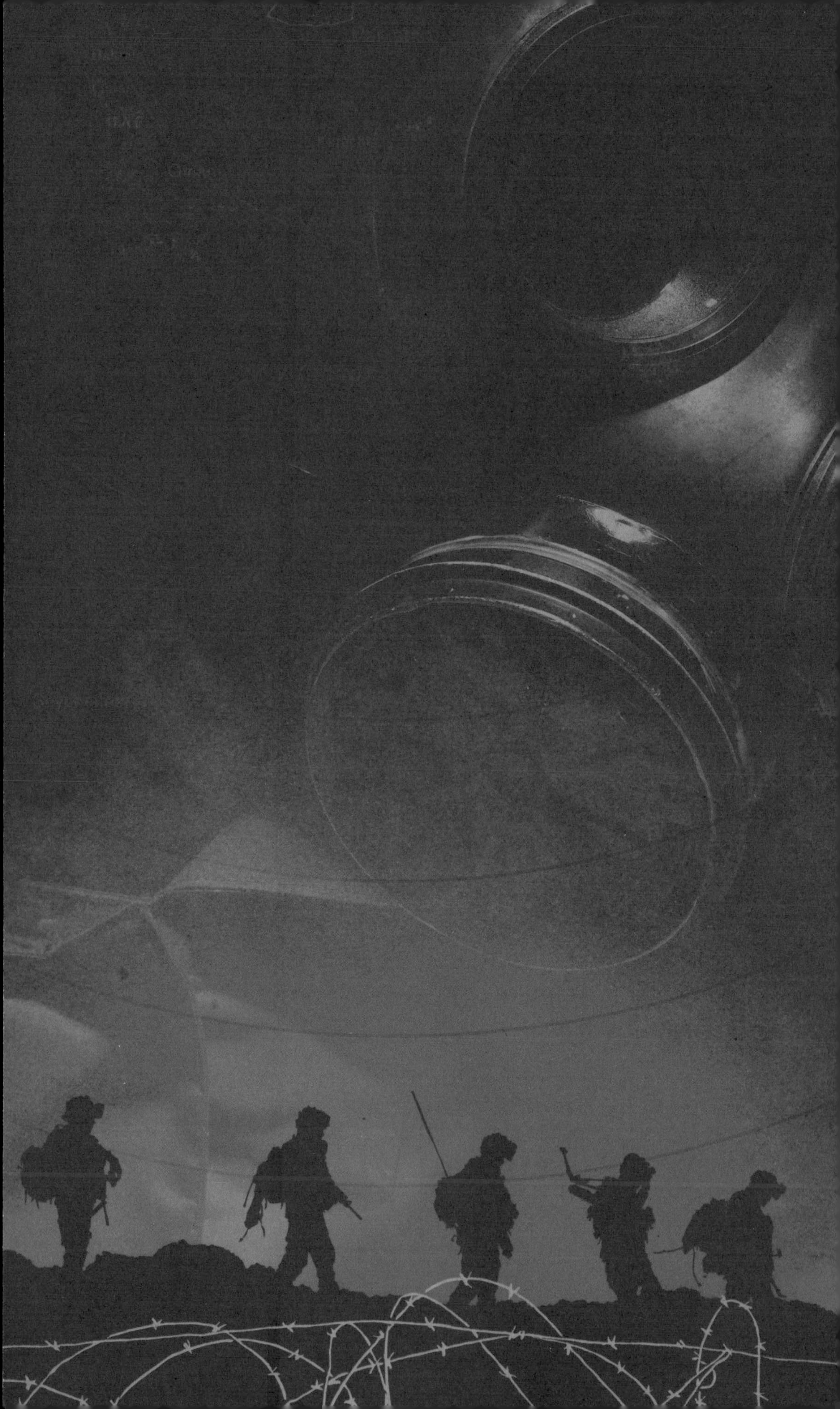

JOHN NEY RIEBER
WRITER

ERIC NGUYEN
ARTIST

LEE LOUGHRIDGE
COLORIST

ROB LEIGH
LETTERER

TIM BRADSTREET
ORIGINAL SERIES COVER ARTIST

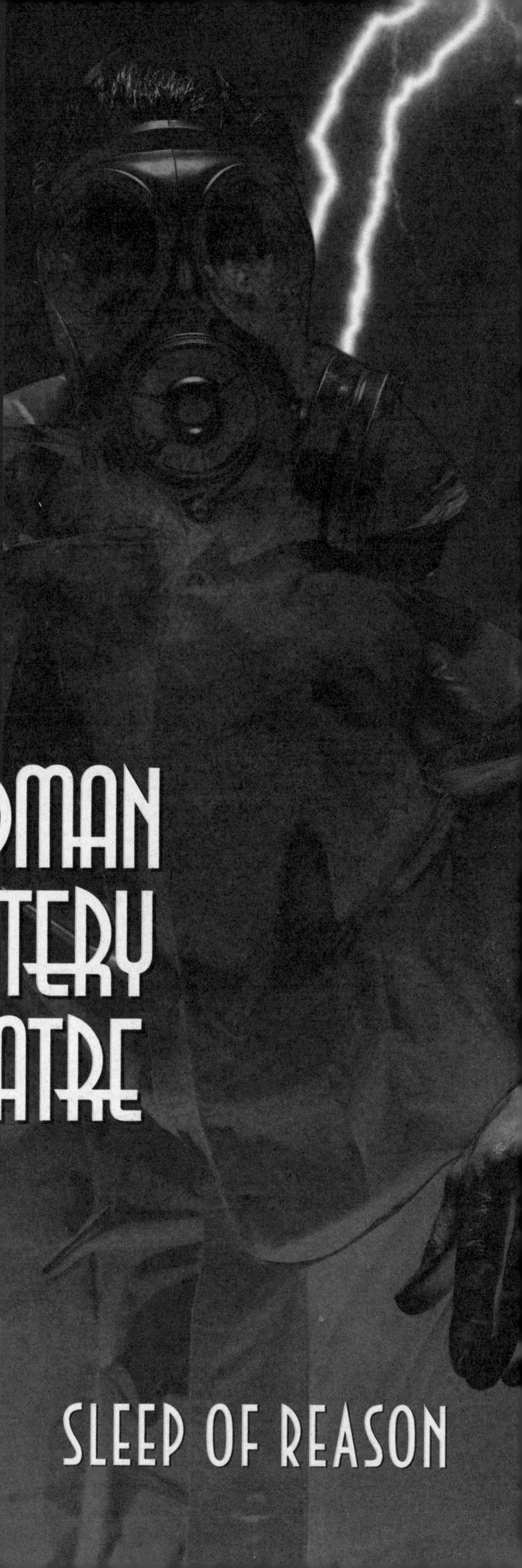

SANDMAN MYSTERY THEATRE

SLEEP OF REASON

Karen Berger
Senior VP-Executive Editor

Jonathan Vankin
Editor-original series

Mark Doyle
Angela Rufino
Assistant Editors-original series

Scott Nybakken
Editor-collected edition

Robbin Brosterman
Senior Art Director

Paul Levitz
President & Publisher

Georg Brewer
VP-Design & DC Direct Creative

Richard Bruning
Senior VP-Creative Director

Patrick Caldon
Executive VP-Finance & Operations

Chris Caramalis
VP-Finance

John Cunningham
VP-Marketing

Terri Cunningham
VP-Managing Editor

Alison Gill
VP-Manufacturing

Hank Kanalz
VP-General Manager, WildStorm

Jim Lee
Editorial Director-WildStorm

Paula Lowitt
Senior VP-Business & Legal Affairs

MaryEllen McLaughlin
VP-Advertising & Custom Publishing

John Nee
VP-Business Development

Gregory Noveck
Senior VP-Creative Affairs

Sue Pohja
VP-Book Trade Sales

Cheryl Rubin
Senior VP-Brand Management

Jeff Trojan
VP-Business Development, DC Direct

Bob Wayne
VP-Sales

Cover illustration by Tim Bradstreet
Publication design by Amelia Grohman

SANDMAN MYSTERY THEATRE: SLEEP OF REASON

DC Comics, 1700 Broadway, New York, NY 10019
A Warner Bros. Entertainment Company

Printed in Canada. First Printing.
ISBN: 1-4012-1454-1   ISBN 13: 978-1-4012-1454-8

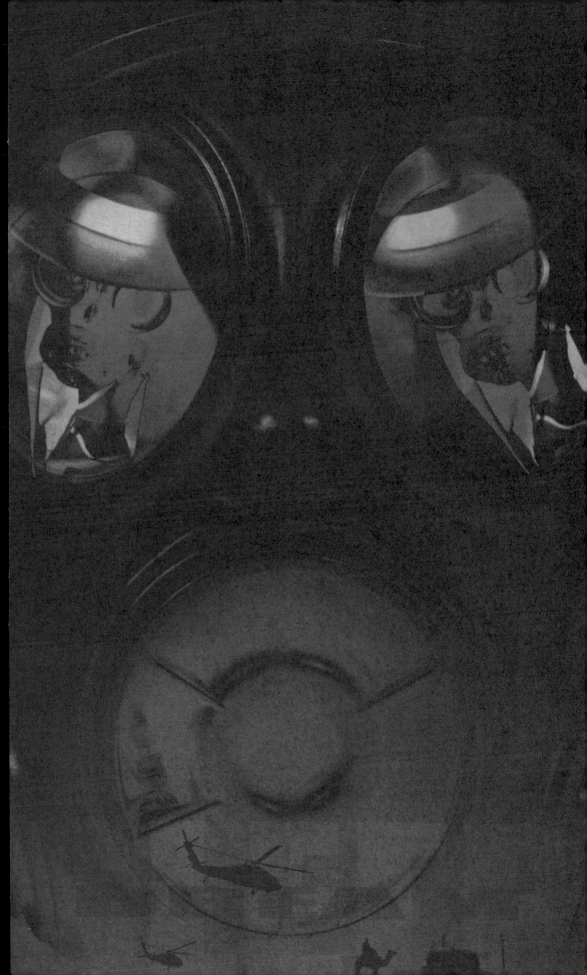

CHAPTER ONE

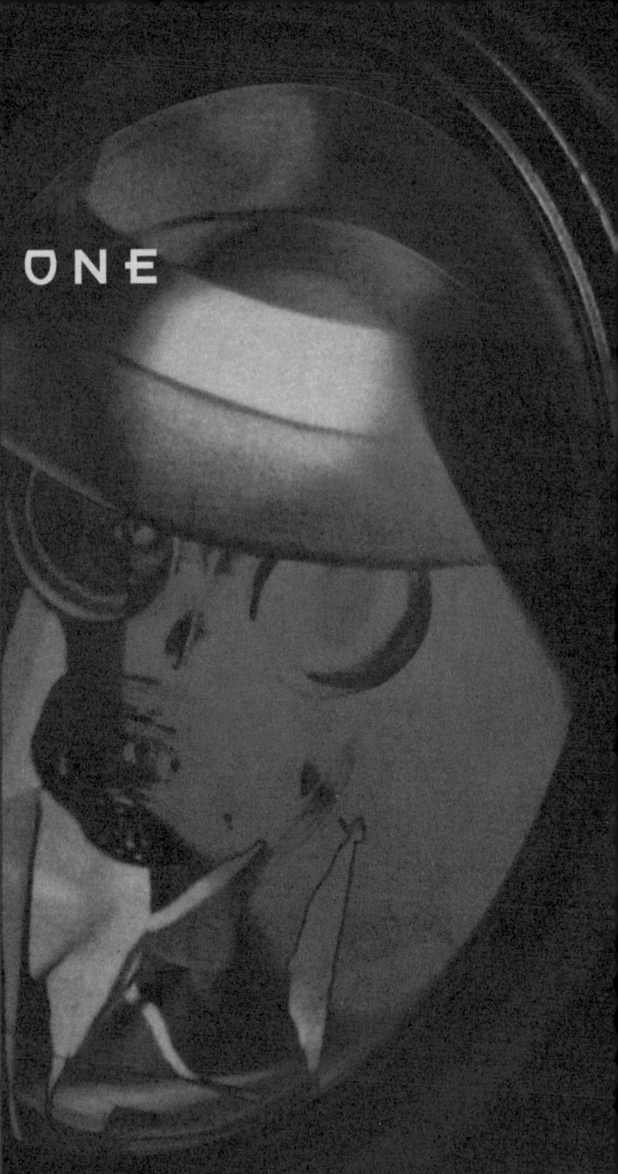

"You've got a lion's heart,
rich man.
But your eyes are weak
and your bones
are old."

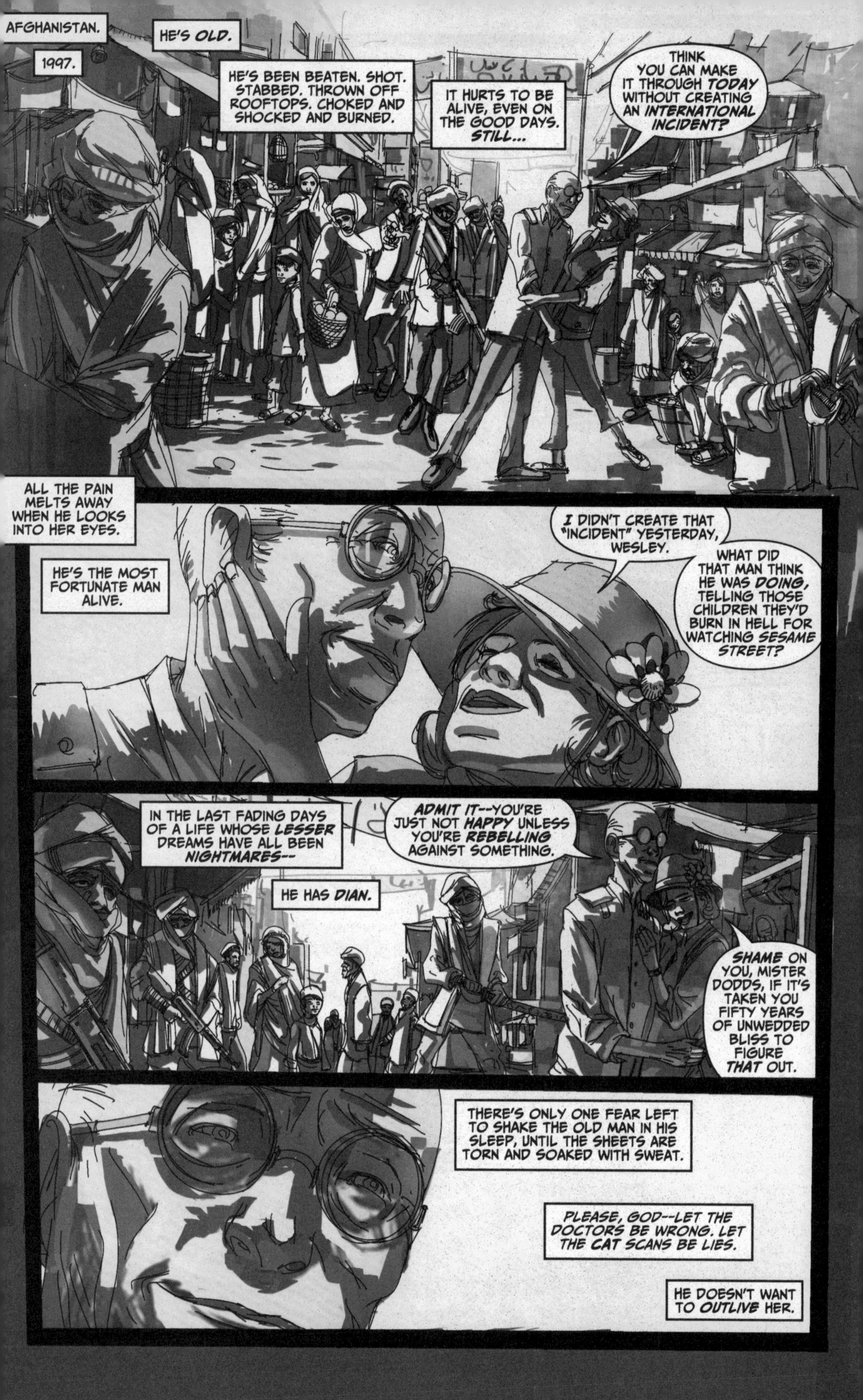
AFGHANISTAN.
1997.
HE'S OLD.
HE'S BEEN BEATEN. SHOT. STABBED. THROWN OFF ROOFTOPS. CHOKED AND SHOCKED AND BURNED.
IT HURTS TO BE ALIVE, EVEN ON THE GOOD DAYS. STILL...
THINK YOU CAN MAKE IT THROUGH TODAY WITHOUT CREATING AN INTERNATIONAL INCIDENT?
ALL THE PAIN MELTS AWAY WHEN HE LOOKS INTO HER EYES.
HE'S THE MOST FORTUNATE MAN ALIVE.
I DIDN'T CREATE THAT "INCIDENT" YESTERDAY, WESLEY.
WHAT DID THAT MAN THINK HE WAS DOING, TELLING THOSE CHILDREN THEY'D BURN IN HELL FOR WATCHING SESAME STREET?
IN THE LAST FADING DAYS OF A LIFE WHOSE LESSER DREAMS HAVE ALL BEEN NIGHTMARES--
ADMIT IT--YOU'RE JUST NOT HAPPY UNLESS YOU'RE REBELLING AGAINST SOMETHING.
HE HAS DIAN.
SHAME ON YOU, MISTER DODDS, IF IT'S TAKEN YOU FIFTY YEARS OF UNWEDDED BLISS TO FIGURE THAT OUT.
THERE'S ONLY ONE FEAR LEFT TO SHAKE THE OLD MAN IN HIS SLEEP, UNTIL THE SHEETS ARE TORN AND SOAKED WITH SWEAT.
PLEASE, GOD--LET THE DOCTORS BE WRONG. LET THE CAT SCANS BE LIES.
HE DOESN'T WANT TO OUTLIVE HER.

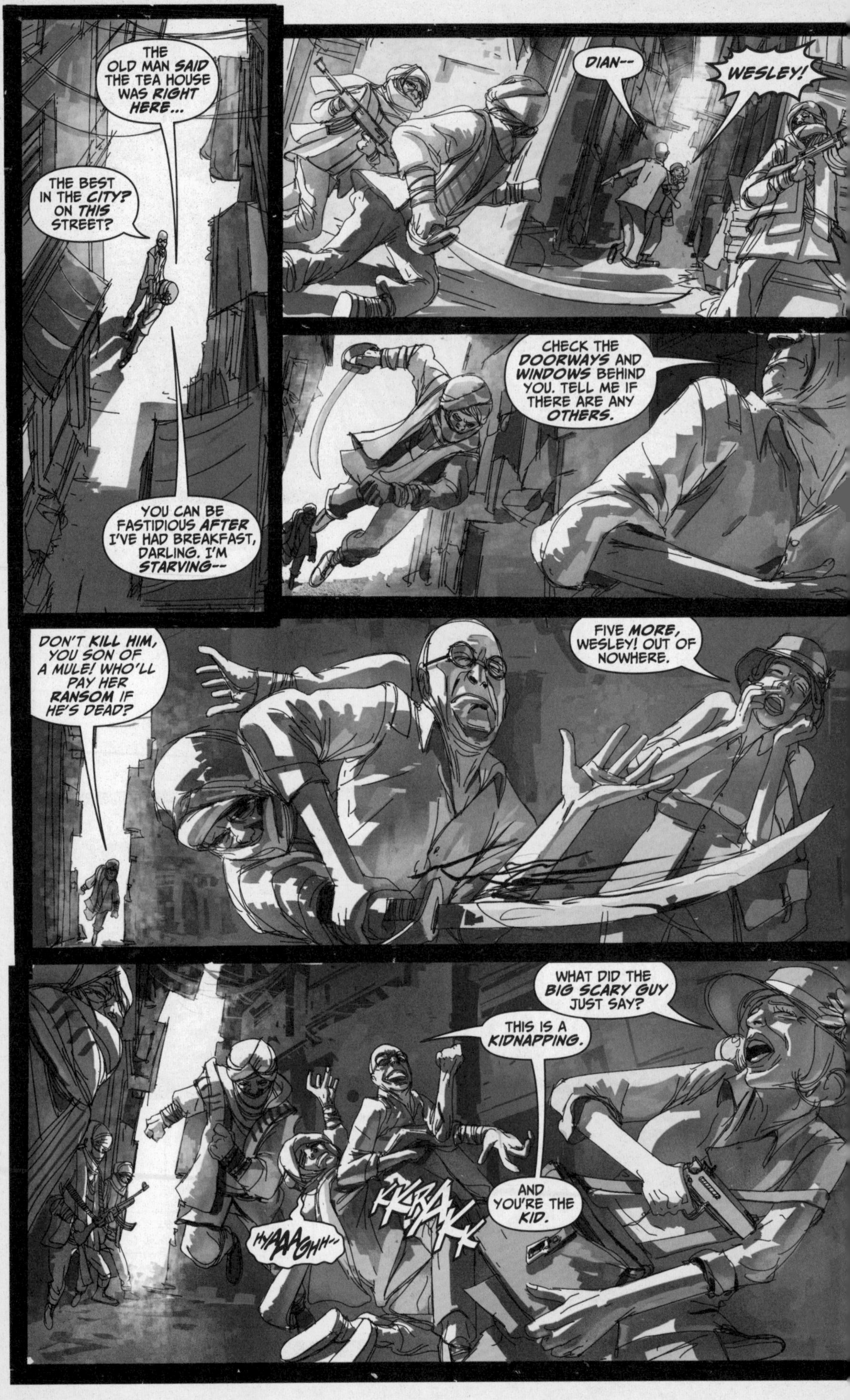
THE OLD MAN *SAID* THE TEA HOUSE WAS *RIGHT HERE*...
THE BEST IN THE *CITY?* ON *THIS* STREET?
YOU CAN BE FASTIDIOUS *AFTER* I'VE HAD BREAKFAST, DARLING. I'M *STARVING*--
DIAN--
WESLEY!
CHECK THE *DOORWAYS* AND *WINDOWS* BEHIND YOU. TELL ME IF THERE ARE ANY *OTHERS*.
DON'T *KILL* HIM, YOU SON OF A MULE! WHO'LL PAY HER *RANSOM* IF HE'S DEAD?
FIVE *MORE*, WESLEY! OUT OF NOWHERE.
WHAT DID THE *BIG SCARY GUY* JUST SAY?
THIS IS A *KIDNAPPING*.
AND YOU'RE THE *KID*.
KKRAKK
HYAAAGHH--

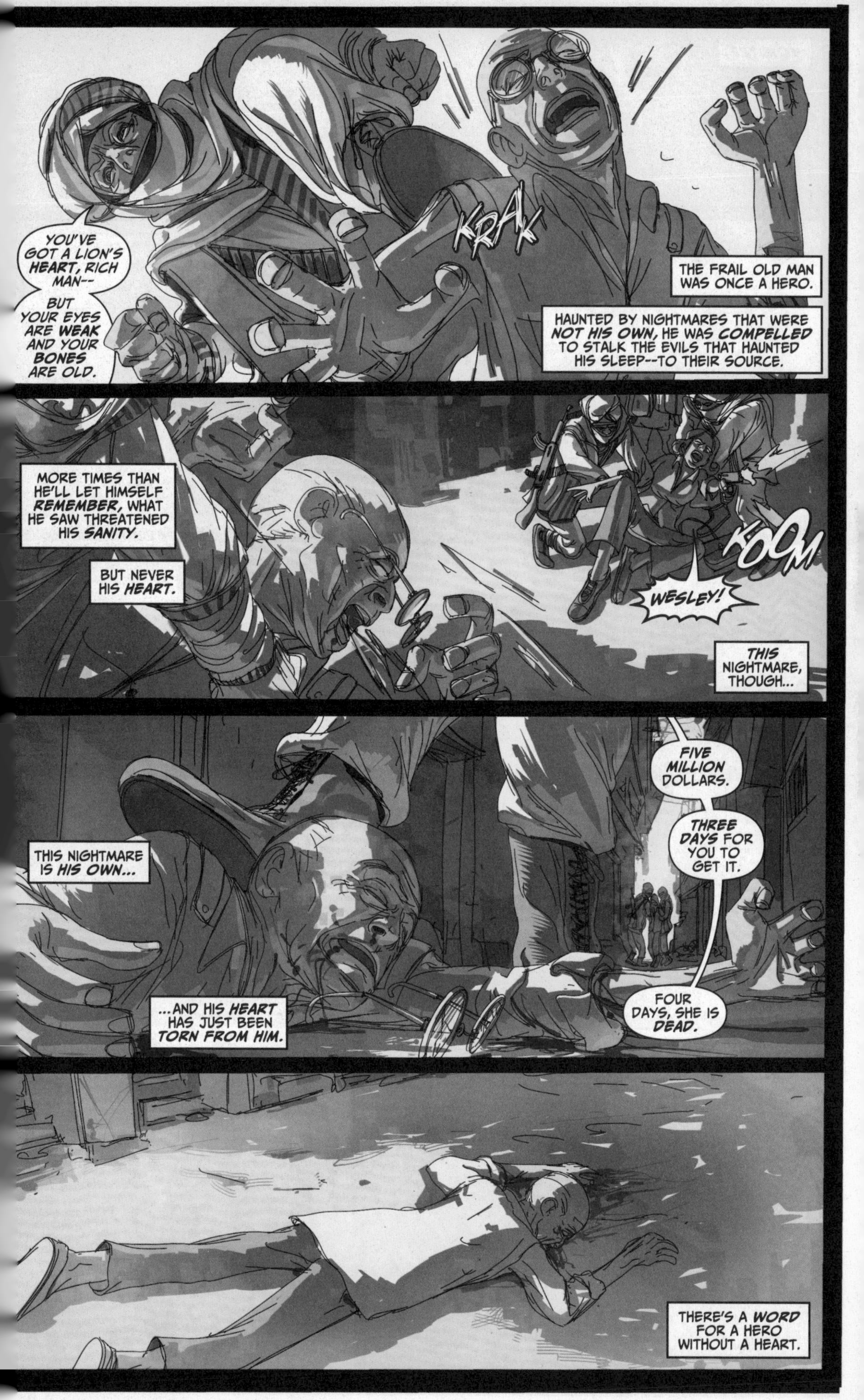
YOU'VE GOT A LION'S HEART, RICH MAN--
BUT YOUR EYES ARE WEAK AND YOUR BONES ARE OLD.
KRAK
THE FRAIL OLD MAN WAS ONCE A HERO.
HAUNTED BY NIGHTMARES THAT WERE NOT HIS OWN, HE WAS COMPELLED TO STALK THE EVILS THAT HAUNTED HIS SLEEP--TO THEIR SOURCE.
MORE TIMES THAN HE'LL LET HIMSELF REMEMBER, WHAT HE SAW THREATENED HIS SANITY.
BUT NEVER HIS HEART.
KOOM
WESLEY!
THIS NIGHTMARE, THOUGH...
THIS NIGHTMARE IS HIS OWN...
...AND HIS HEART HAS JUST BEEN TORN FROM HIM.
FIVE MILLION DOLLARS.
THREE DAYS FOR YOU TO GET IT.
FOUR DAYS, SHE IS DEAD.
THERE'S A WORD FOR A HERO WITHOUT A HEART.

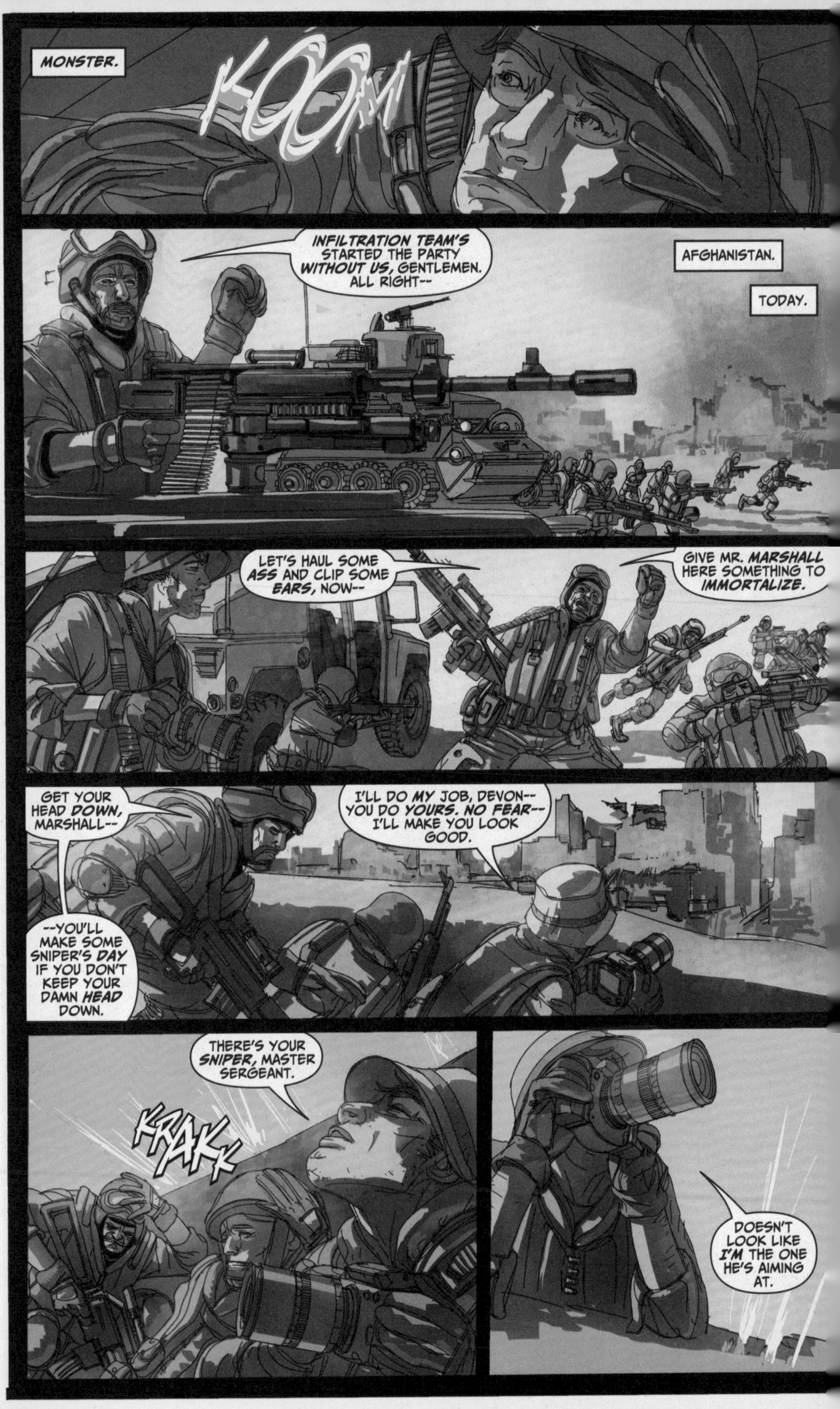
MONSTER.
KOOM
INFILTRATION TEAM'S STARTED THE PARTY WITHOUT US, GENTLEMEN. ALL RIGHT--
AFGHANISTAN.
TODAY.
LET'S HAUL SOME ASS AND CLIP SOME EARS, NOW--
GIVE MR. MARSHALL HERE SOMETHING TO IMMORTALIZE.
GET YOUR HEAD DOWN, MARSHALL--
--YOU'LL MAKE SOME SNIPER'S DAY IF YOU DON'T KEEP YOUR DAMN HEAD DOWN.
I'LL DO MY JOB, DEVON-- YOU DO YOURS. NO FEAR-- I'LL MAKE YOU LOOK GOOD.
THERE'S YOUR SNIPER, MASTER SERGEANT.
KRAKK
DOESN'T LOOK LIKE I'M THE ONE HE'S AIMING AT.

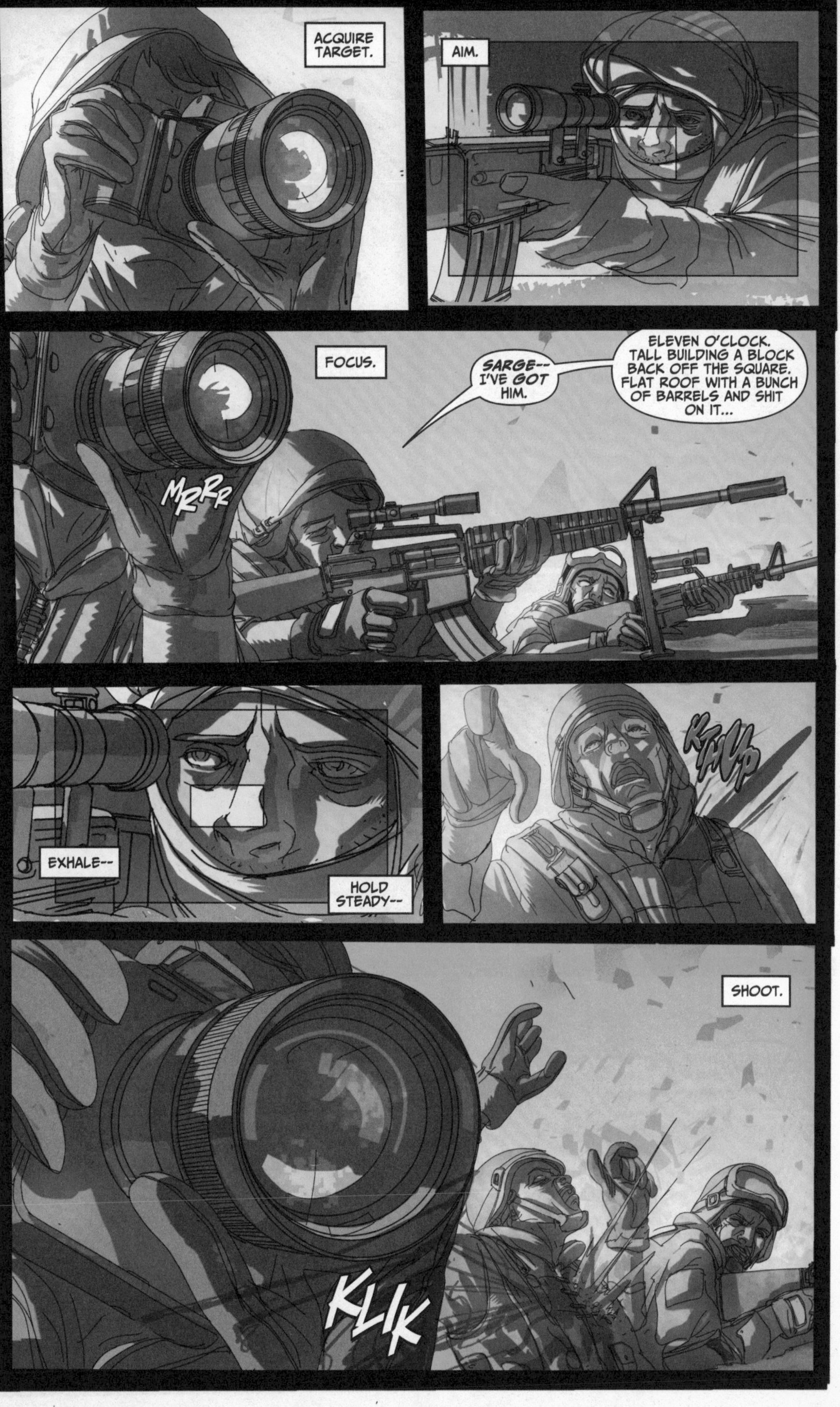
ACQUIRE TARGET.
AIM.
FOCUS.
SARGE-- I'VE GOT HIM.
ELEVEN O'CLOCK. TALL BUILDING A BLOCK BACK OFF THE SQUARE. FLAT ROOF WITH A BUNCH OF BARRELS AND SHIT ON IT...
MRRR
EXHALE--
HOLD STEADY--
KTHUP
SHOOT.
KLIK

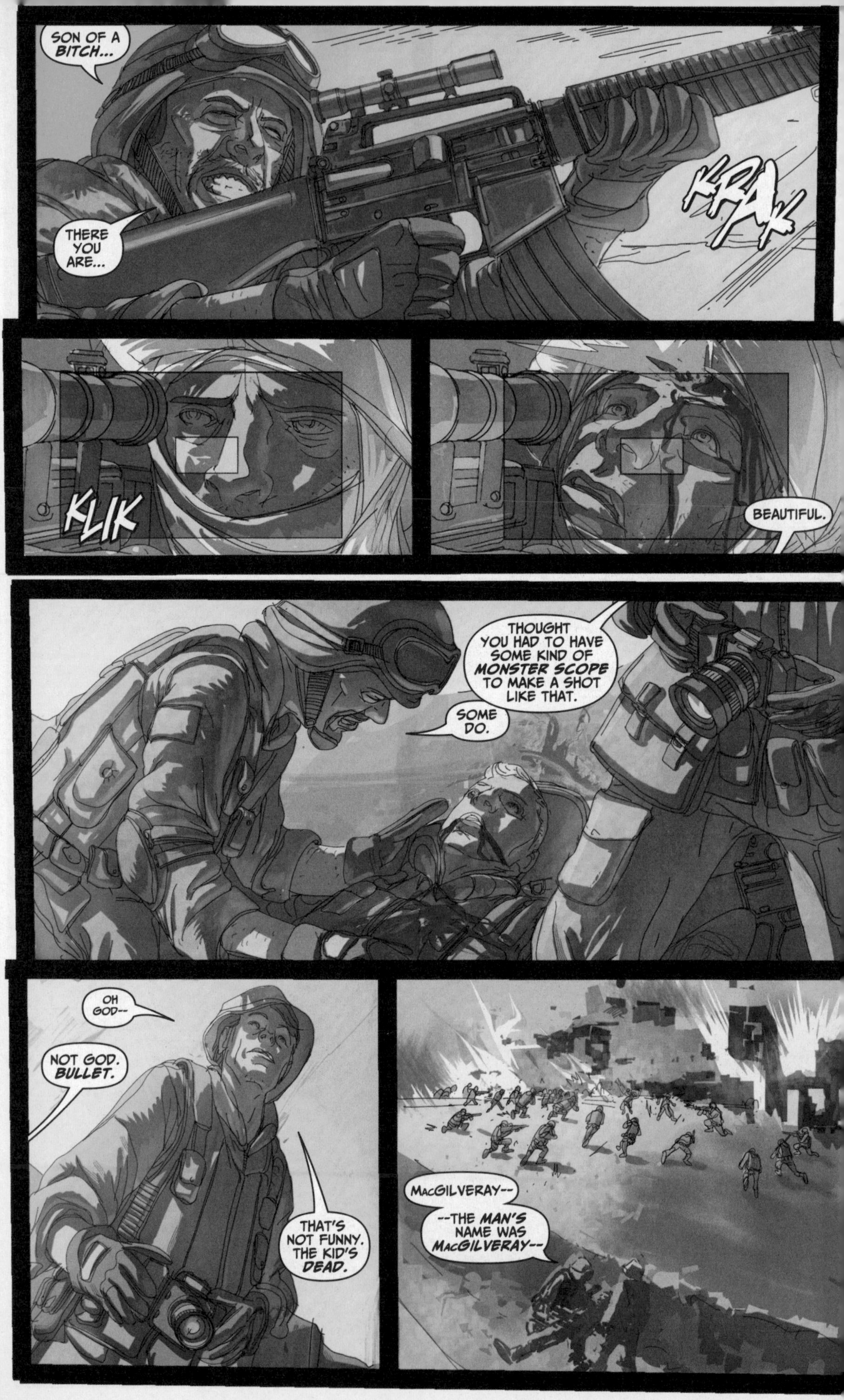
SON OF A BITCH...
THERE YOU ARE...
KRAK
KLIK
BEAUTIFUL.
THOUGHT YOU HAD TO HAVE SOME KIND OF MONSTER SCOPE TO MAKE A SHOT LIKE THAT.
SOME DO.
OH GOD--
NOT GOD. BULLET.
THAT'S NOT FUNNY. THE KID'S DEAD.
MacGILVERAY--
--THE MAN'S NAME WAS MacGILVERAY--

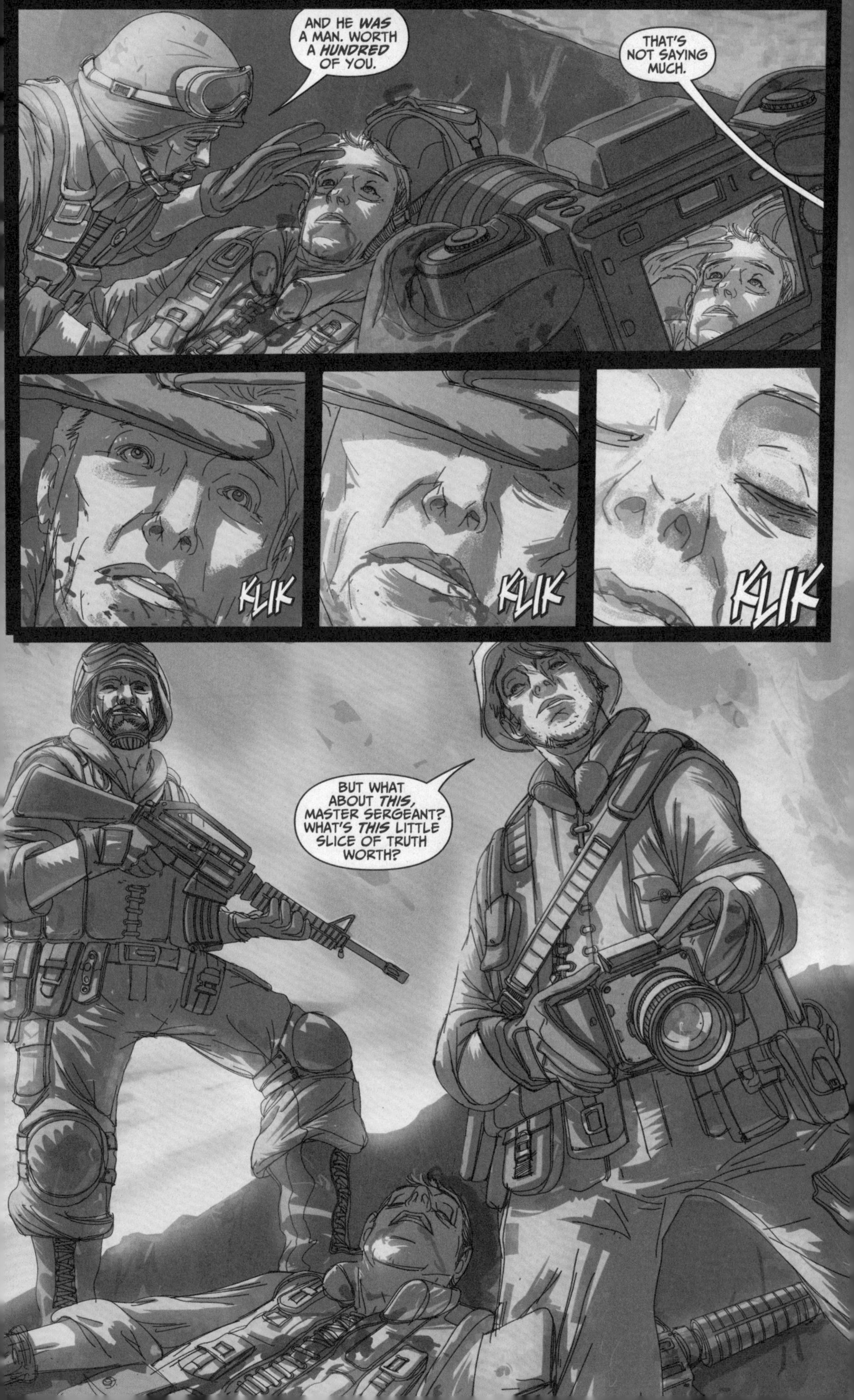
AND HE *WAS* A MAN. WORTH A *HUNDRED* OF YOU.
THAT'S NOT SAYING MUCH.
KLIK
KLIK
KLIK
BUT WHAT ABOUT *THIS*, MASTER SERGEANT? WHAT'S *THIS* LITTLE SLICE OF TRUTH WORTH?

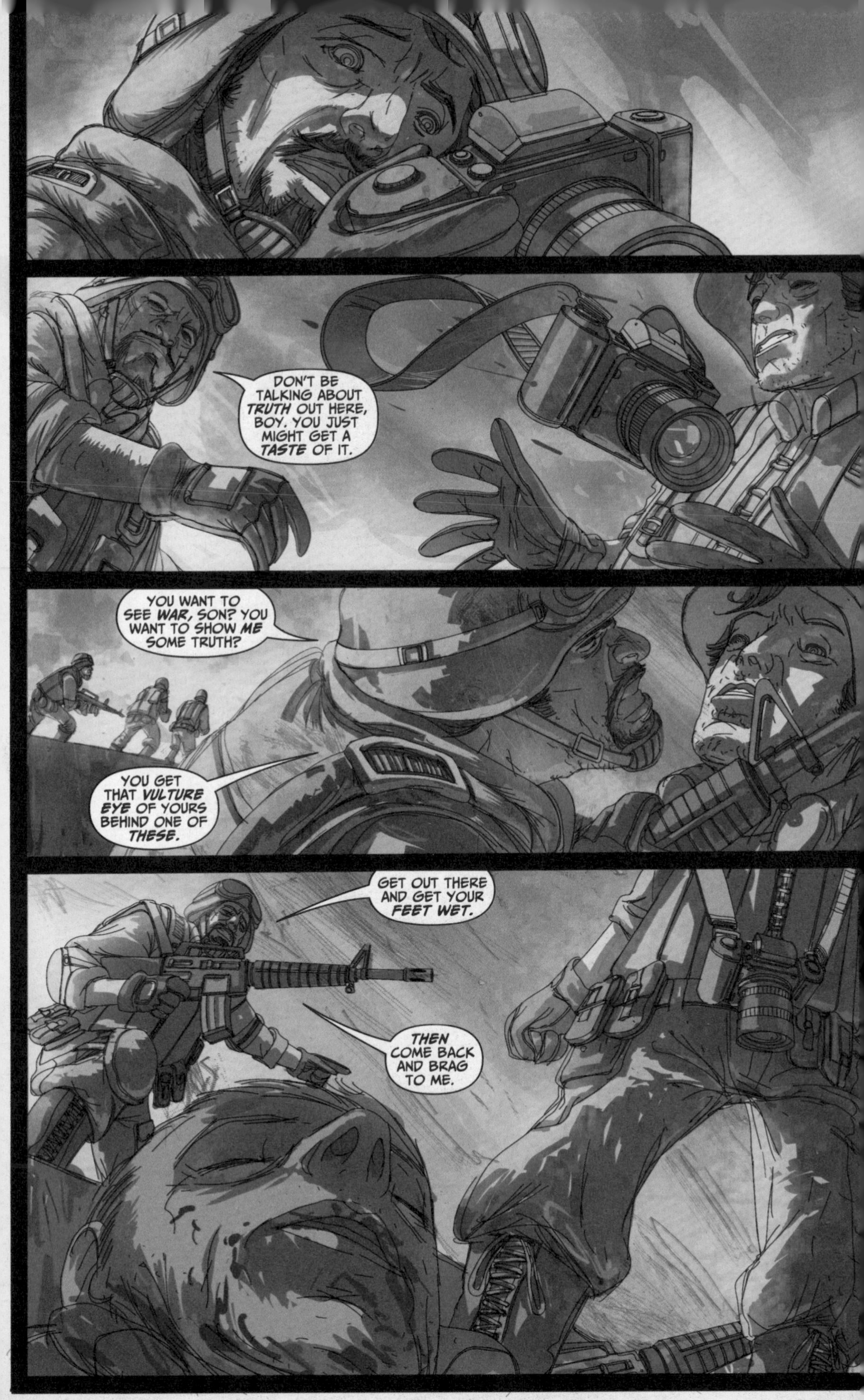
DON'T BE TALKING ABOUT *TRUTH* OUT HERE, BOY. YOU JUST MIGHT GET A *TASTE* OF IT.
YOU WANT TO SEE *WAR,* SON? YOU WANT TO SHOW *ME* SOME TRUTH?
YOU GET THAT *VULTURE EYE* OF YOURS BEHIND ONE OF *THESE.*
GET OUT THERE AND GET YOUR *FEET WET.*
THEN COME BACK AND BRAG TO ME.

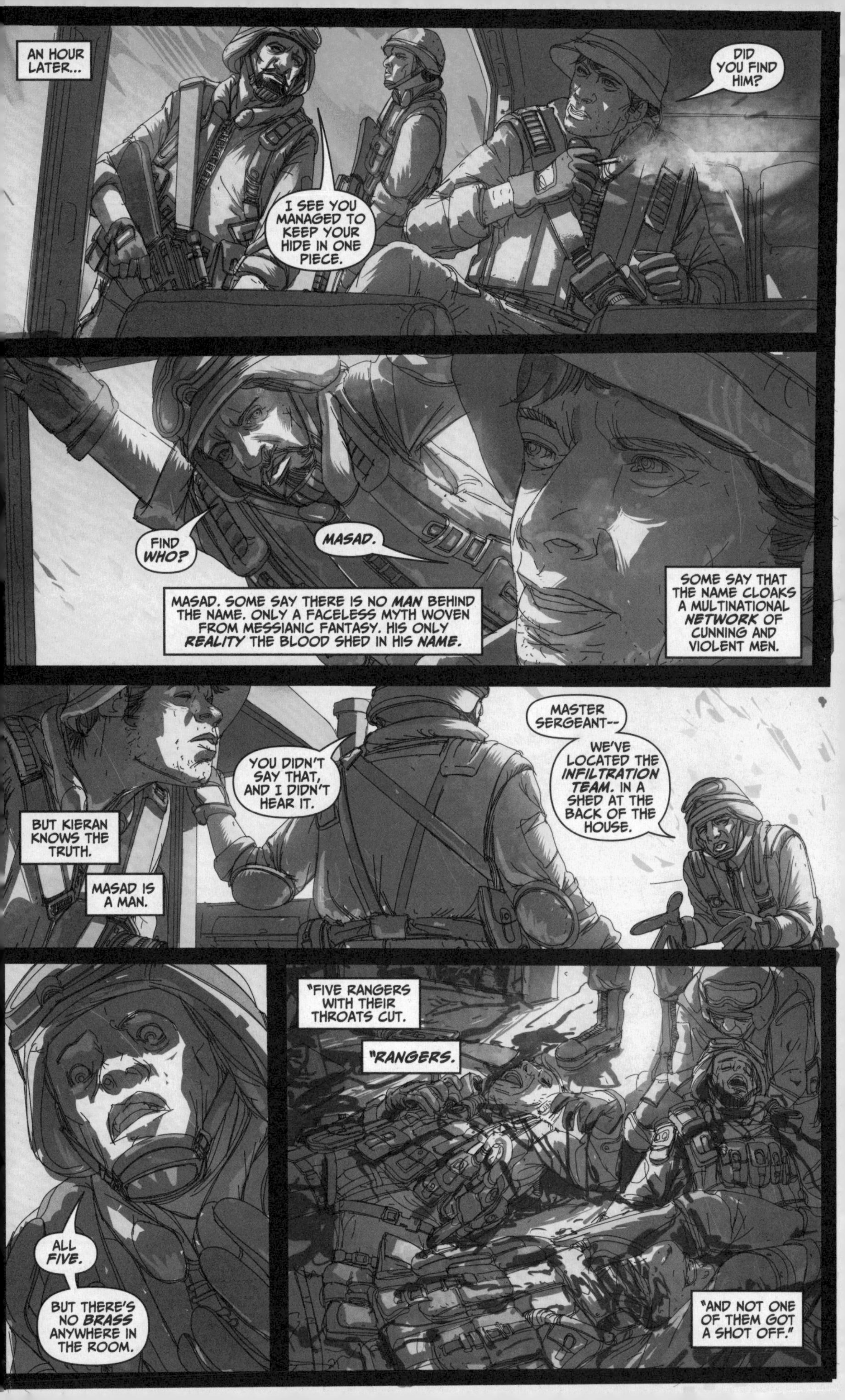
AN HOUR LATER...
DID YOU FIND HIM?
I SEE YOU MANAGED TO KEEP YOUR HIDE IN ONE PIECE.
FIND WHO?
MASAD.
MASAD. SOME SAY THERE IS NO MAN BEHIND THE NAME. ONLY A FACELESS MYTH WOVEN FROM MESSIANIC FANTASY. HIS ONLY REALITY THE BLOOD SHED IN HIS NAME.
SOME SAY THAT THE NAME CLOAKS A MULTINATIONAL NETWORK OF CUNNING AND VIOLENT MEN.
YOU DIDN'T SAY THAT, AND I DIDN'T HEAR IT.
BUT KIERAN KNOWS THE TRUTH.
MASAD IS A MAN.
MASTER SERGEANT--
WE'VE LOCATED THE INFILTRATION TEAM. IN A SHED AT THE BACK OF THE HOUSE.
ALL FIVE.
BUT THERE'S NO BRASS ANYWHERE IN THE ROOM.
"FIVE RANGERS WITH THEIR THROATS CUT.
"RANGERS.
"AND NOT ONE OF THEM GOT A SHOT OFF."

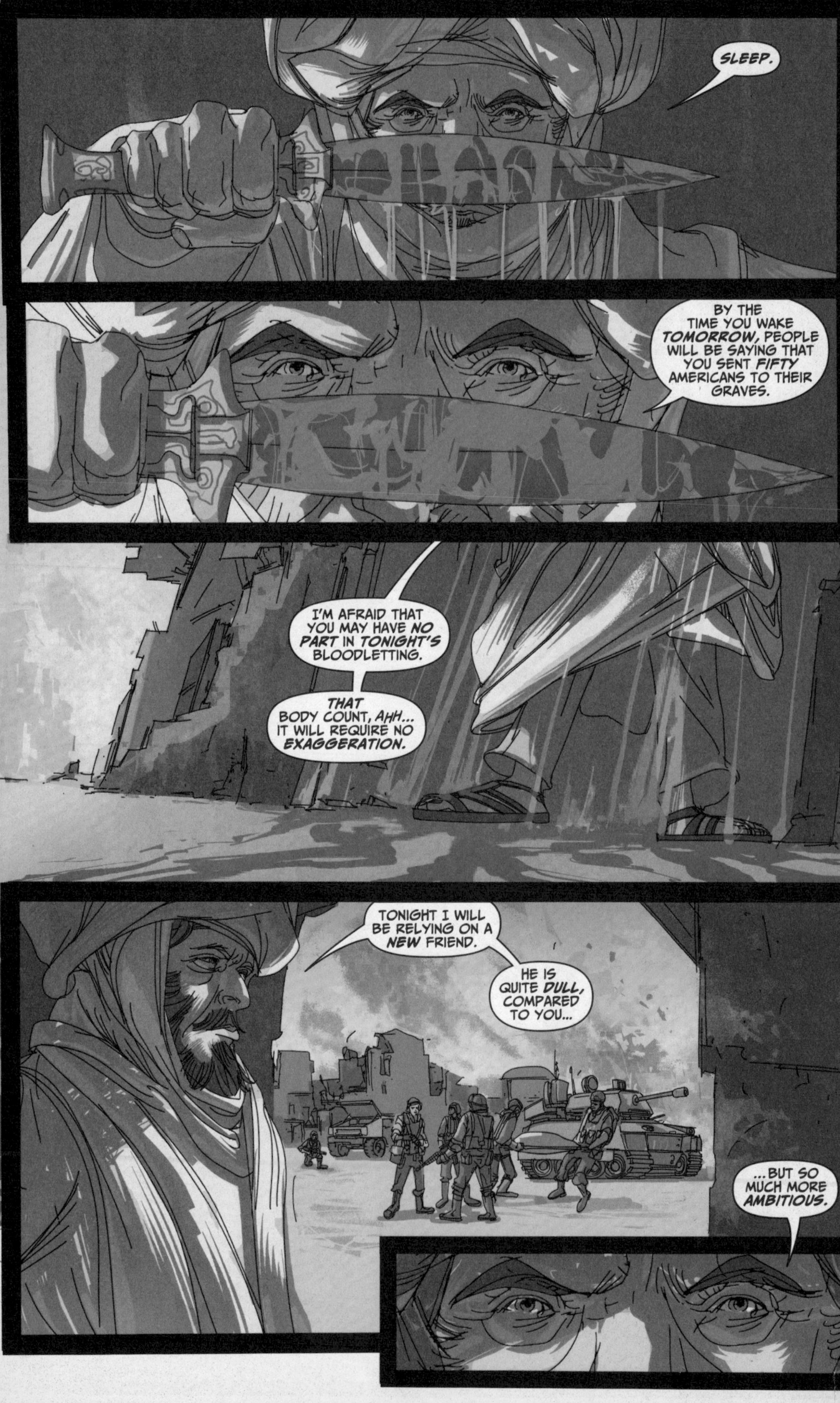
SLEEP.
BY THE TIME YOU WAKE TOMORROW, PEOPLE WILL BE SAYING THAT YOU SENT FIFTY AMERICANS TO THEIR GRAVES.
I'M AFRAID THAT YOU MAY HAVE NO PART IN TONIGHT'S BLOODLETTING.
THAT BODY COUNT, AHH... IT WILL REQUIRE NO EXAGGERATION.
TONIGHT I WILL BE RELYING ON A NEW FRIEND.
HE IS QUITE DULL, COMPARED TO YOU...
...BUT SO MUCH MORE AMBITIOUS.

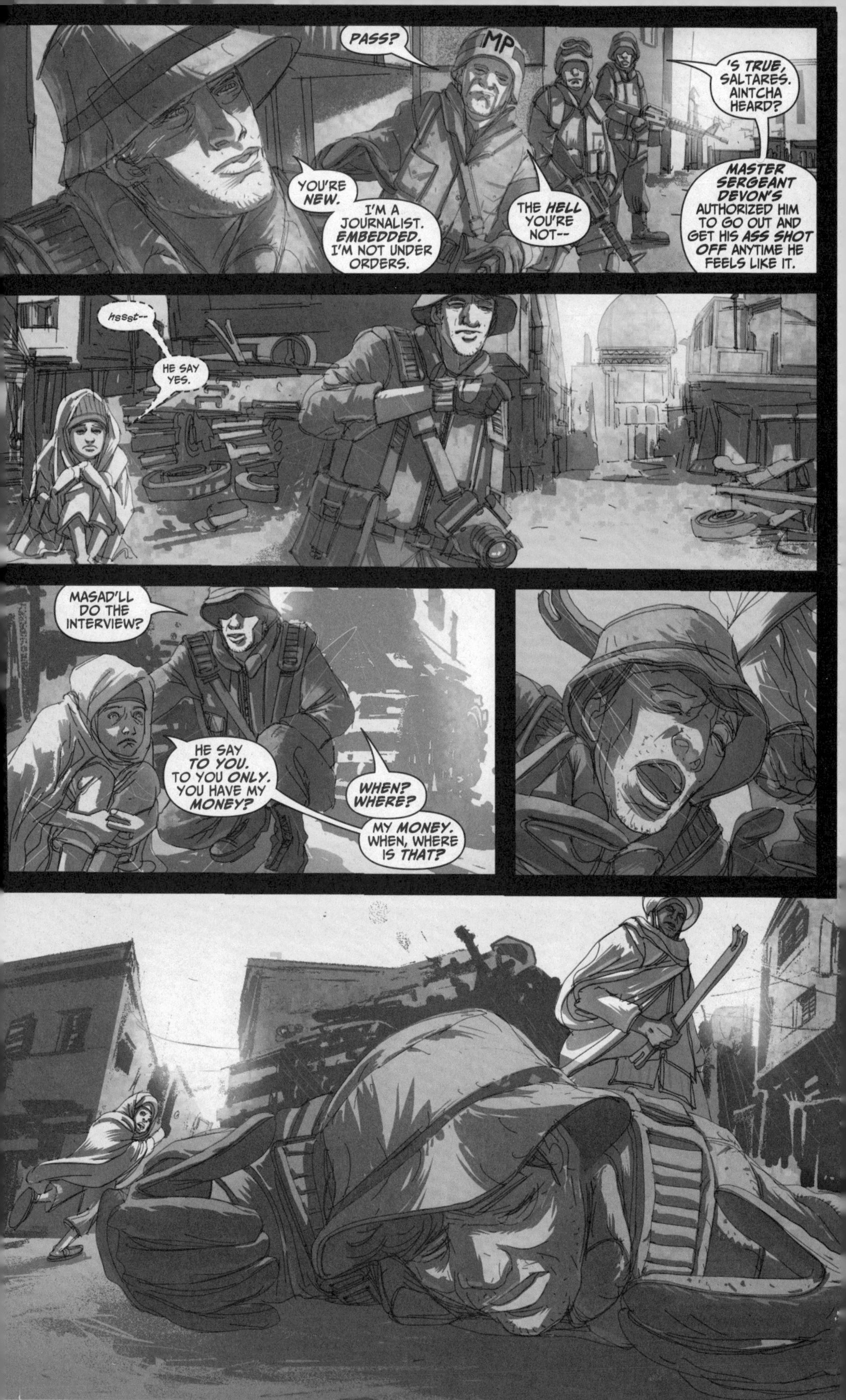
PASS?
YOU'RE NEW.
I'M A JOURNALIST. EMBEDDED. I'M NOT UNDER ORDERS.
THE HELL YOU'RE NOT--
'S TRUE, SALTARES. AINTCHA HEARD?
MASTER SERGEANT DEVON'S AUTHORIZED HIM TO GO OUT AND GET HIS ASS SHOT OFF ANYTIME HE FEELS LIKE IT.
hssst--
HE SAY YES.
MASAD'LL DO THE INTERVIEW?
HE SAY TO YOU. TO YOU ONLY. YOU HAVE MY MONEY?
WHEN? WHERE?
MY MONEY. WHEN, WHERE IS THAT?

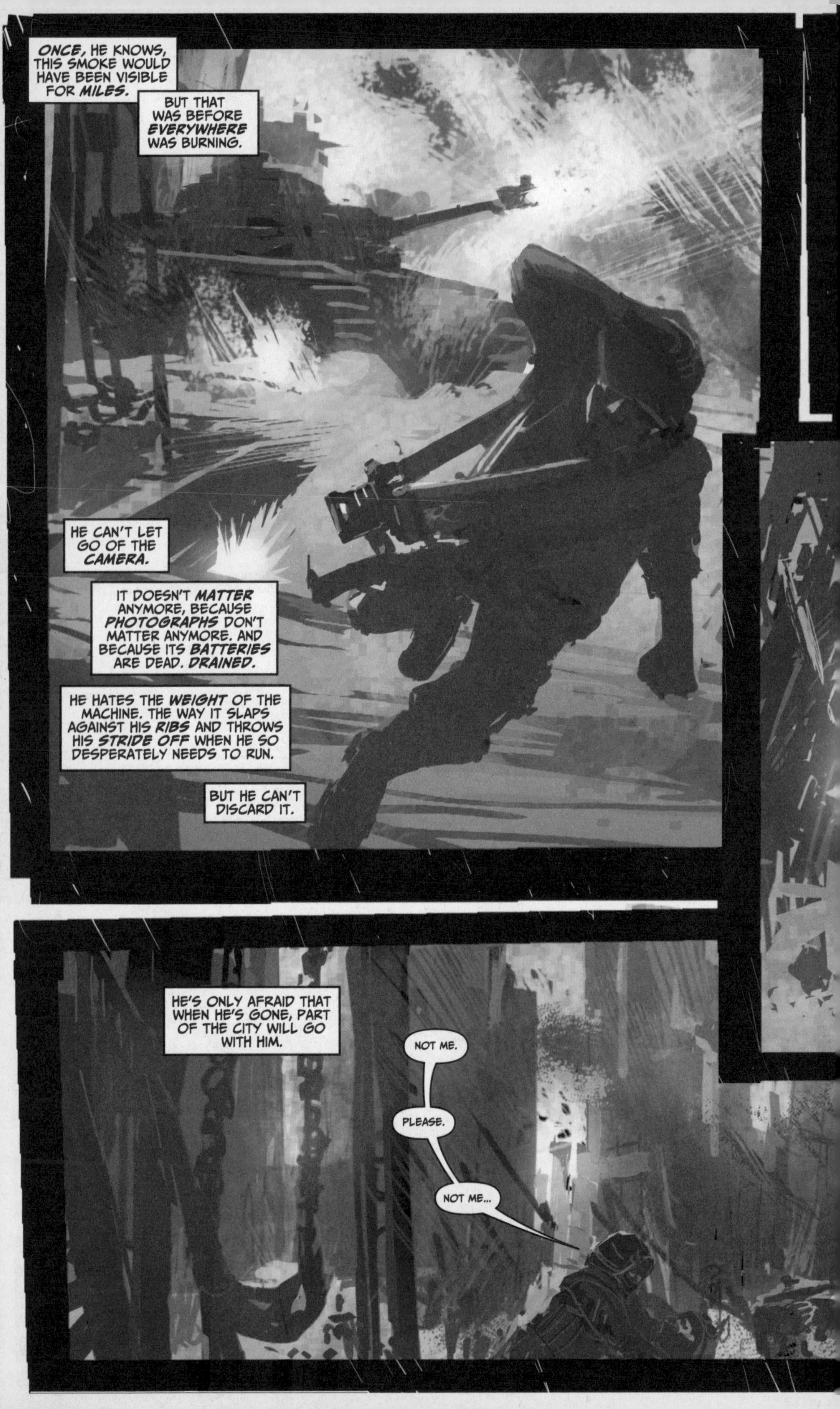
ONCE, HE KNOWS, THIS SMOKE WOULD HAVE BEEN VISIBLE FOR *MILES.*
BUT THAT WAS BEFORE *EVERYWHERE* WAS BURNING.
HE CAN'T LET GO OF THE *CAMERA.*
IT DOESN'T *MATTER* ANYMORE, BECAUSE *PHOTOGRAPHS* DON'T MATTER ANYMORE. AND BECAUSE ITS *BATTERIES* ARE DEAD. *DRAINED.*
HE HATES THE *WEIGHT* OF THE MACHINE. THE WAY IT SLAPS AGAINST HIS *RIBS* AND THROWS HIS *STRIDE OFF* WHEN HE SO DESPERATELY NEEDS TO RUN.
BUT HE CAN'T DISCARD IT.
HE'S ONLY AFRAID THAT WHEN HE'S GONE, PART OF THE CITY WILL GO WITH HIM.
NOT ME.
PLEASE.
NOT ME...

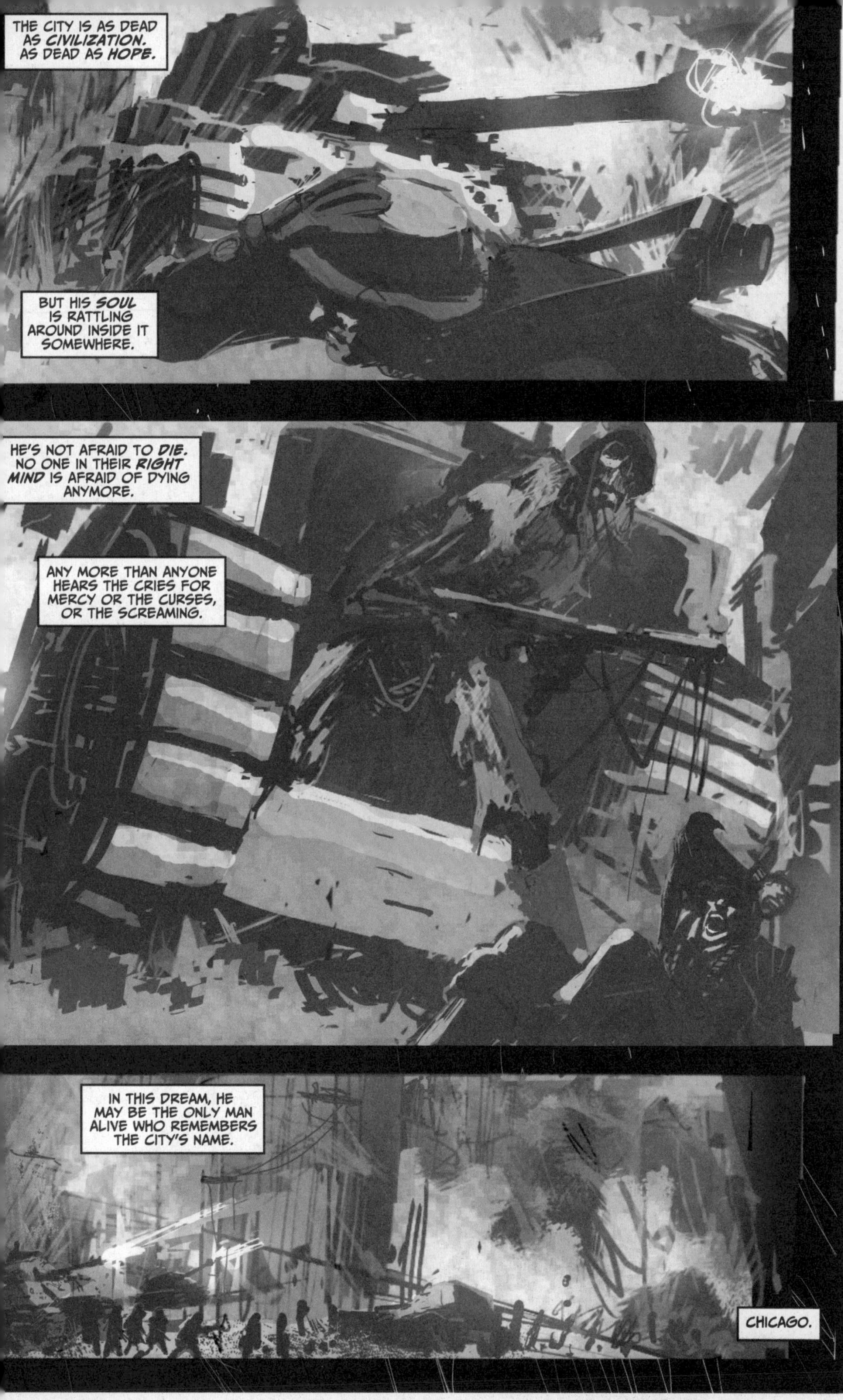
THE CITY IS AS DEAD AS CIVILIZATION. AS DEAD AS HOPE.
BUT HIS SOUL IS RATTLING AROUND INSIDE IT SOMEWHERE.
HE'S NOT AFRAID TO DIE. NO ONE IN THEIR RIGHT MIND IS AFRAID OF DYING ANYMORE.
ANY MORE THAN ANYONE HEARS THE CRIES FOR MERCY OR THE CURSES, OR THE SCREAMING.
IN THIS DREAM, HE MAY BE THE ONLY MAN ALIVE WHO REMEMBERS THE CITY'S NAME.
CHICAGO.

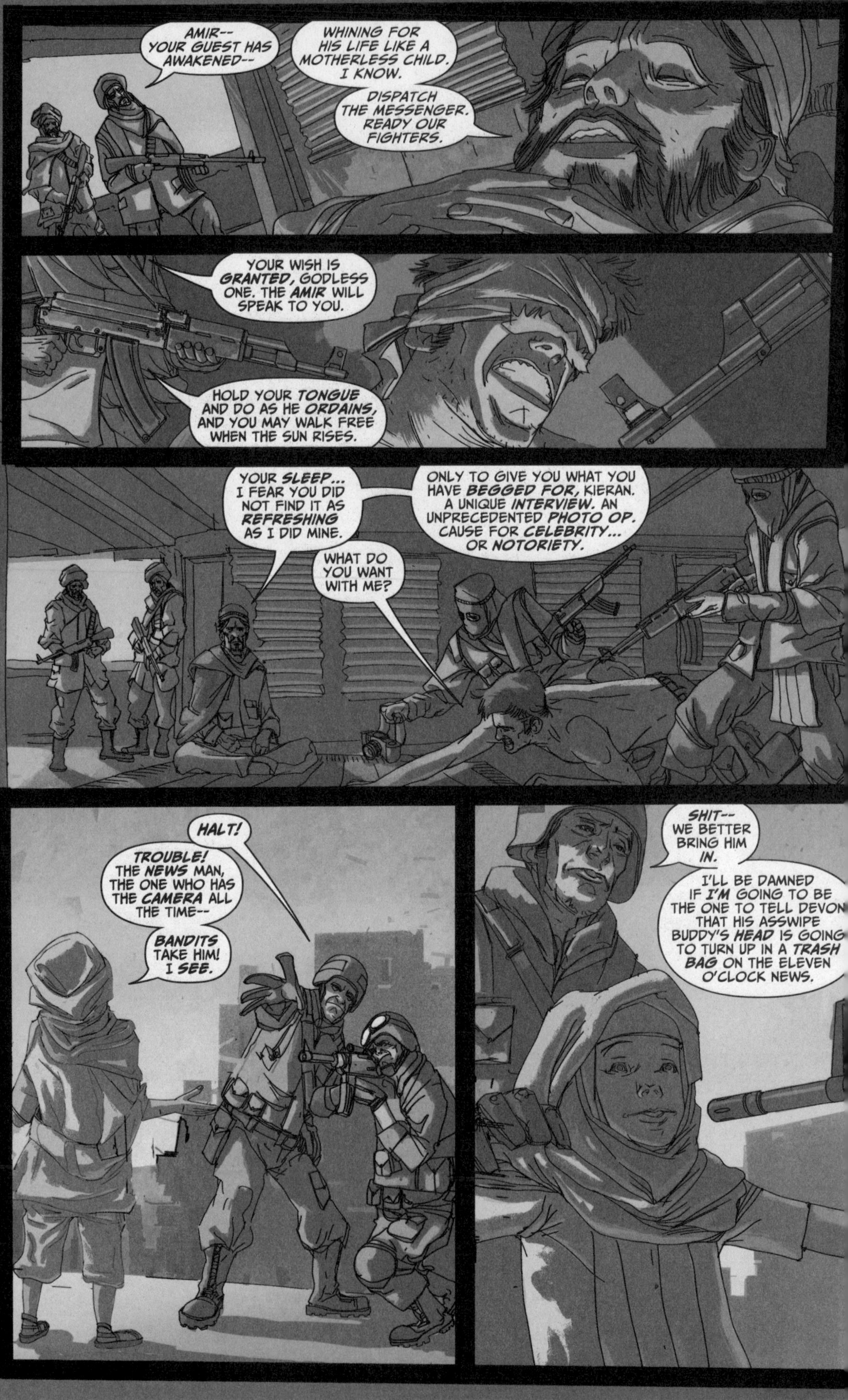
AMIR-- YOUR GUEST HAS AWAKENED--
WHINING FOR HIS LIFE LIKE A MOTHERLESS CHILD. I KNOW.
DISPATCH THE MESSENGER. READY OUR FIGHTERS.
YOUR WISH IS GRANTED, GODLESS ONE. THE AMIR WILL SPEAK TO YOU.
HOLD YOUR TONGUE AND DO AS HE ORDAINS, AND YOU MAY WALK FREE WHEN THE SUN RISES.
YOUR SLEEP... I FEAR YOU DID NOT FIND IT AS REFRESHING AS I DID MINE.
ONLY TO GIVE YOU WHAT YOU HAVE BEGGED FOR, KIERAN. A UNIQUE INTERVIEW. AN UNPRECEDENTED PHOTO OP. CAUSE FOR CELEBRITY... OR NOTORIETY.
WHAT DO YOU WANT WITH ME?
HALT!
TROUBLE! THE NEWS MAN, THE ONE WHO HAS THE CAMERA ALL THE TIME--
BANDITS TAKE HIM! I SEE.
SHIT-- WE BETTER BRING HIM IN.
I'LL BE DAMNED IF I'M GOING TO BE THE ONE TO TELL DEVON THAT HIS ASSWIPE BUDDY'S HEAD IS GOING TO TURN UP IN A TRASH BAG ON THE ELEVEN O'CLOCK NEWS.

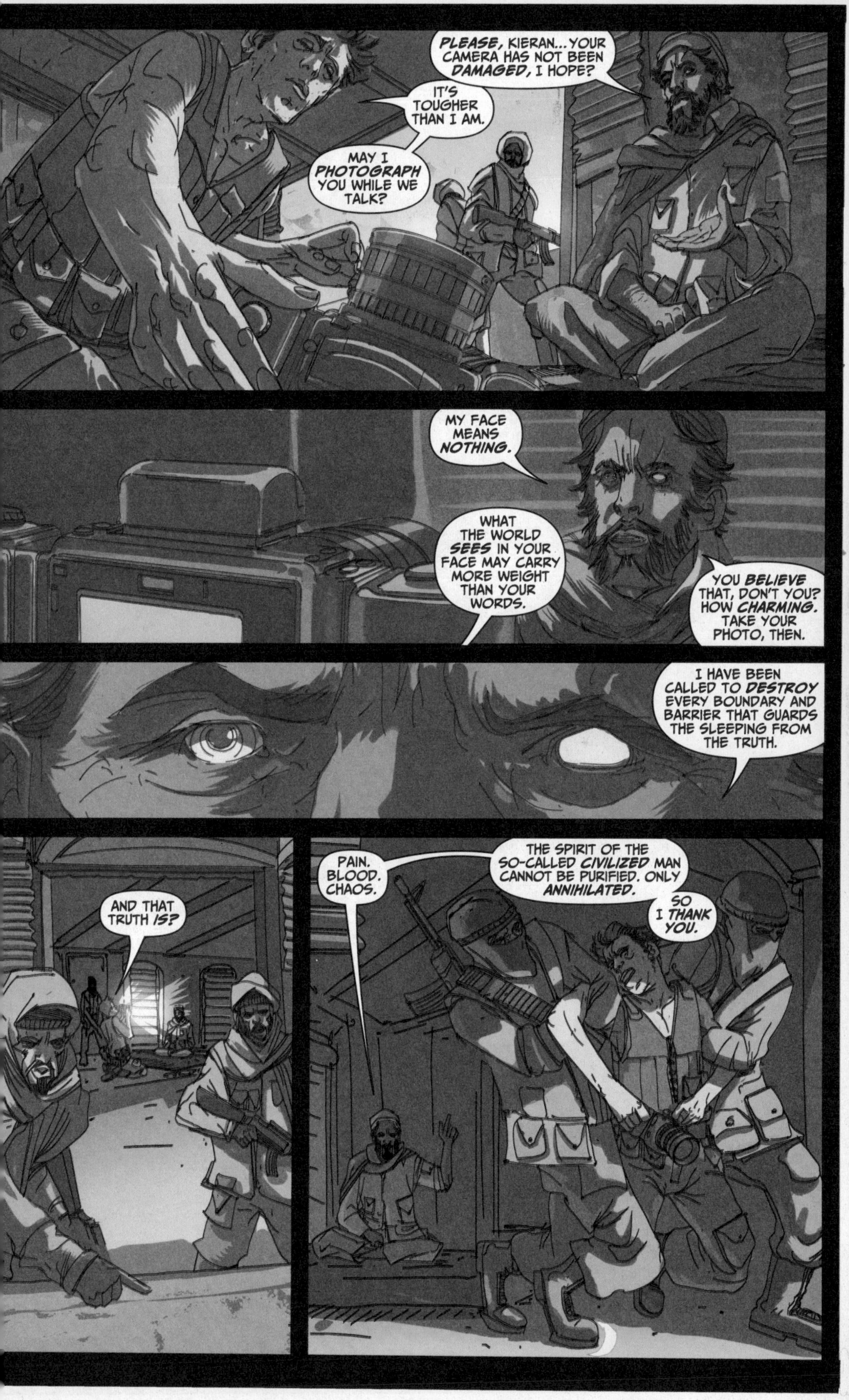
PLEASE, KIERAN... YOUR CAMERA HAS NOT BEEN DAMAGED, I HOPE?
IT'S TOUGHER THAN I AM.
MAY I PHOTOGRAPH YOU WHILE WE TALK?
MY FACE MEANS NOTHING.
WHAT THE WORLD SEES IN YOUR FACE MAY CARRY MORE WEIGHT THAN YOUR WORDS.
YOU BELIEVE THAT, DON'T YOU? HOW CHARMING. TAKE YOUR PHOTO, THEN.
I HAVE BEEN CALLED TO DESTROY EVERY BOUNDARY AND BARRIER THAT GUARDS THE SLEEPING FROM THE TRUTH.
AND THAT TRUTH IS?
PAIN. BLOOD. CHAOS.
THE SPIRIT OF THE SO-CALLED CIVILIZED MAN CANNOT BE PURIFIED. ONLY ANNIHILATED.
SO I THANK YOU.

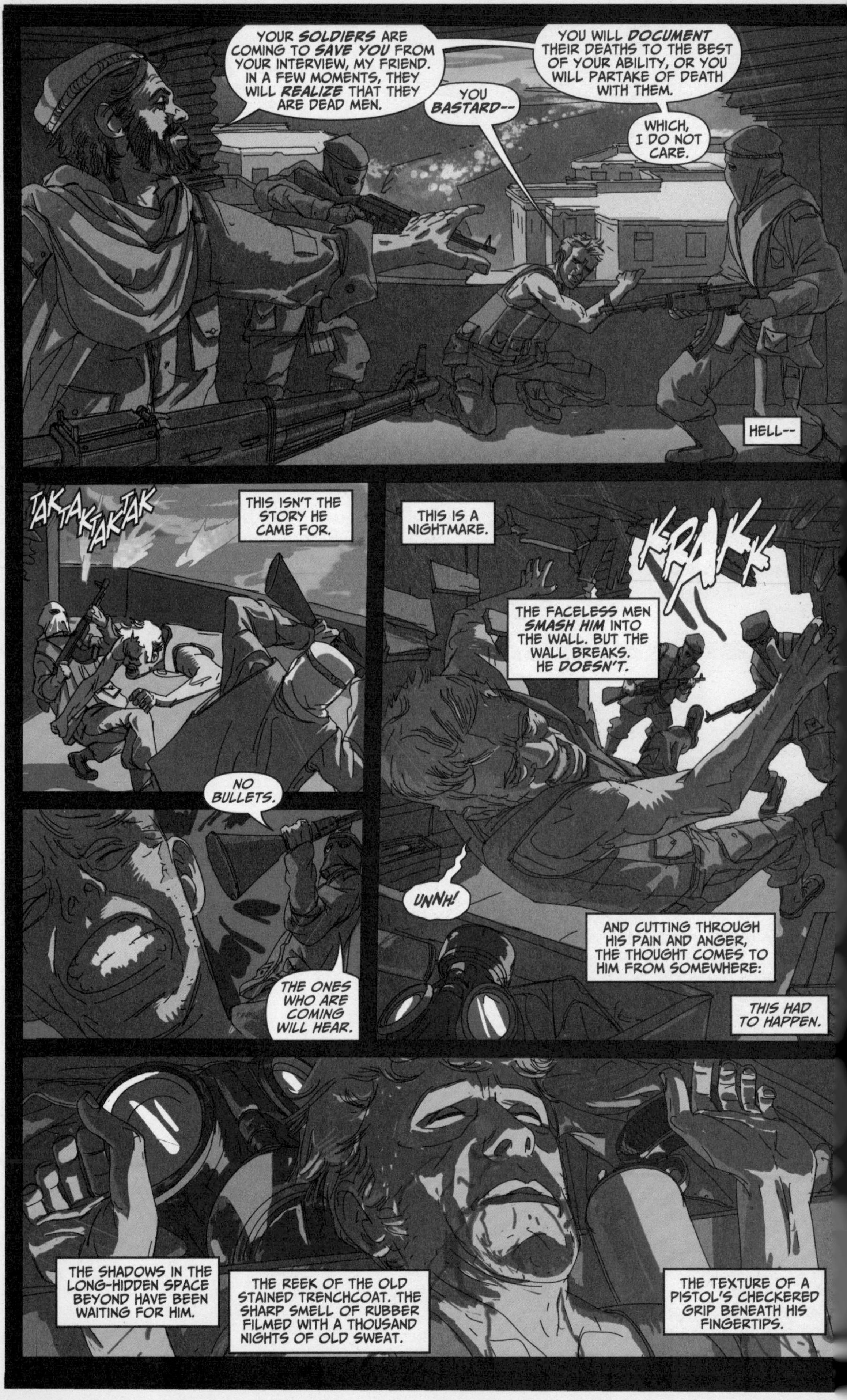

YOUR SOLDIERS ARE COMING TO SAVE YOU FROM YOUR INTERVIEW, MY FRIEND. IN A FEW MOMENTS, THEY WILL REALIZE THAT THEY ARE DEAD MEN.
YOU BASTARD--
YOU WILL DOCUMENT THEIR DEATHS TO THE BEST OF YOUR ABILITY, OR YOU WILL PARTAKE OF DEATH WITH THEM.
WHICH, I DO NOT CARE.
HELL--
TAKTAKTAKTAK
THIS ISN'T THE STORY HE CAME FOR.
NO BULLETS.
THE ONES WHO ARE COMING WILL HEAR.
THIS IS A NIGHTMARE.
KRAKK
THE FACELESS MEN SMASH HIM INTO THE WALL. BUT THE WALL BREAKS. HE DOESN'T.
UNNH!
AND CUTTING THROUGH HIS PAIN AND ANGER, THE THOUGHT COMES TO HIM FROM SOMEWHERE:
THIS HAD TO HAPPEN.
THE SHADOWS IN THE LONG-HIDDEN SPACE BEYOND HAVE BEEN WAITING FOR HIM.
THE REEK OF THE OLD STAINED TRENCHCOAT. THE SHARP SMELL OF RUBBER FILMED WITH A THOUSAND NIGHTS OF OLD SWEAT.
THE TEXTURE OF A PISTOL'S CHECKERED GRIP BENEATH HIS FINGERTIPS.

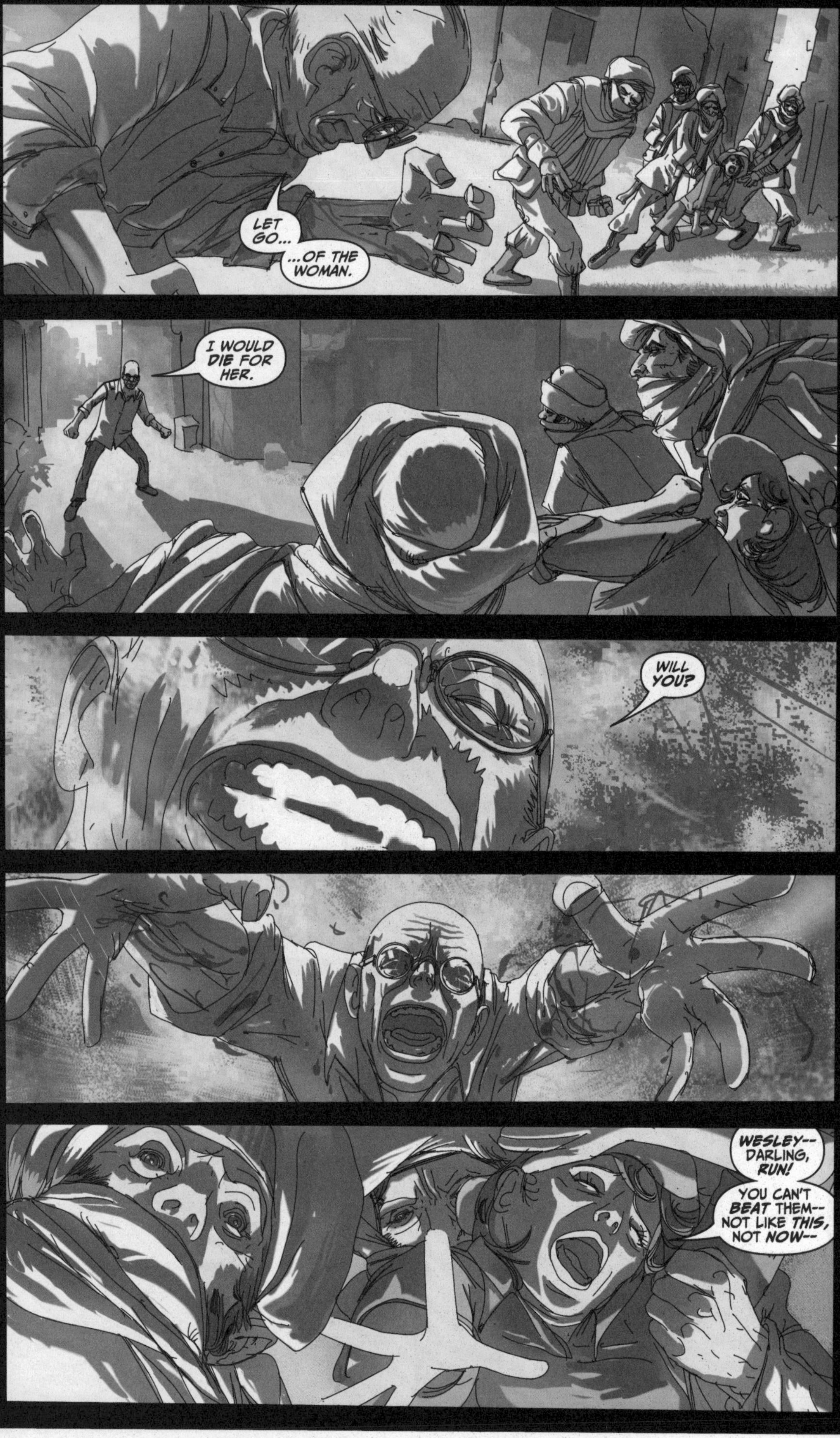
LET GO...
...OF THE WOMAN.
I WOULD DIE FOR HER.
WILL YOU?
WESLEY--DARLING, RUN!
YOU CAN'T BEAT THEM--NOT LIKE THIS, NOT NOW--

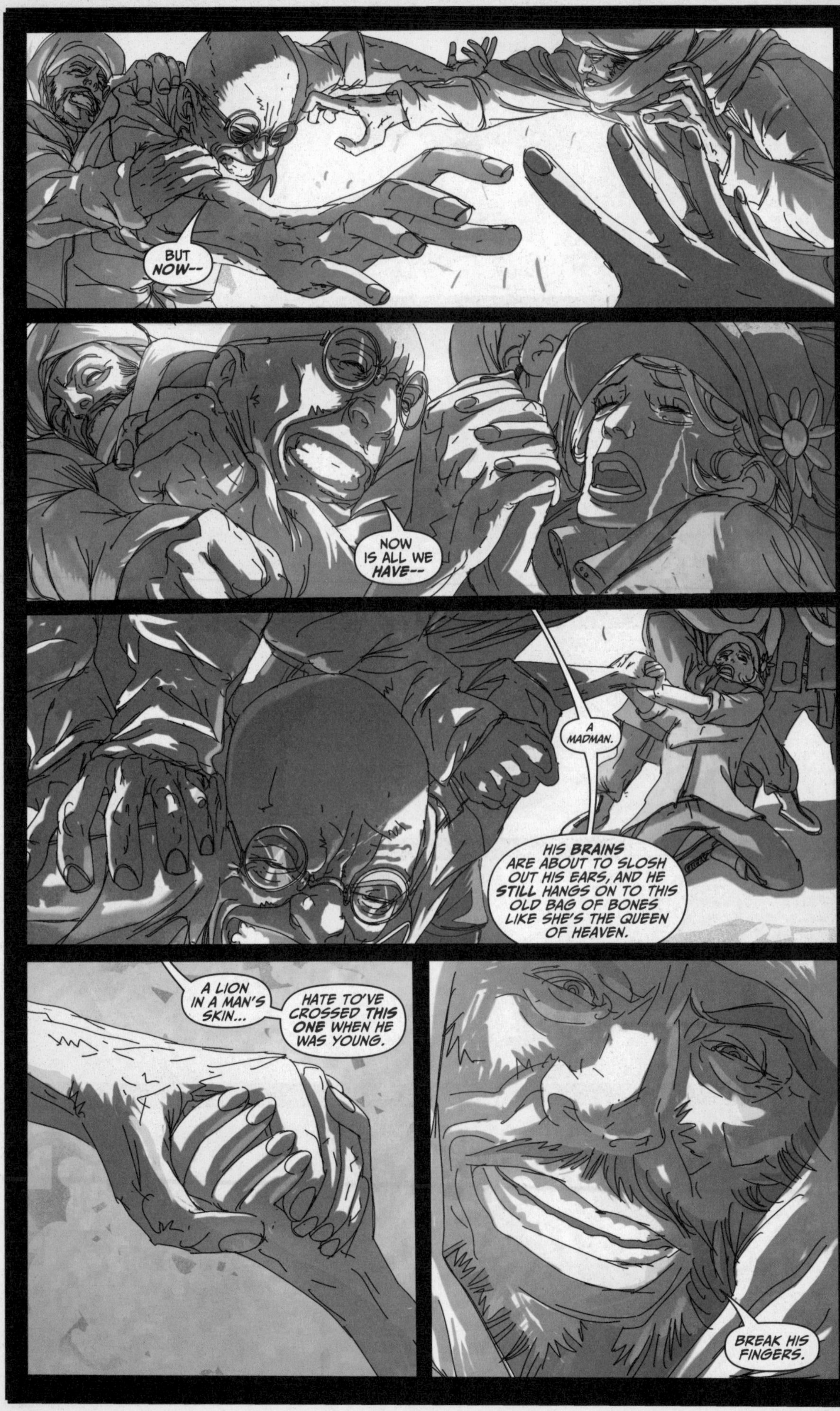

BUT NOW--
NOW IS ALL WE HAVE--
A MADMAN.
HIS BRAINS ARE ABOUT TO SLOSH OUT HIS EARS, AND HE STILL HANGS ON TO THIS OLD BAG OF BONES LIKE SHE'S THE QUEEN OF HEAVEN.
A LION IN A MAN'S SKIN...
HATE TO'VE CROSSED THIS ONE WHEN HE WAS YOUNG.
BREAK HIS FINGERS.

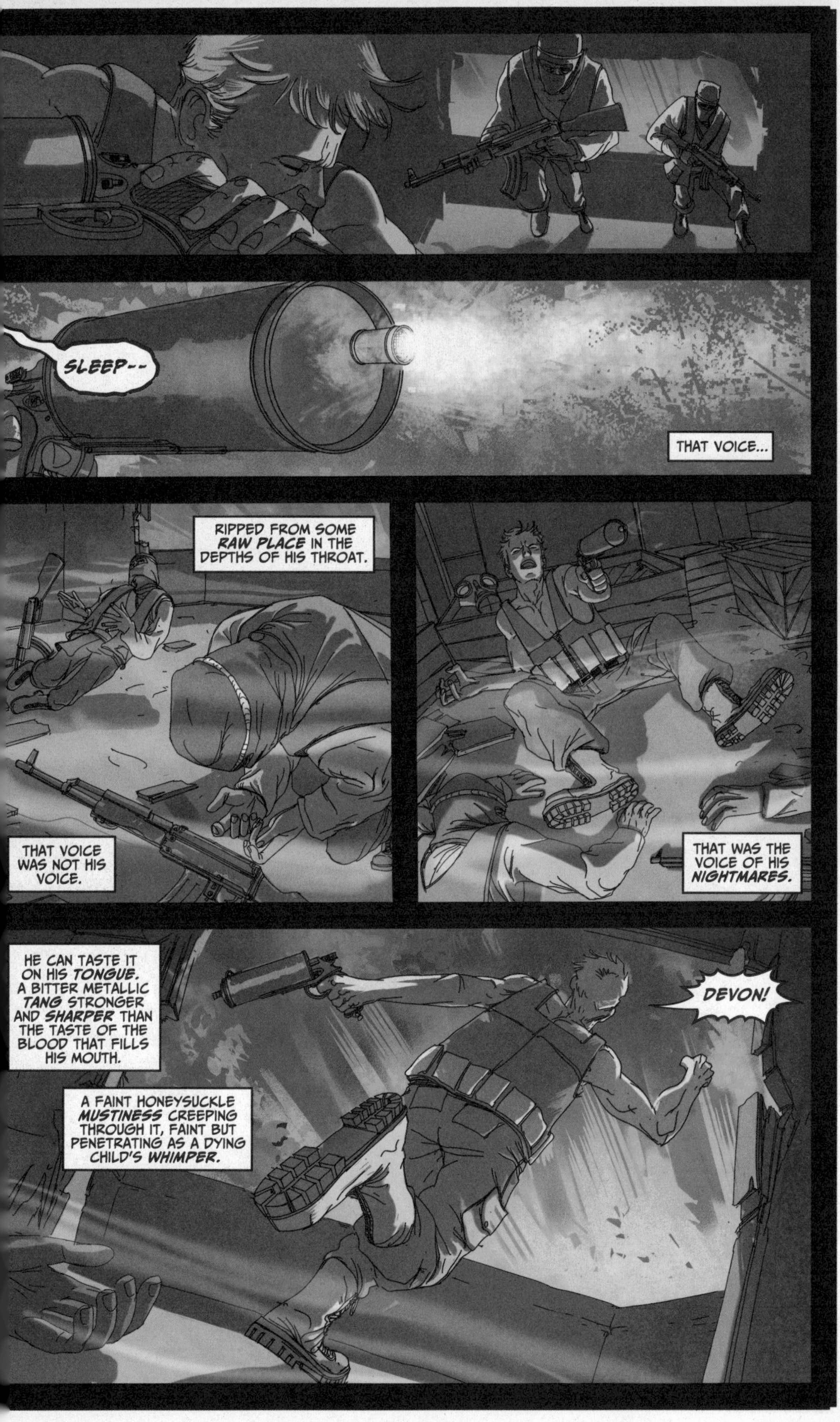
SLEEP--
THAT VOICE...
RIPPED FROM SOME RAW PLACE IN THE DEPTHS OF HIS THROAT.
THAT VOICE WAS NOT HIS VOICE.
THAT WAS THE VOICE OF HIS NIGHTMARES.
HE CAN TASTE IT ON HIS TONGUE. A BITTER METALLIC TANG STRONGER AND SHARPER THAN THE TASTE OF THE BLOOD THAT FILLS HIS MOUTH.
DEVON!
A FAINT HONEYSUCKLE MUSTINESS CREEPING THROUGH IT, FAINT BUT PENETRATING AS A DYING CHILD'S WHIMPER.

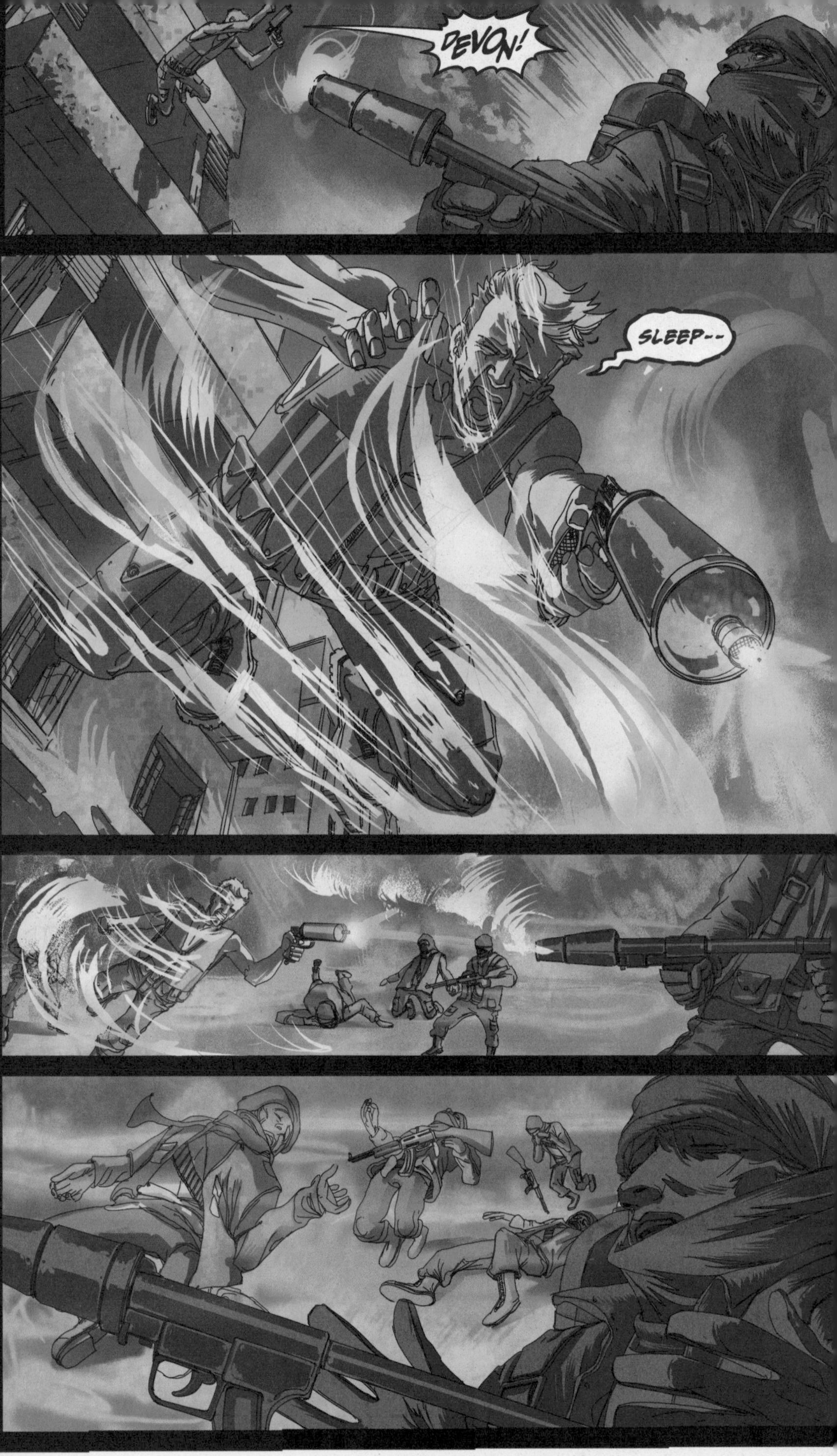
DEVON!
SLEEP--

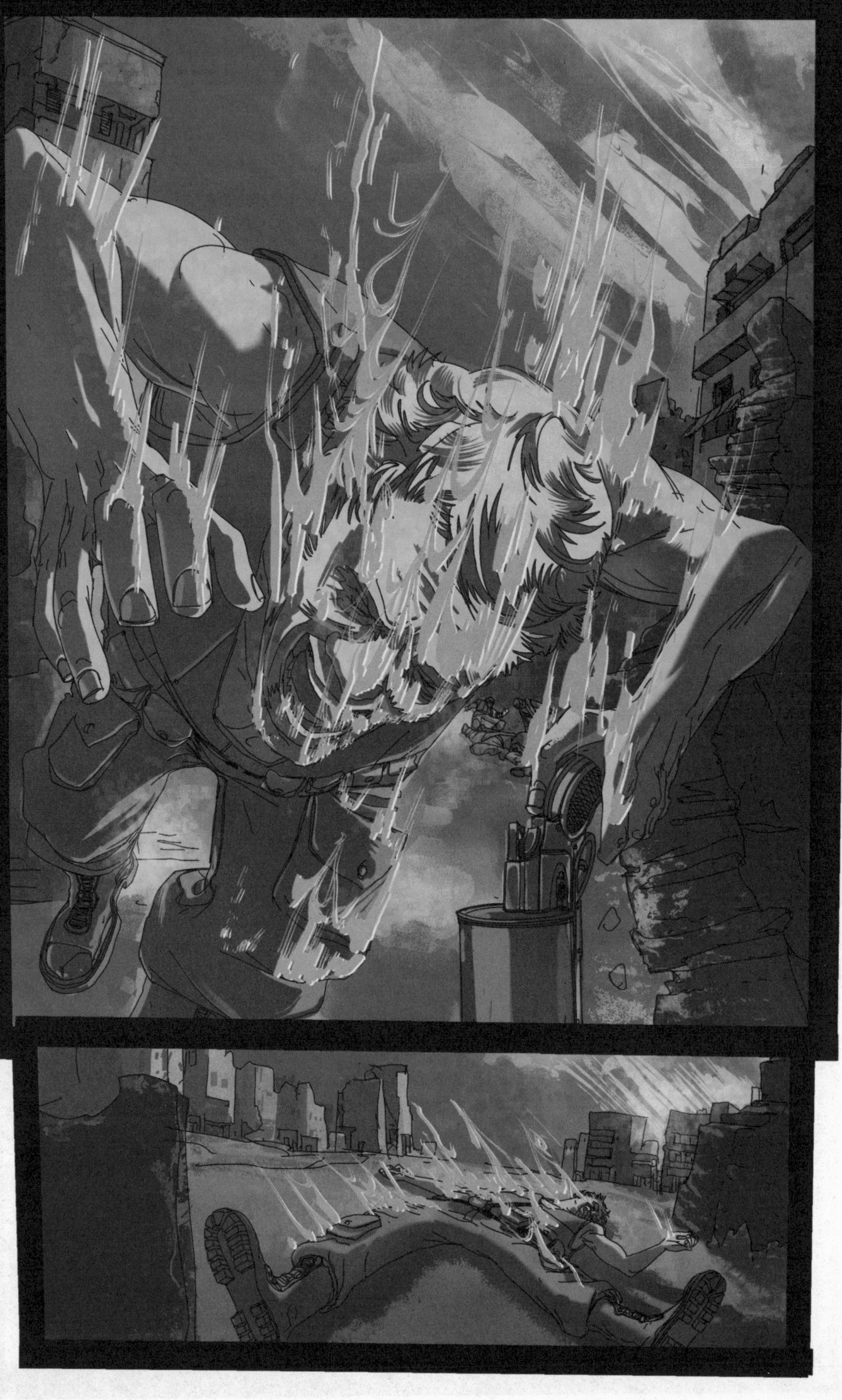

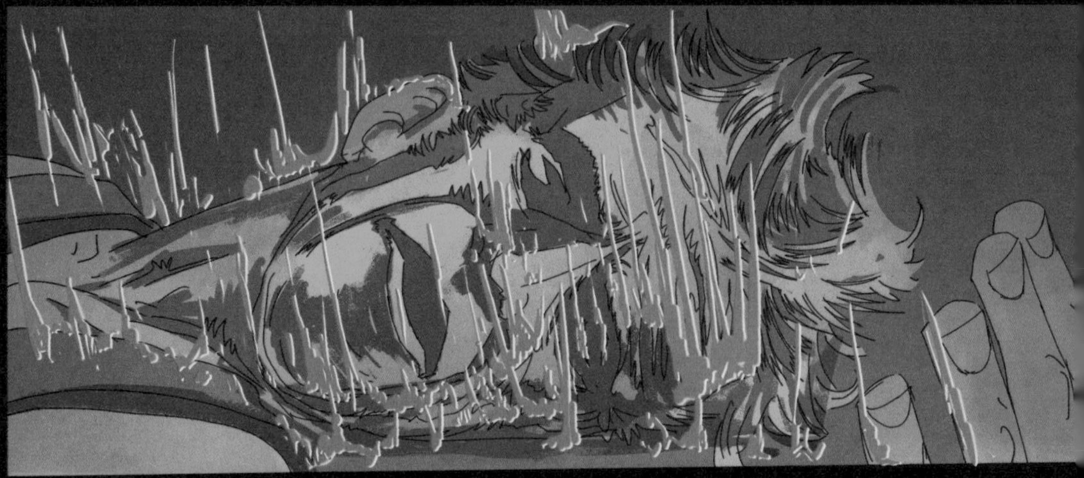

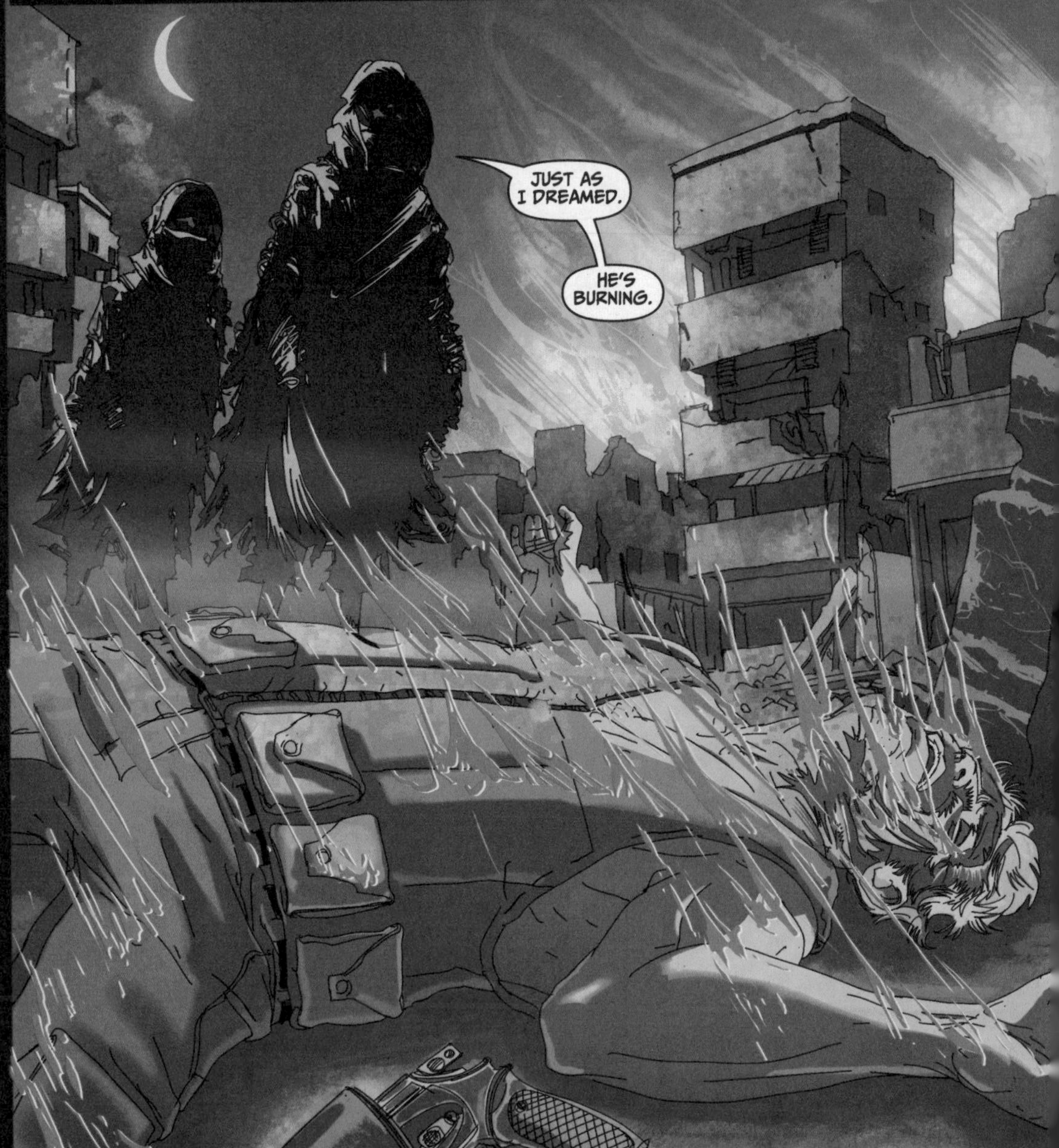
JUST AS I DREAMED.
HE'S BURNING.

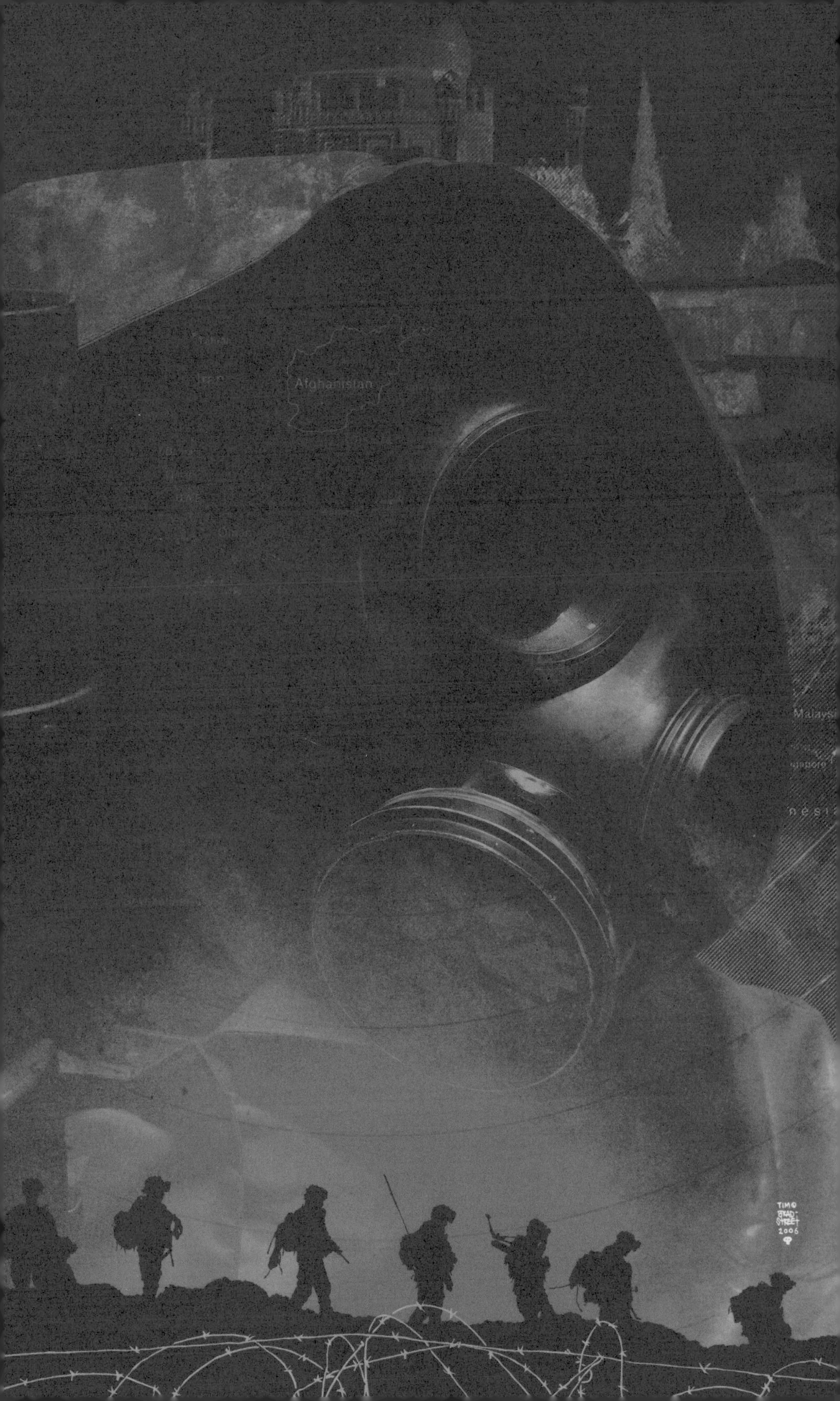
Afghanistan

CHAPTER TWO

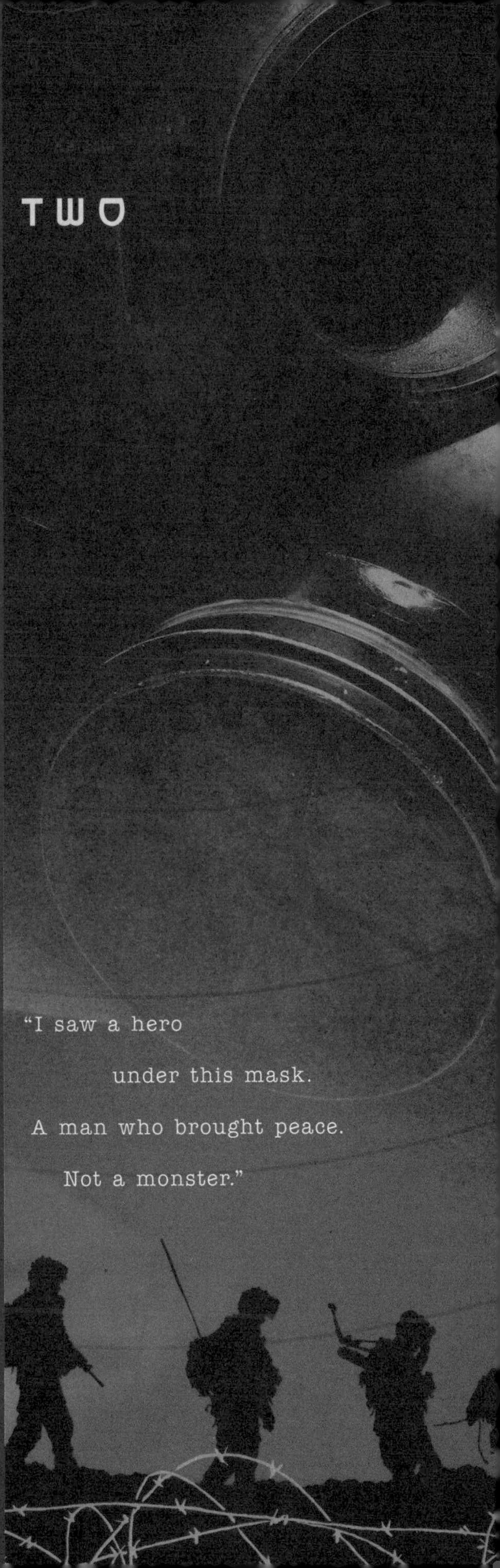

"I saw a hero
under this mask.
A man who brought peace.
Not a monster."

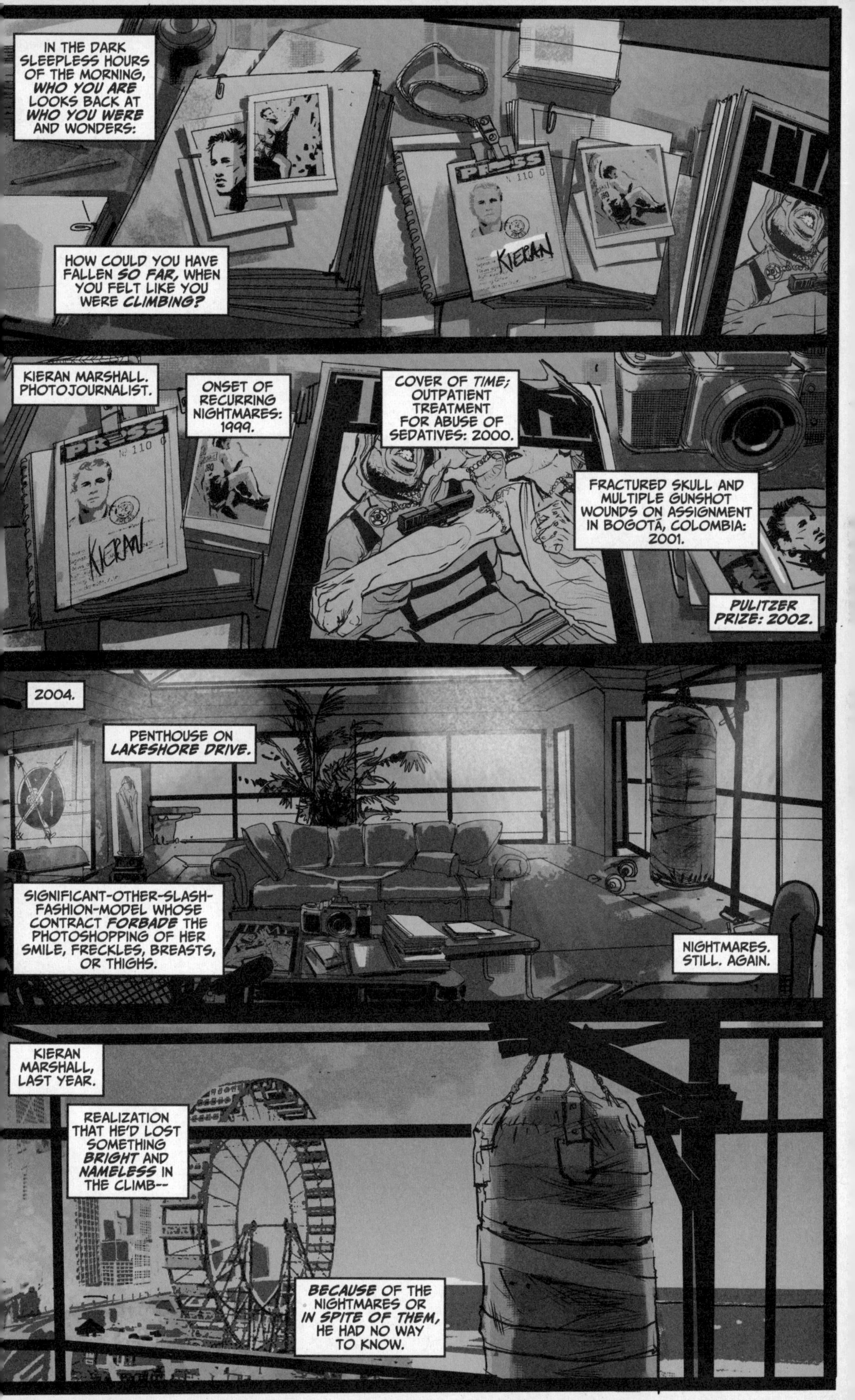

IN THE DARK SLEEPLESS HOURS OF THE MORNING, *WHO YOU ARE* LOOKS BACK AT *WHO YOU WERE* AND WONDERS:
HOW COULD YOU HAVE FALLEN *SO FAR,* WHEN YOU FELT LIKE YOU WERE *CLIMBING?*
PRESS
KIERAN
KIERAN MARSHALL. PHOTOJOURNALIST.
ONSET OF RECURRING NIGHTMARES: 1999.
COVER OF *TIME;* OUTPATIENT TREATMENT FOR ABUSE OF SEDATIVES: 2000.
FRACTURED SKULL AND MULTIPLE GUNSHOT WOUNDS ON ASSIGNMENT IN BOGOTÁ, COLOMBIA: 2001.
PULITZER PRIZE: 2002.
2004.
PENTHOUSE ON *LAKESHORE DRIVE.*
SIGNIFICANT-OTHER-SLASH-FASHION-MODEL WHOSE CONTRACT *FORBADE* THE PHOTOSHOPPING OF HER SMILE, FRECKLES, BREASTS, OR THIGHS.
NIGHTMARES. STILL. AGAIN.
KIERAN MARSHALL, LAST YEAR.
REALIZATION THAT HE'D LOST SOMETHING *BRIGHT* AND *NAMELESS* IN THE CLIMB--
BECAUSE OF THE NIGHTMARES OR *IN SPITE OF THEM,* HE HAD NO WAY TO KNOW.

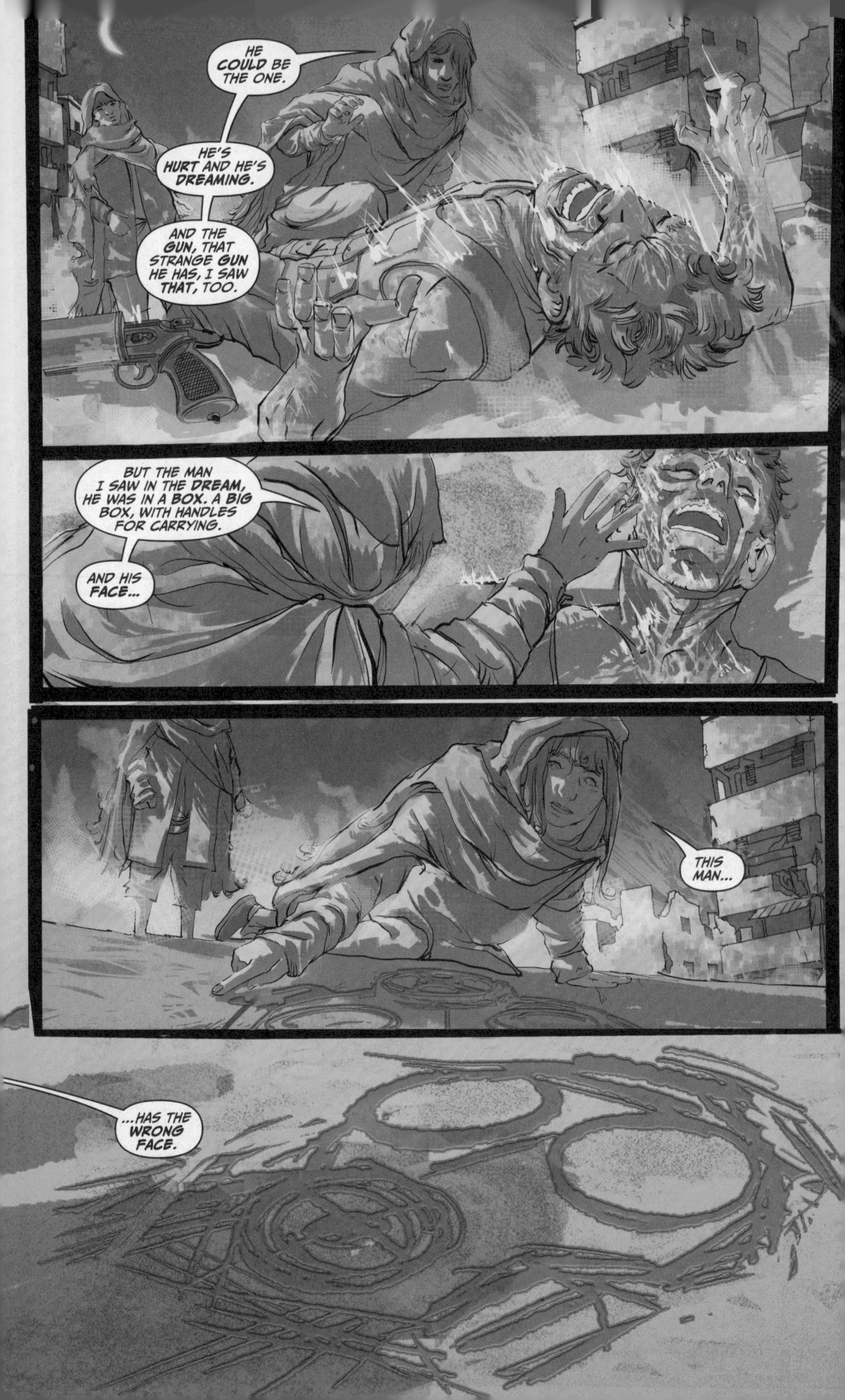
HE COULD BE THE ONE.
HE'S HURT AND HE'S DREAMING.
AND THE GUN, THAT STRANGE GUN HE HAS, I SAW THAT, TOO.
BUT THE MAN I SAW IN THE DREAM, HE WAS IN A BOX. A BIG BOX, WITH HANDLES FOR CARRYING.
AND HIS FACE...
THIS MAN...
...HAS THE WRONG FACE.

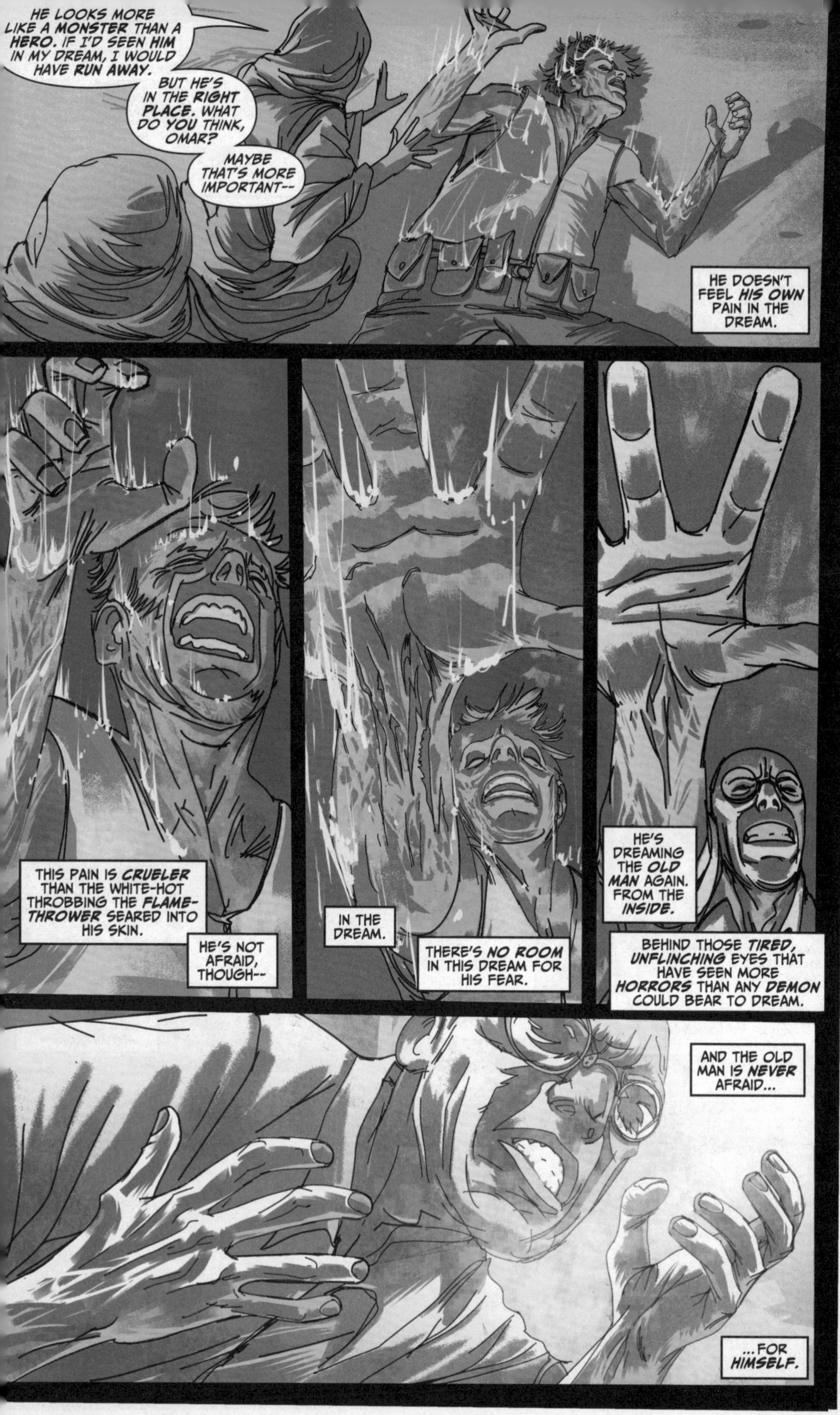
HE LOOKS MORE LIKE A MONSTER THAN A HERO. IF I'D SEEN HIM IN MY DREAM, I WOULD HAVE RUN AWAY.
BUT HE'S IN THE RIGHT PLACE. WHAT DO YOU THINK, OMAR?
MAYBE THAT'S MORE IMPORTANT--
HE DOESN'T FEEL HIS OWN PAIN IN THE DREAM.
THIS PAIN IS CRUELER THAN THE WHITE-HOT THROBBING THE FLAME-THROWER SEARED INTO HIS SKIN.
HE'S NOT AFRAID, THOUGH--
IN THE DREAM.
THERE'S NO ROOM IN THIS DREAM FOR HIS FEAR.
HE'S DREAMING THE OLD MAN AGAIN. FROM THE INSIDE.
BEHIND THOSE TIRED, UNFLINCHING EYES THAT HAVE SEEN MORE HORRORS THAN ANY DEMON COULD BEAR TO DREAM.
AND THE OLD MAN IS NEVER AFRAID...
...FOR HIMSELF.

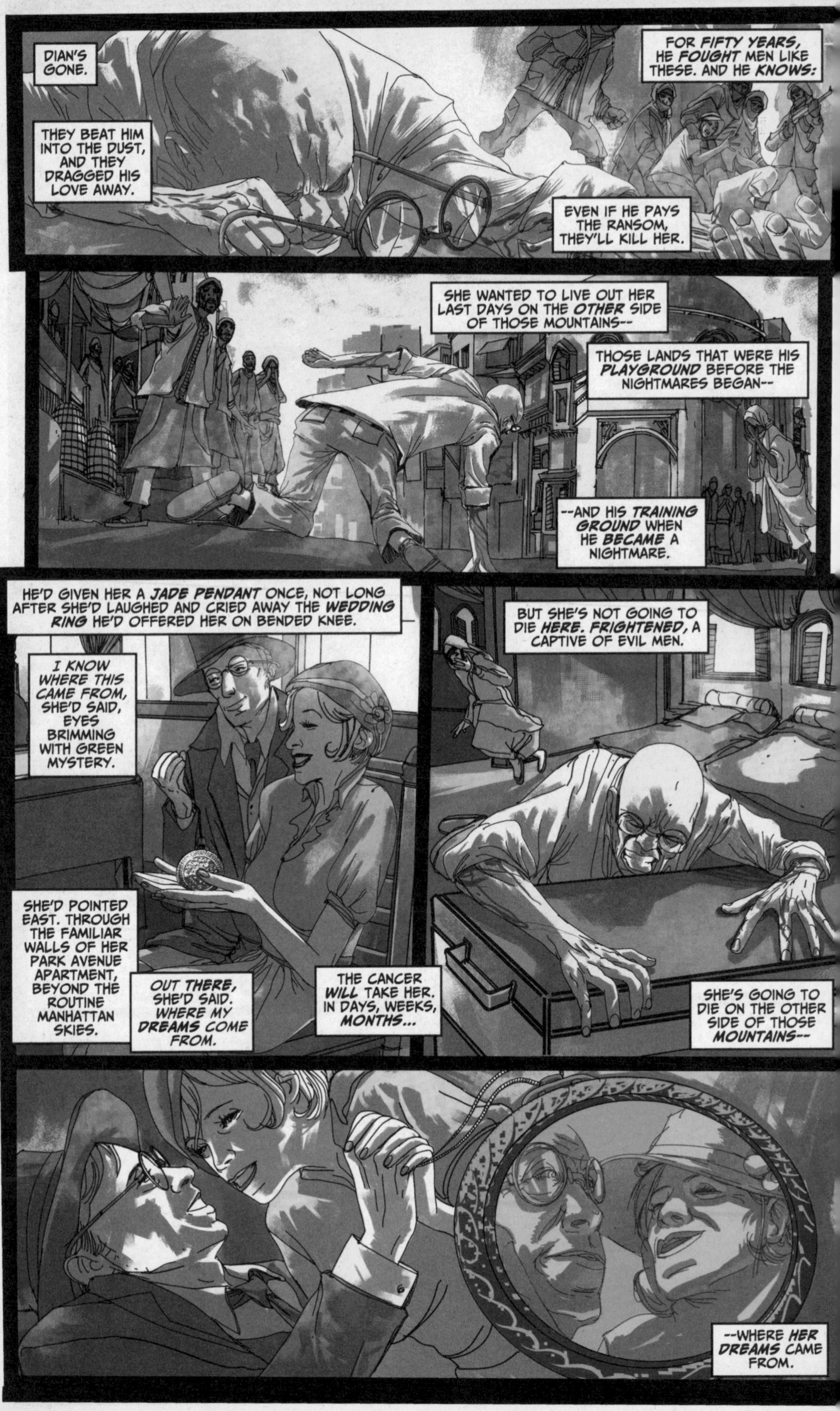

DIAN'S GONE.
THEY BEAT HIM INTO THE DUST, AND THEY DRAGGED HIS LOVE AWAY.
FOR FIFTY YEARS, HE FOUGHT MEN LIKE THESE. AND HE KNOWS:
EVEN IF HE PAYS THE RANSOM, THEY'LL KILL HER.
SHE WANTED TO LIVE OUT HER LAST DAYS ON THE OTHER SIDE OF THOSE MOUNTAINS--
THOSE LANDS THAT WERE HIS PLAYGROUND BEFORE THE NIGHTMARES BEGAN--
--AND HIS TRAINING GROUND WHEN HE BECAME A NIGHTMARE.
HE'D GIVEN HER A JADE PENDANT ONCE, NOT LONG AFTER SHE'D LAUGHED AND CRIED AWAY THE WEDDING RING HE'D OFFERED HER ON BENDED KNEE.
I KNOW WHERE THIS CAME FROM, SHE'D SAID, EYES BRIMMING WITH GREEN MYSTERY.
SHE'D POINTED EAST. THROUGH THE FAMILIAR WALLS OF HER PARK AVENUE APARTMENT, BEYOND THE ROUTINE MANHATTAN SKIES.
OUT THERE, SHE'D SAID. WHERE MY DREAMS COME FROM.
THE CANCER WILL TAKE HER. IN DAYS, WEEKS, MONTHS...
BUT SHE'S NOT GOING TO DIE HERE. FRIGHTENED, A CAPTIVE OF EVIL MEN.
SHE'S GOING TO DIE ON THE OTHER SIDE OF THOSE MOUNTAINS--
--WHERE HER DREAMS CAME FROM.

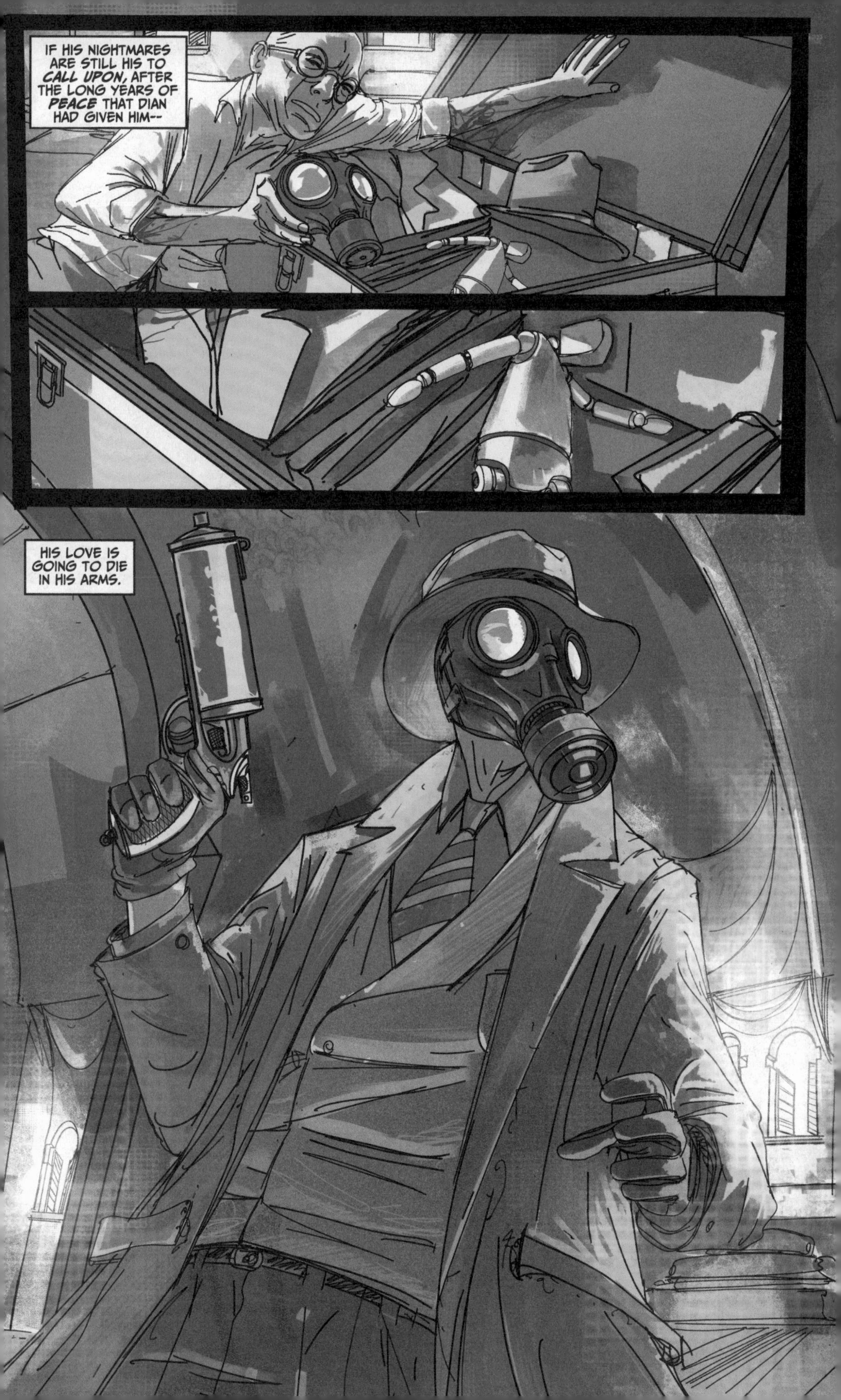
IF HIS NIGHTMARES ARE STILL HIS TO CALL UPON, AFTER THE LONG YEARS OF PEACE THAT DIAN HAD GIVEN HIM--
HIS LOVE IS GOING TO DIE IN HIS ARMS.

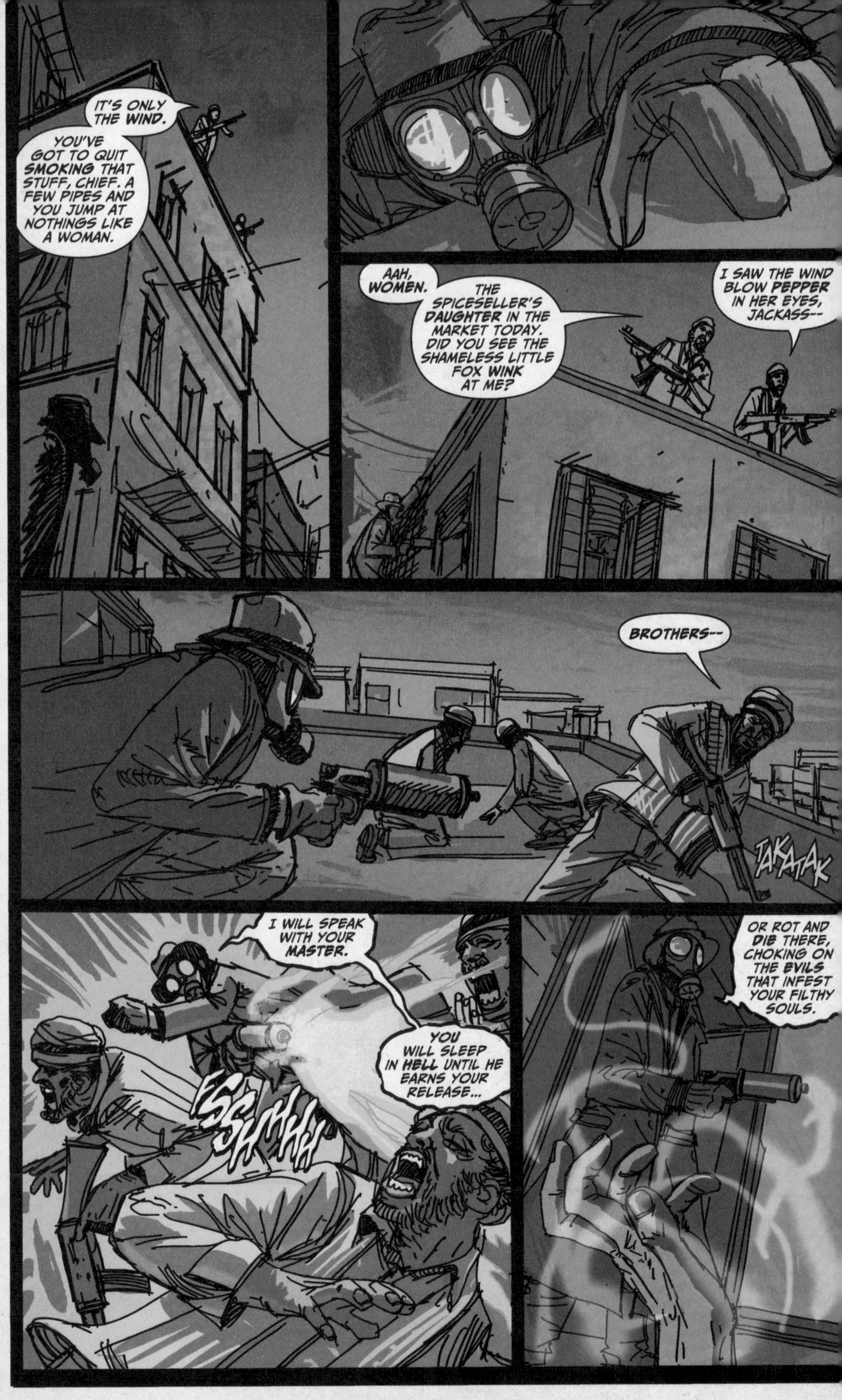
IT'S ONLY THE WIND.
YOU'VE GOT TO QUIT SMOKING THAT STUFF, CHIEF. A FEW PIPES AND YOU JUMP AT NOTHINGS LIKE A WOMAN.
AAH, WOMEN.
THE SPICESELLER'S DAUGHTER IN THE MARKET TODAY. DID YOU SEE THE SHAMELESS LITTLE FOX WINK AT ME?
I SAW THE WIND BLOW PEPPER IN HER EYES, JACKASS--
BROTHERS--
TAKATAK
I WILL SPEAK WITH YOUR MASTER.
YOU WILL SLEEP IN HELL UNTIL HE EARNS YOUR RELEASE...
FSSHHHH
OR ROT AND DIE THERE, CHOKING ON THE EVILS THAT INFEST YOUR FILTHY SOULS.

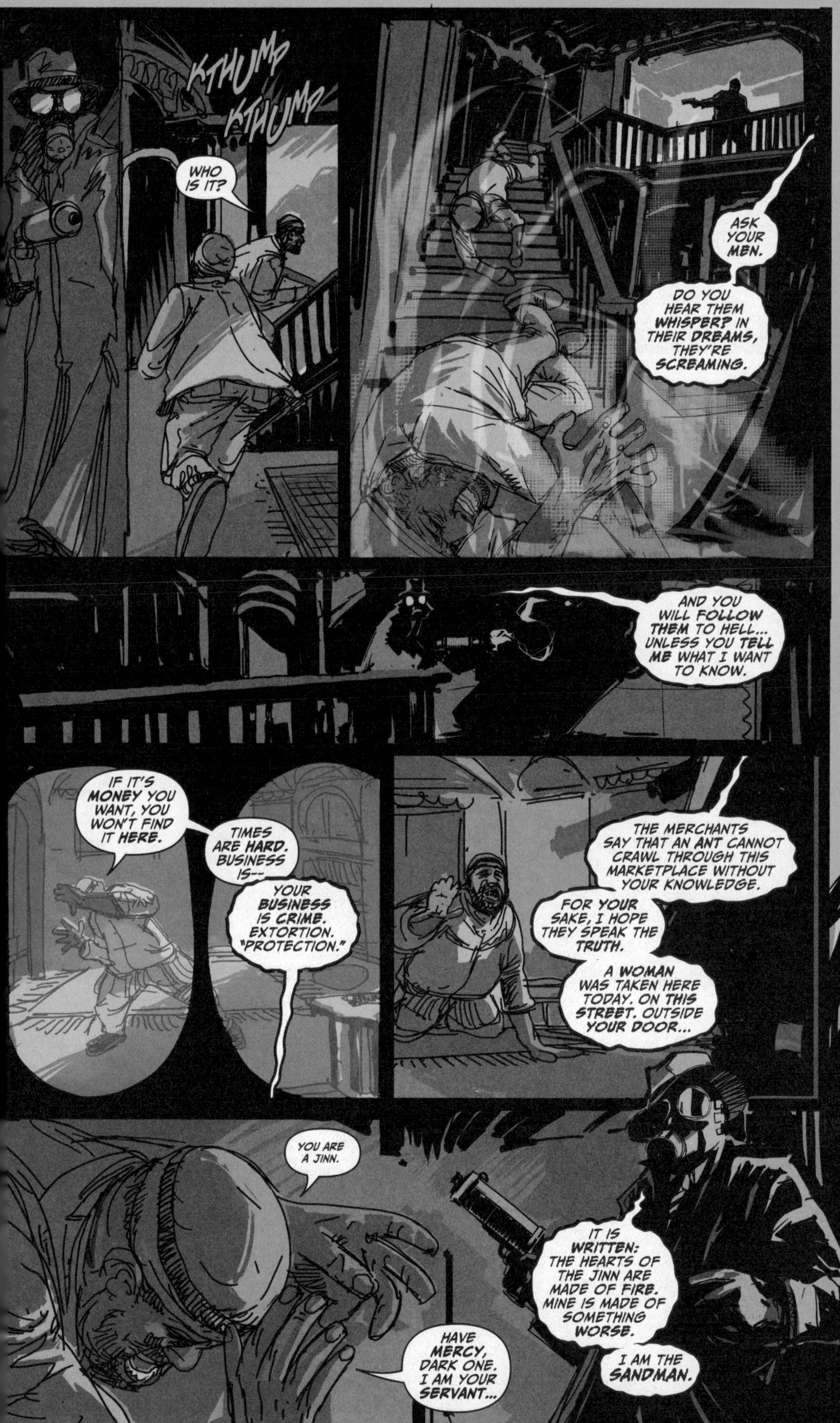
KTHUMP
KTHUMP
WHO IS IT?
ASK YOUR MEN.
DO YOU HEAR THEM WHISPER? IN THEIR DREAMS, THEY'RE SCREAMING.
AND YOU WILL FOLLOW THEM TO HELL... UNLESS YOU TELL ME WHAT I WANT TO KNOW.
IF IT'S MONEY YOU WANT, YOU WON'T FIND IT HERE.
TIMES ARE HARD. BUSINESS IS--
YOUR BUSINESS IS CRIME. EXTORTION. "PROTECTION."
THE MERCHANTS SAY THAT AN ANT CANNOT CRAWL THROUGH THIS MARKETPLACE WITHOUT YOUR KNOWLEDGE.
FOR YOUR SAKE, I HOPE THEY SPEAK THE TRUTH.
A WOMAN WAS TAKEN HERE TODAY. ON THIS STREET. OUTSIDE YOUR DOOR...
YOU ARE A JINN.
HAVE MERCY, DARK ONE. I AM YOUR SERVANT...
IT IS WRITTEN: THE HEARTS OF THE JINN ARE MADE OF FIRE. MINE IS MADE OF SOMETHING WORSE.
I AM THE SANDMAN.

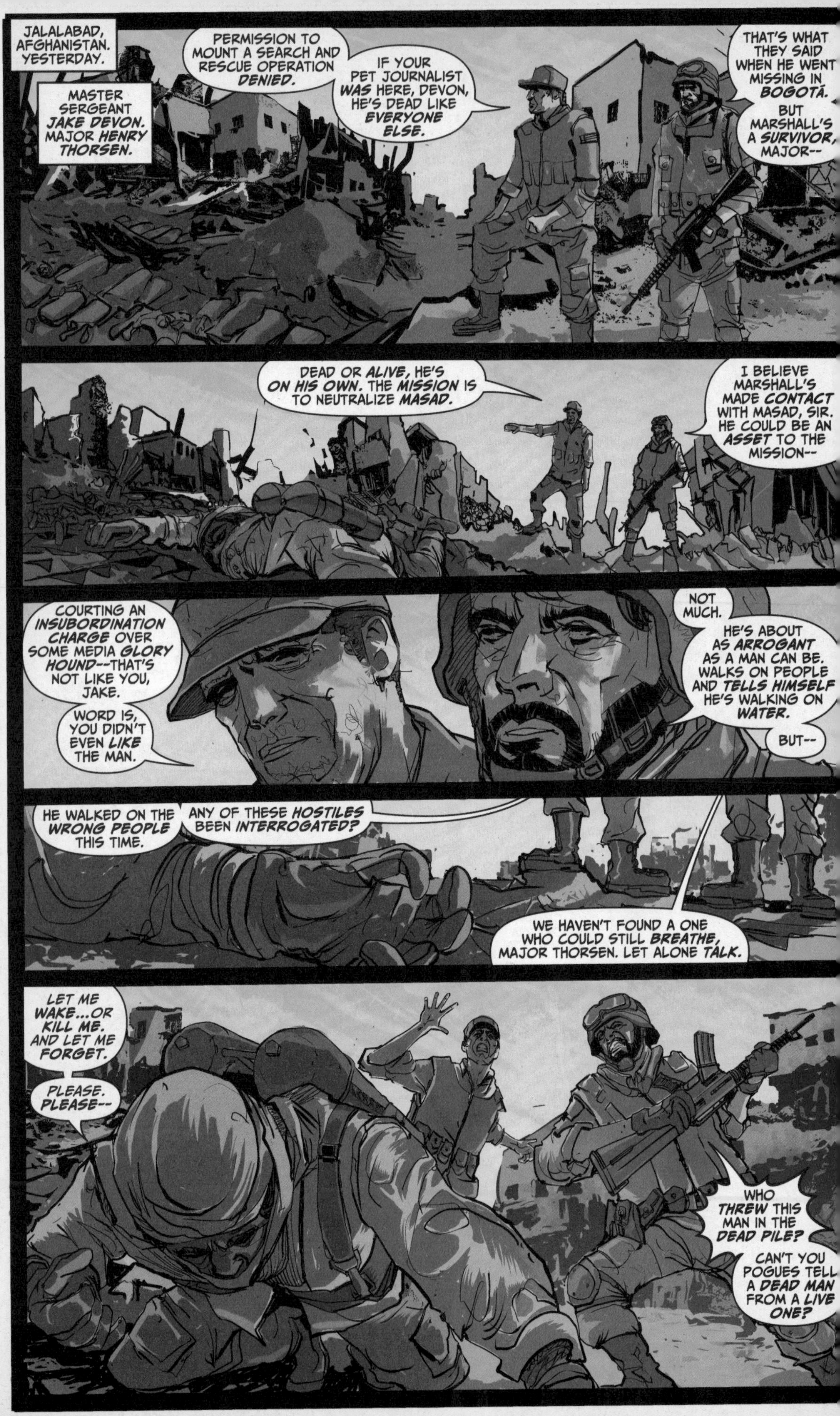

JALALABAD, AFGHANISTAN. YESTERDAY.
MASTER SERGEANT JAKE DEVON. MAJOR HENRY THORSEN.
PERMISSION TO MOUNT A SEARCH AND RESCUE OPERATION DENIED.
IF YOUR PET JOURNALIST WAS HERE, DEVON, HE'S DEAD LIKE EVERYONE ELSE.
THAT'S WHAT THEY SAID WHEN HE WENT MISSING IN BOGOTÁ.
BUT MARSHALL'S A SURVIVOR, MAJOR--
DEAD OR ALIVE, HE'S ON HIS OWN. THE MISSION IS TO NEUTRALIZE MASAD.
I BELIEVE MARSHALL'S MADE CONTACT WITH MASAD, SIR. HE COULD BE AN ASSET TO THE MISSION--
COURTING AN INSUBORDINATION CHARGE OVER SOME MEDIA GLORY HOUND--THAT'S NOT LIKE YOU, JAKE.
WORD IS, YOU DIDN'T EVEN LIKE THE MAN.
NOT MUCH.
HE'S ABOUT AS ARROGANT AS A MAN CAN BE. WALKS ON PEOPLE AND TELLS HIMSELF HE'S WALKING ON WATER.
BUT--
HE WALKED ON THE WRONG PEOPLE THIS TIME.
ANY OF THESE HOSTILES BEEN INTERROGATED?
WE HAVEN'T FOUND A ONE WHO COULD STILL BREATHE, MAJOR THORSEN. LET ALONE TALK.
LET ME WAKE...OR KILL ME. AND LET ME FORGET.
PLEASE. PLEASE--
WHO THREW THIS MAN IN THE DEAD PILE?
CAN'T YOU POGUES TELL A DEAD MAN FROM A LIVE ONE?

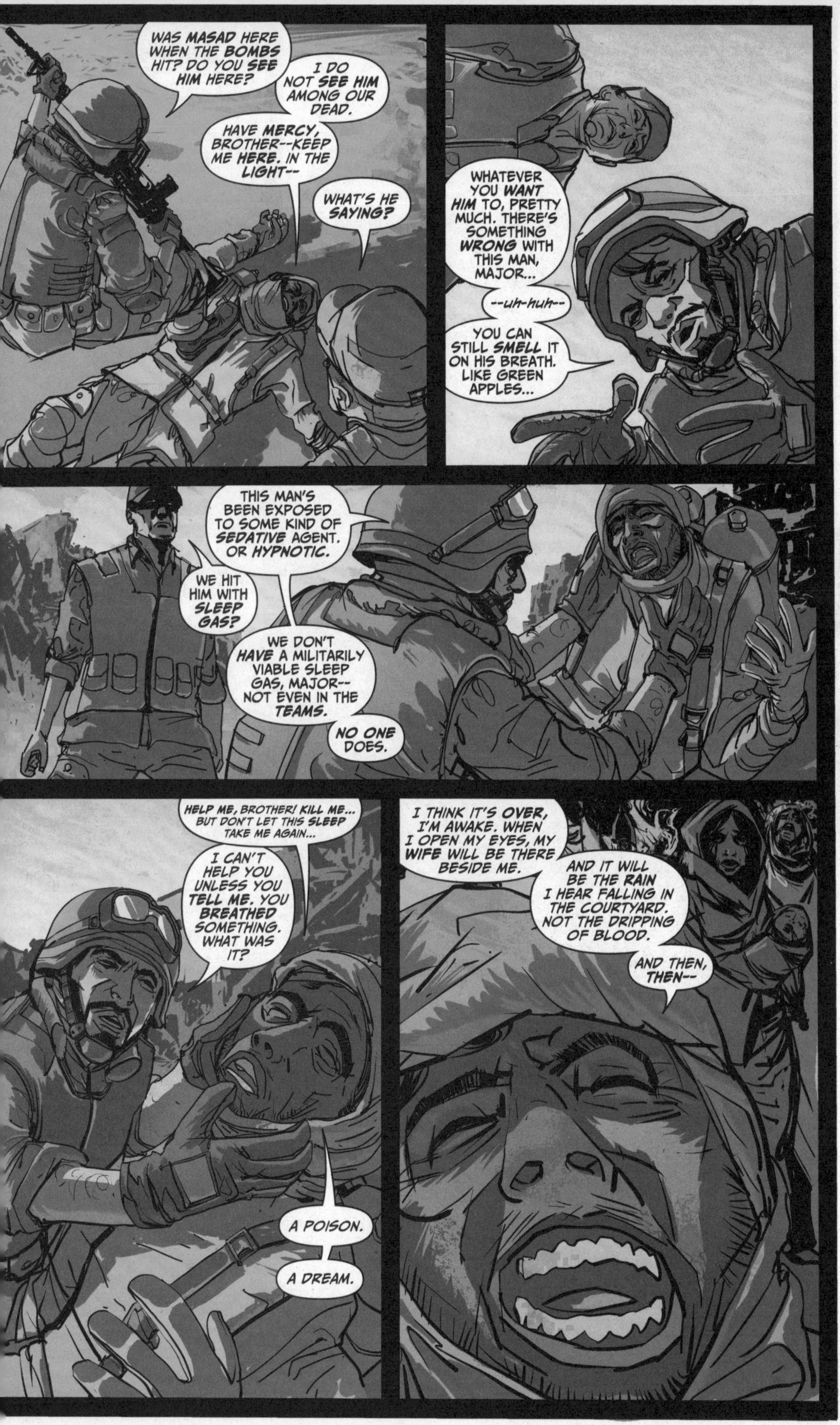
WAS MASAD HERE WHEN THE BOMBS HIT? DO YOU SEE HIM HERE?
I DO NOT SEE HIM AMONG OUR DEAD.
HAVE MERCY, BROTHER--KEEP ME HERE. IN THE LIGHT--
WHAT'S HE SAYING?
WHATEVER YOU WANT HIM TO, PRETTY MUCH. THERE'S SOMETHING WRONG WITH THIS MAN, MAJOR...
--uh-huh--
YOU CAN STILL SMELL IT ON HIS BREATH. LIKE GREEN APPLES...
THIS MAN'S BEEN EXPOSED TO SOME KIND OF SEDATIVE AGENT. OR HYPNOTIC.
WE HIT HIM WITH SLEEP GAS?
WE DON'T HAVE A MILITARILY VIABLE SLEEP GAS, MAJOR-- NOT EVEN IN THE TEAMS.
NO ONE DOES.
HELP ME, BROTHER! KILL ME... BUT DON'T LET THIS SLEEP TAKE ME AGAIN...
I CAN'T HELP YOU UNLESS YOU TELL ME. YOU BREATHED SOMETHING. WHAT WAS IT?
A POISON.
A DREAM.
I THINK IT'S OVER, I'M AWAKE. WHEN I OPEN MY EYES, MY WIFE WILL BE THERE BESIDE ME.
AND IT WILL BE THE RAIN I HEAR FALLING IN THE COURTYARD. NOT THE DRIPPING OF BLOOD.
AND THEN, THEN--

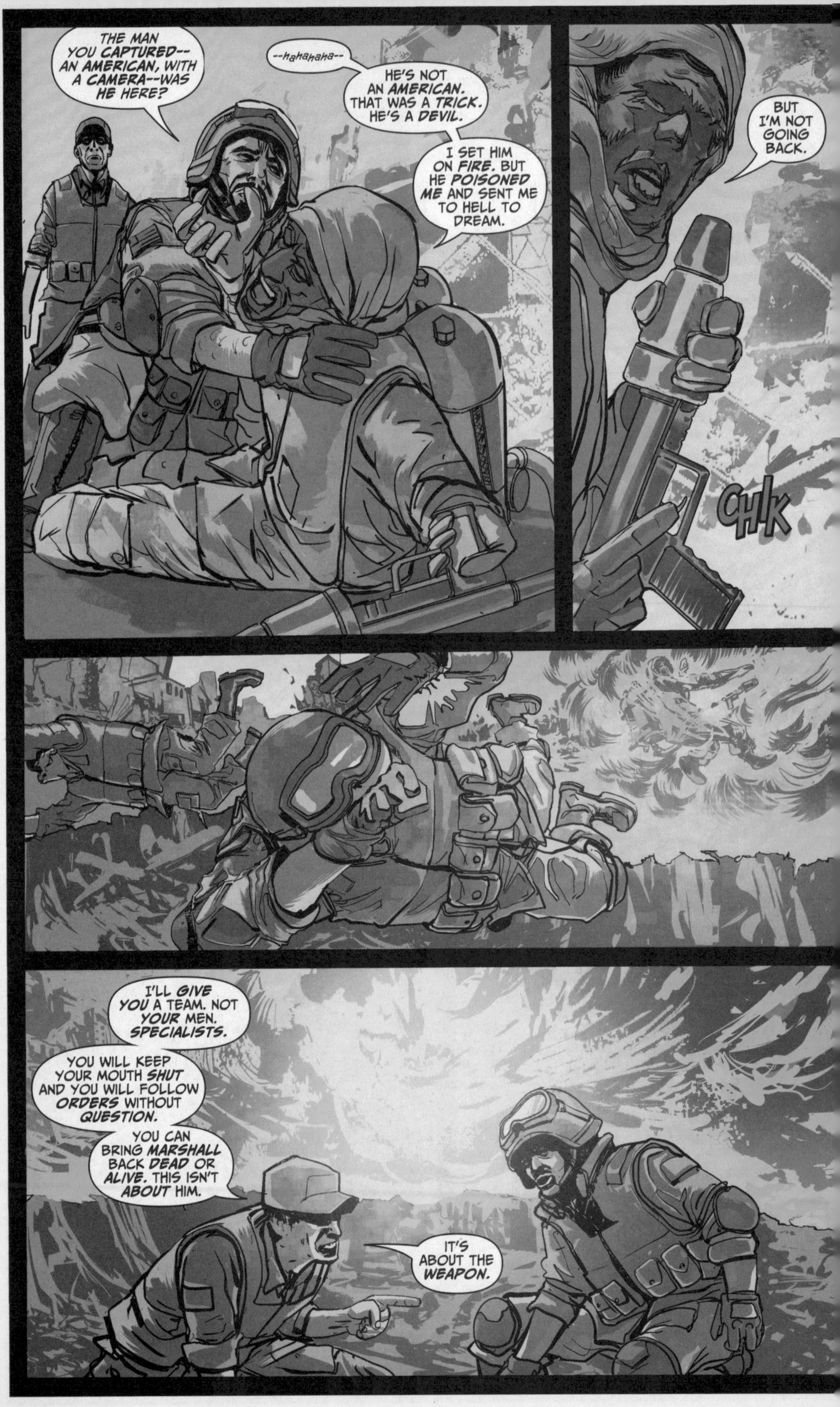
THE MAN YOU CAPTURED-- AN AMERICAN, WITH A CAMERA--WAS HE HERE?
--hahahaha--
HE'S NOT AN AMERICAN. THAT WAS A TRICK. HE'S A DEVIL.
I SET HIM ON FIRE. BUT HE POISONED ME AND SENT ME TO HELL TO DREAM.
BUT I'M NOT GOING BACK.
CHIK
I'LL GIVE YOU A TEAM. NOT YOUR MEN. SPECIALISTS.
YOU WILL KEEP YOUR MOUTH SHUT AND YOU WILL FOLLOW ORDERS WITHOUT QUESTION.
YOU CAN BRING MARSHALL BACK DEAD OR ALIVE. THIS ISN'T ABOUT HIM.
IT'S ABOUT THE WEAPON.

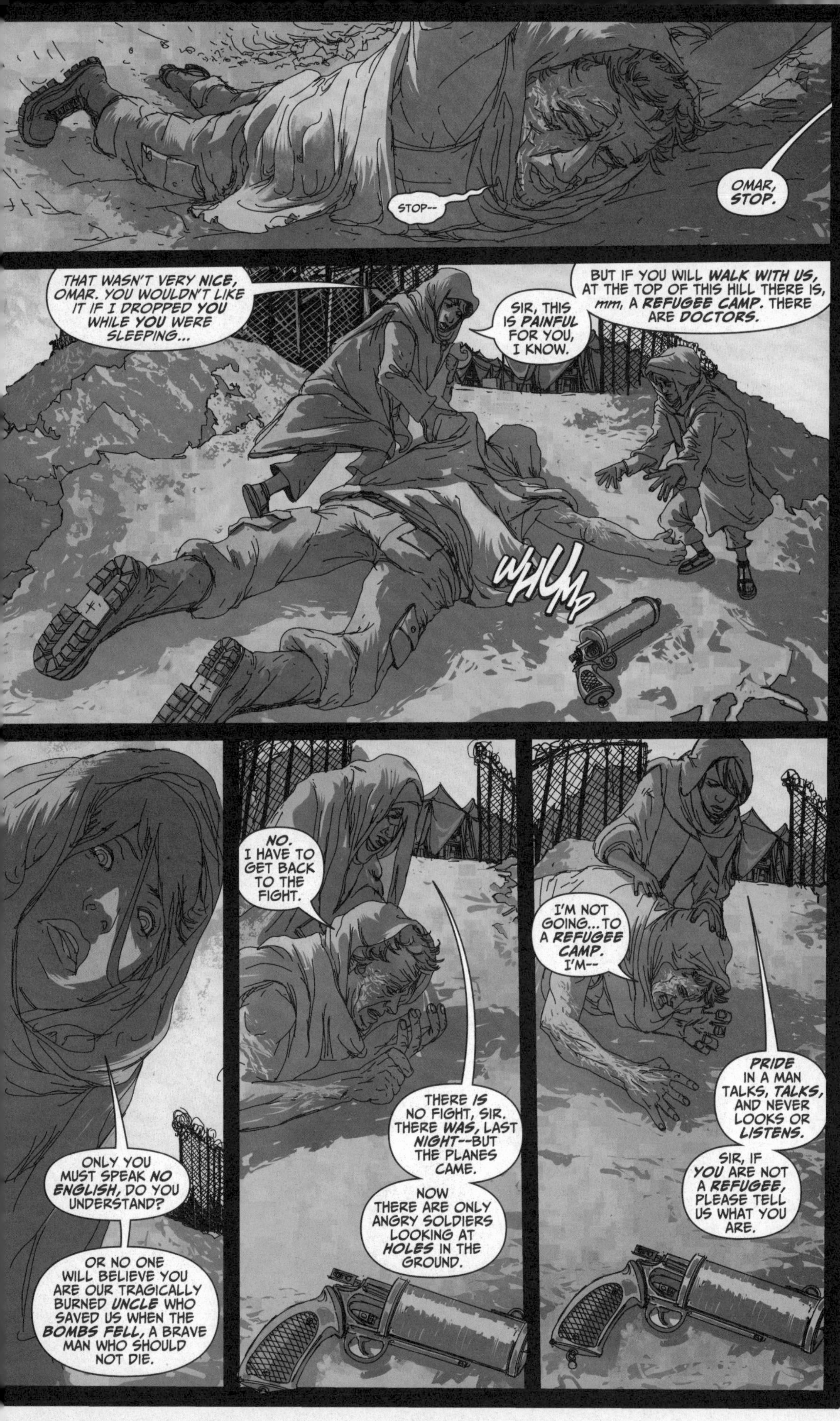
STOP--
OMAR, STOP.
THAT WASN'T VERY NICE, OMAR. YOU WOULDN'T LIKE IT IF I DROPPED YOU WHILE YOU WERE SLEEPING...
SIR, THIS IS PAINFUL FOR YOU, I KNOW.
BUT IF YOU WILL WALK WITH US, AT THE TOP OF THIS HILL THERE IS, mm, A REFUGEE CAMP. THERE ARE DOCTORS.
WHUMP
ONLY YOU MUST SPEAK NO ENGLISH, DO YOU UNDERSTAND?
OR NO ONE WILL BELIEVE YOU ARE OUR TRAGICALLY BURNED UNCLE WHO SAVED US WHEN THE BOMBS FELL, A BRAVE MAN WHO SHOULD NOT DIE.
NO. I HAVE TO GET BACK TO THE FIGHT.
THERE IS NO FIGHT, SIR. THERE WAS, LAST NIGHT--BUT THE PLANES CAME.
NOW THERE ARE ONLY ANGRY SOLDIERS LOOKING AT HOLES IN THE GROUND.
I'M NOT GOING...TO A REFUGEE CAMP. I'M--
PRIDE IN A MAN TALKS, TALKS, AND NEVER LOOKS OR LISTENS.
SIR, IF YOU ARE NOT A REFUGEE, PLEASE TELL US WHAT YOU ARE.

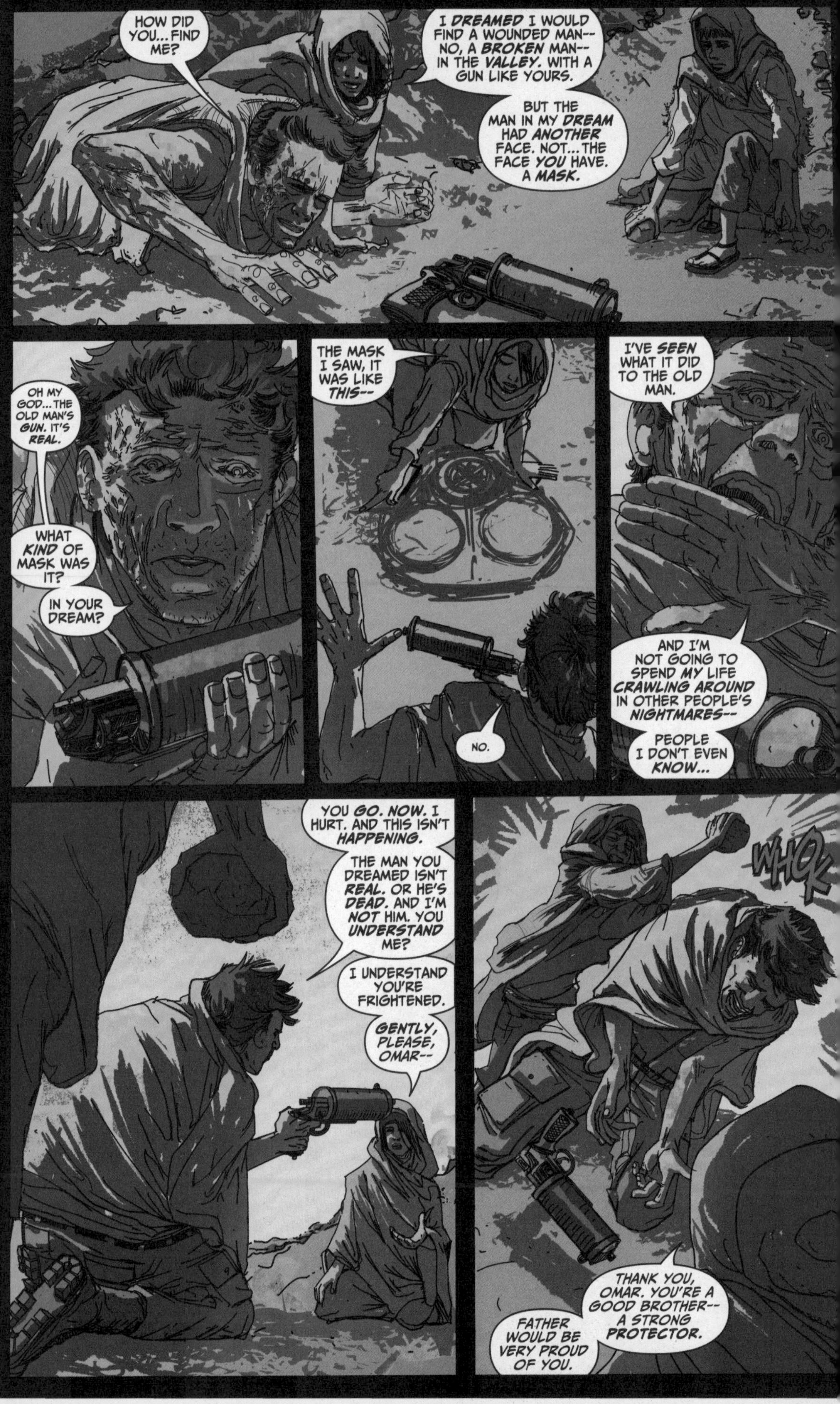

HOW DID YOU... FIND ME?
I DREAMED I WOULD FIND A WOUNDED MAN-- NO, A BROKEN MAN-- IN THE VALLEY. WITH A GUN LIKE YOURS.
BUT THE MAN IN MY DREAM HAD ANOTHER FACE. NOT... THE FACE YOU HAVE. A MASK.
OH MY GOD... THE OLD MAN'S GUN. IT'S REAL.
WHAT KIND OF MASK WAS IT?
IN YOUR DREAM?
THE MASK I SAW, IT WAS LIKE THIS--
NO.
I'VE SEEN WHAT IT DID TO THE OLD MAN.
AND I'M NOT GOING TO SPEND MY LIFE CRAWLING AROUND IN OTHER PEOPLE'S NIGHTMARES--
PEOPLE I DON'T EVEN KNOW...
YOU GO. NOW. I HURT. AND THIS ISN'T HAPPENING.
THE MAN YOU DREAMED ISN'T REAL. OR HE'S DEAD. AND I'M NOT HIM. YOU UNDERSTAND ME?
I UNDERSTAND YOU'RE FRIGHTENED.
GENTLY, PLEASE, OMAR--
WHQK
THANK YOU, OMAR. YOU'RE A GOOD BROTHER-- A STRONG PROTECTOR.
FATHER WOULD BE VERY PROUD OF YOU.

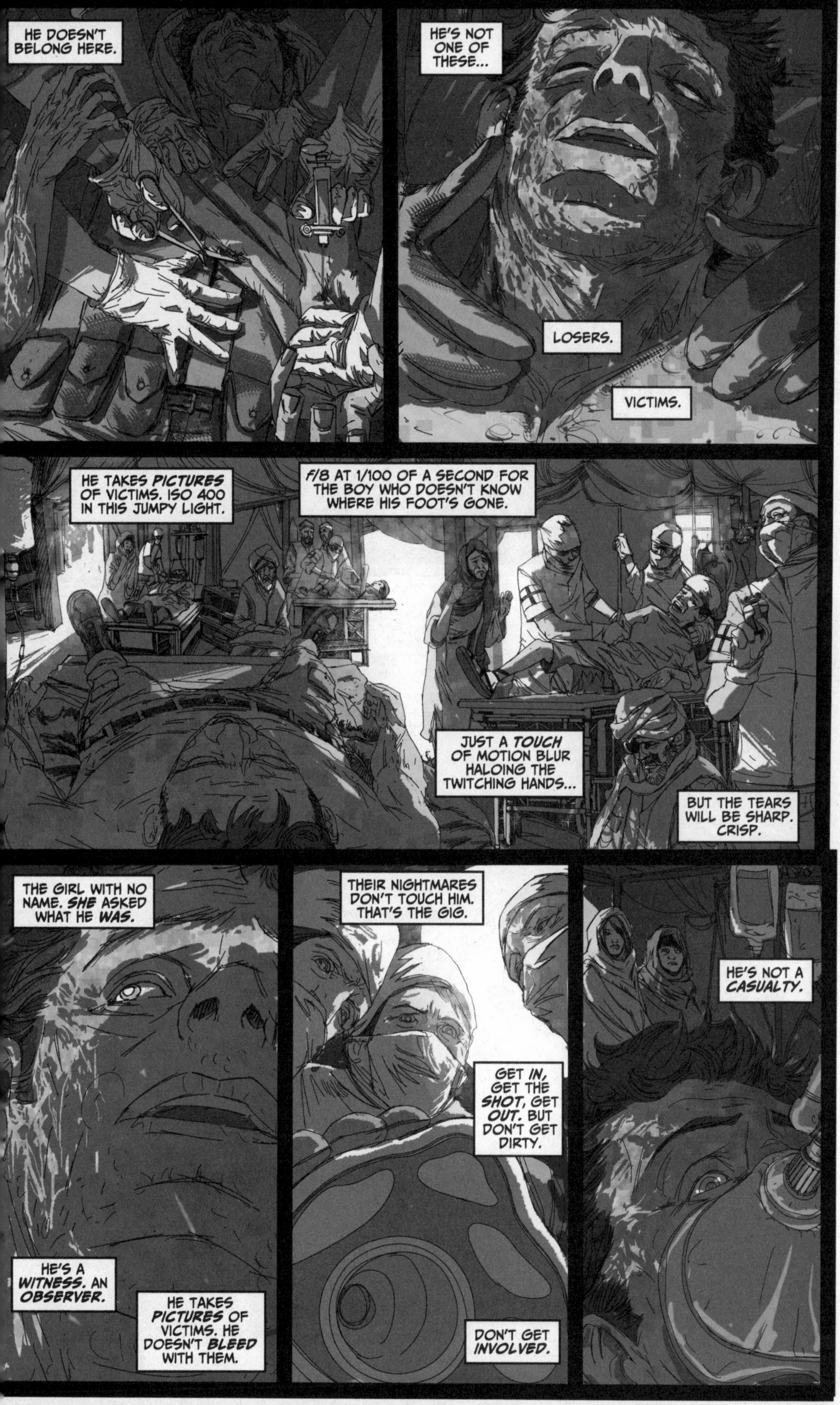
HE DOESN'T BELONG HERE.
HE'S NOT ONE OF THESE...
LOSERS.
VICTIMS.
HE TAKES PICTURES OF VICTIMS. ISO 400 IN THIS JUMPY LIGHT.
F/8 AT 1/100 OF A SECOND FOR THE BOY WHO DOESN'T KNOW WHERE HIS FOOT'S GONE.
JUST A TOUCH OF MOTION BLUR HALOING THE TWITCHING HANDS...
BUT THE TEARS WILL BE SHARP. CRISP.
THE GIRL WITH NO NAME. SHE ASKED WHAT HE WAS.
HE'S A WITNESS. AN OBSERVER.
HE TAKES PICTURES OF VICTIMS. HE DOESN'T BLEED WITH THEM.
THEIR NIGHTMARES DON'T TOUCH HIM. THAT'S THE GIG.
GET IN, GET THE SHOT, GET OUT. BUT DON'T GET DIRTY.
DON'T GET INVOLVED.
HE'S NOT A CASUALTY.

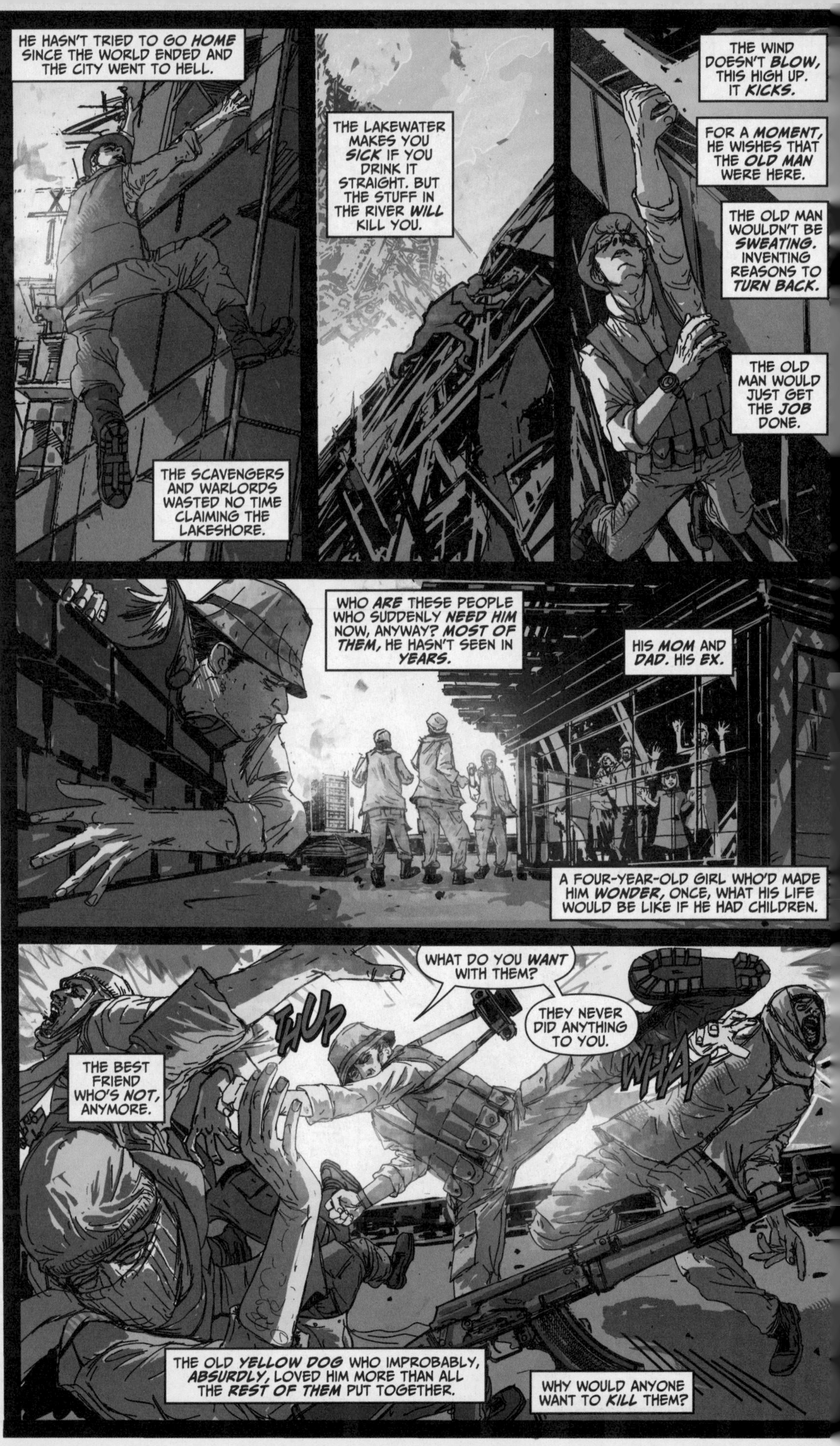
HE HASN'T TRIED TO GO HOME SINCE THE WORLD ENDED AND THE CITY WENT TO HELL.
THE SCAVENGERS AND WARLORDS WASTED NO TIME CLAIMING THE LAKESHORE.
THE LAKEWATER MAKES YOU SICK IF YOU DRINK IT STRAIGHT. BUT THE STUFF IN THE RIVER WILL KILL YOU.
THE WIND DOESN'T BLOW, THIS HIGH UP. IT KICKS.
FOR A MOMENT, HE WISHES THAT THE OLD MAN WERE HERE.
THE OLD MAN WOULDN'T BE SWEATING. INVENTING REASONS TO TURN BACK.
THE OLD MAN WOULD JUST GET THE JOB DONE.
WHO ARE THESE PEOPLE WHO SUDDENLY NEED HIM NOW, ANYWAY? MOST OF THEM, HE HASN'T SEEN IN YEARS.
HIS MOM AND DAD. HIS EX.
A FOUR-YEAR-OLD GIRL WHO'D MADE HIM WONDER, ONCE, WHAT HIS LIFE WOULD BE LIKE IF HE HAD CHILDREN.
THE BEST FRIEND WHO'S NOT, ANYMORE.
WHAT DO YOU WANT WITH THEM?
THUP
THEY NEVER DID ANYTHING TO YOU.
WHAP
THE OLD YELLOW DOG WHO IMPROBABLY, ABSURDLY, LOVED HIM MORE THAN ALL THE REST OF THEM PUT TOGETHER.
WHY WOULD ANYONE WANT TO KILL THEM?

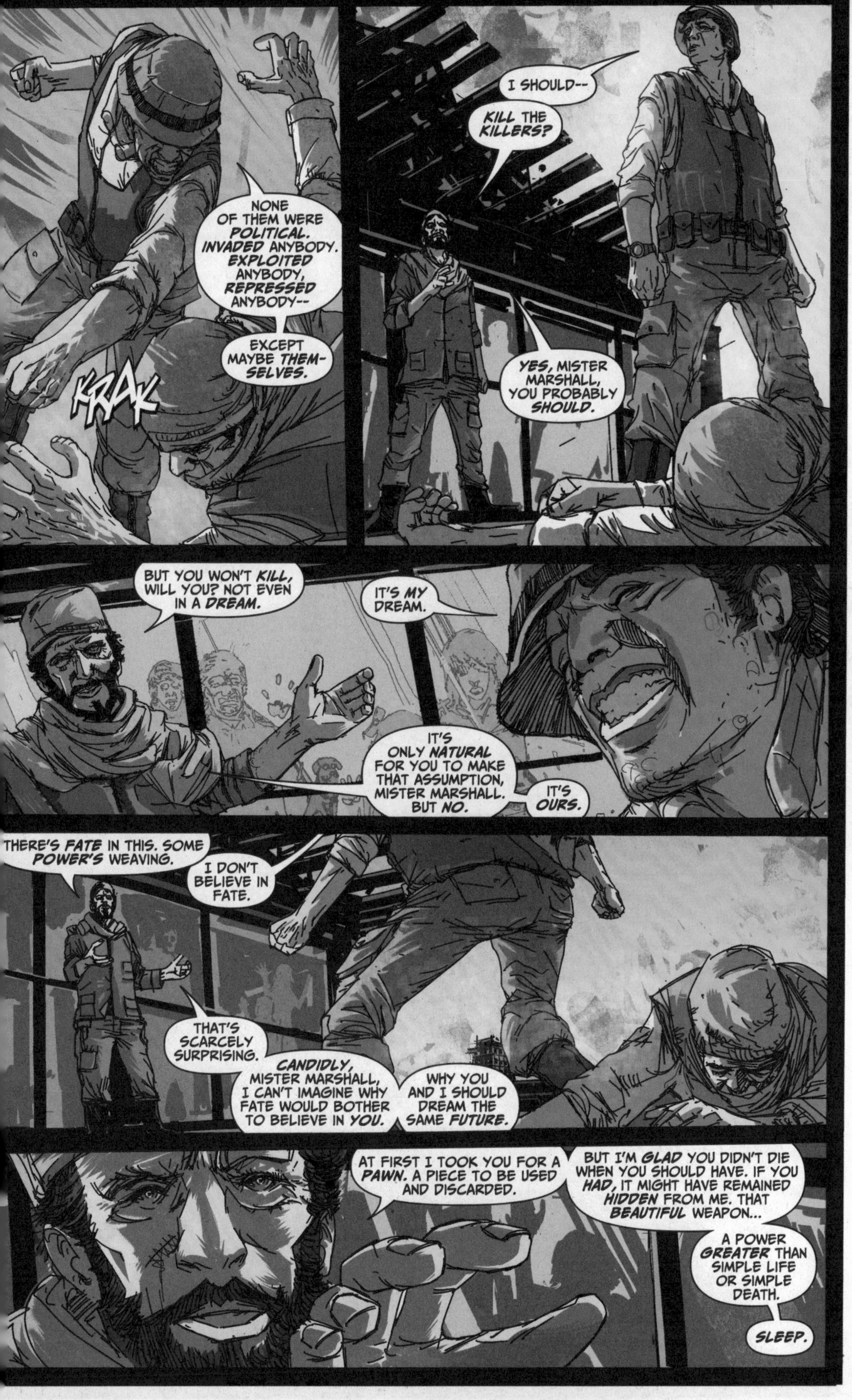
NONE OF THEM WERE POLITICAL. INVADED ANYBODY. EXPLOITED ANYBODY, REPRESSED ANYBODY--
EXCEPT MAYBE THEMSELVES.
KRAK
I SHOULD--
KILL THE KILLERS?
YES, MISTER MARSHALL, YOU PROBABLY SHOULD.
BUT YOU WON'T KILL, WILL YOU? NOT EVEN IN A DREAM.
IT'S MY DREAM.
IT'S ONLY NATURAL FOR YOU TO MAKE THAT ASSUMPTION, MISTER MARSHALL. BUT NO.
IT'S OURS.
THERE'S FATE IN THIS. SOME POWER'S WEAVING.
I DON'T BELIEVE IN FATE.
THAT'S SCARCELY SURPRISING.
CANDIDLY, MISTER MARSHALL, I CAN'T IMAGINE WHY FATE WOULD BOTHER TO BELIEVE IN YOU.
WHY YOU AND I SHOULD DREAM THE SAME FUTURE.
AT FIRST I TOOK YOU FOR A PAWN. A PIECE TO BE USED AND DISCARDED.
BUT I'M GLAD YOU DIDN'T DIE WHEN YOU SHOULD HAVE. IF YOU HAD, IT MIGHT HAVE REMAINED HIDDEN FROM ME. THAT BEAUTIFUL WEAPON...
A POWER GREATER THAN SIMPLE LIFE OR SIMPLE DEATH.
SLEEP.

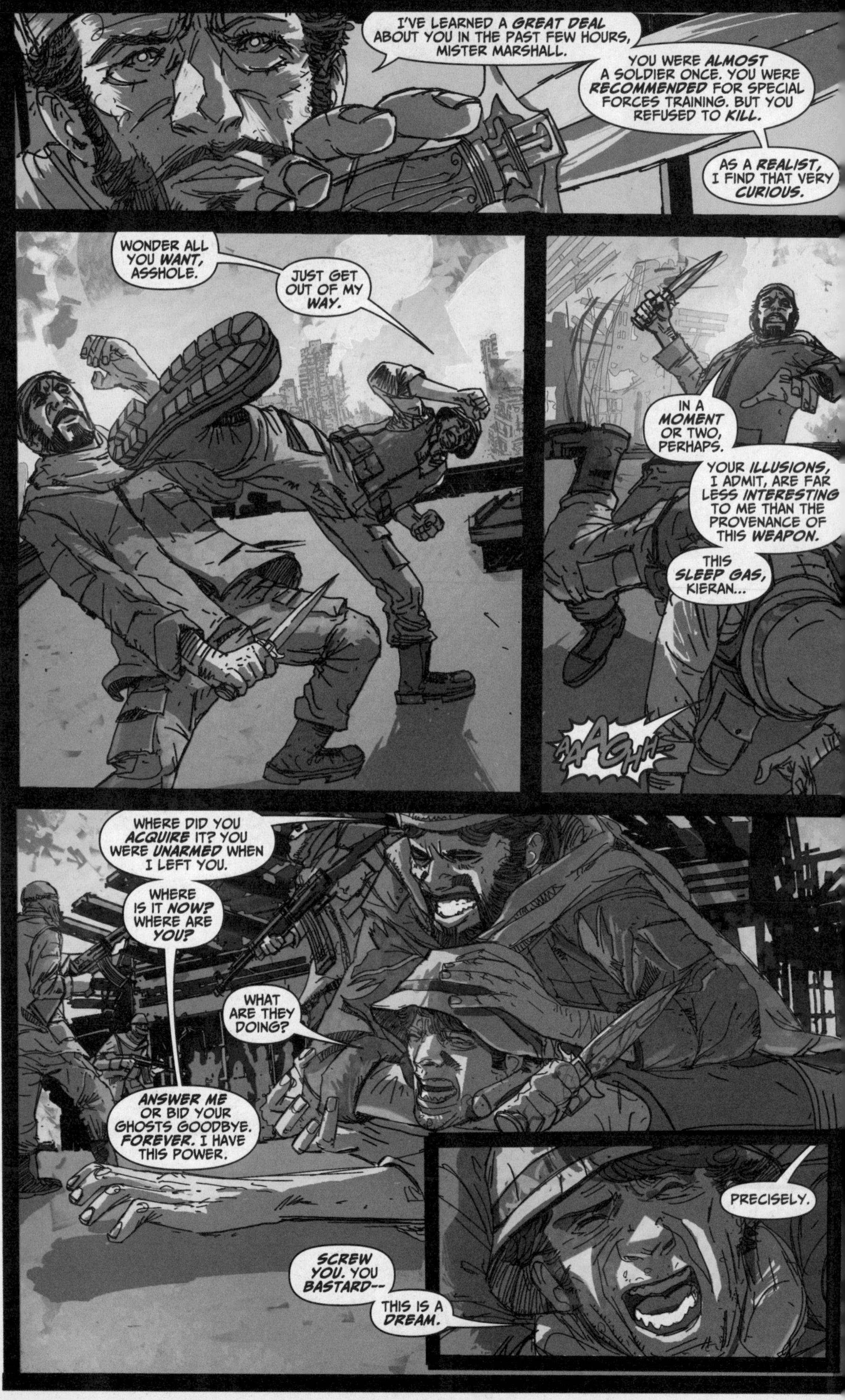
I'VE LEARNED A GREAT DEAL ABOUT YOU IN THE PAST FEW HOURS, MISTER MARSHALL.
YOU WERE ALMOST A SOLDIER ONCE. YOU WERE RECOMMENDED FOR SPECIAL FORCES TRAINING. BUT YOU REFUSED TO KILL.
AS A REALIST, I FIND THAT VERY CURIOUS.
WONDER ALL YOU WANT, ASSHOLE.
JUST GET OUT OF MY WAY.
IN A MOMENT OR TWO, PERHAPS.
YOUR ILLUSIONS, I ADMIT, ARE FAR LESS INTERESTING TO ME THAN THE PROVENANCE OF THIS WEAPON.
THIS SLEEP GAS, KIERAN...
AAAGHH--
WHERE DID YOU ACQUIRE IT? YOU WERE UNARMED WHEN I LEFT YOU.
WHERE IS IT NOW? WHERE ARE YOU?
WHAT ARE THEY DOING?
ANSWER ME OR BID YOUR GHOSTS GOODBYE. FOREVER. I HAVE THIS POWER.
SCREW YOU. YOU BASTARD--
THIS IS A DREAM.
PRECISELY.

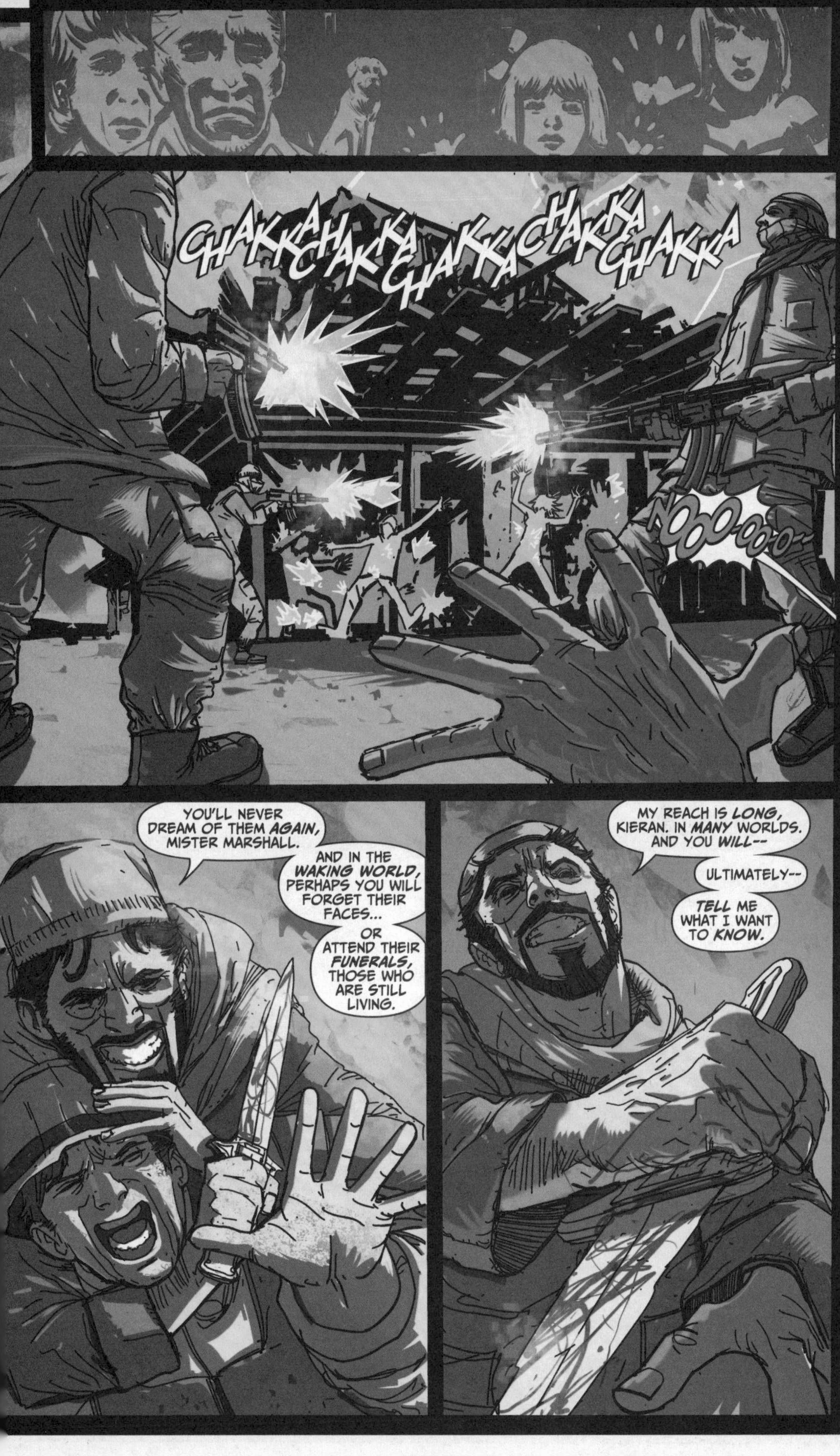
CHAKKA CHAKKA CHAKKA CHAKKA CHAKKA
NOOO-OO-O--
YOU'LL NEVER DREAM OF THEM AGAIN, MISTER MARSHALL.
AND IN THE WAKING WORLD, PERHAPS YOU WILL FORGET THEIR FACES...
OR ATTEND THEIR FUNERALS, THOSE WHO ARE STILL LIVING.
MY REACH IS LONG, KIERAN. IN MANY WORLDS. AND YOU WILL--
ULTIMATELY--
TELL ME WHAT I WANT TO KNOW.

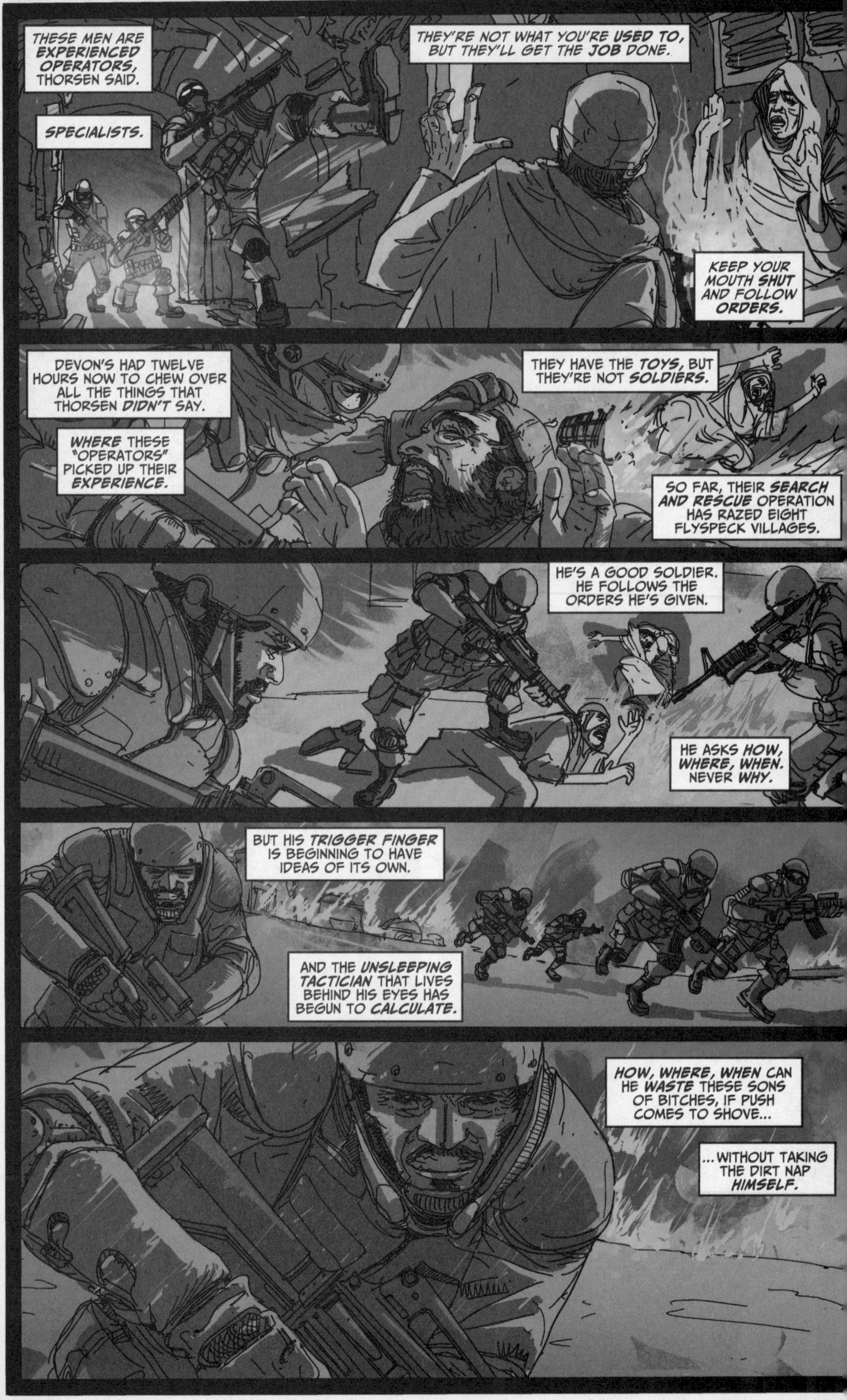
THESE MEN ARE EXPERIENCED OPERATORS, THORSEN SAID.
SPECIALISTS.
THEY'RE NOT WHAT YOU'RE USED TO, BUT THEY'LL GET THE JOB DONE.
KEEP YOUR MOUTH SHUT AND FOLLOW ORDERS.
DEVON'S HAD TWELVE HOURS NOW TO CHEW OVER ALL THE THINGS THAT THORSEN DIDN'T SAY.
WHERE THESE "OPERATORS" PICKED UP THEIR EXPERIENCE.
THEY HAVE THE TOYS, BUT THEY'RE NOT SOLDIERS.
SO FAR, THEIR SEARCH AND RESCUE OPERATION HAS RAZED EIGHT FLYSPECK VILLAGES.
HE'S A GOOD SOLDIER. HE FOLLOWS THE ORDERS HE'S GIVEN.
HE ASKS HOW, WHERE, WHEN. NEVER WHY.
BUT HIS TRIGGER FINGER IS BEGINNING TO HAVE IDEAS OF ITS OWN.
AND THE UNSLEEPING TACTICIAN THAT LIVES BEHIND HIS EYES HAS BEGUN TO CALCULATE.
HOW, WHERE, WHEN CAN HE WASTE THESE SONS OF BITCHES, IF PUSH COMES TO SHOVE...
...WITHOUT TAKING THE DIRT NAP HIMSELF.

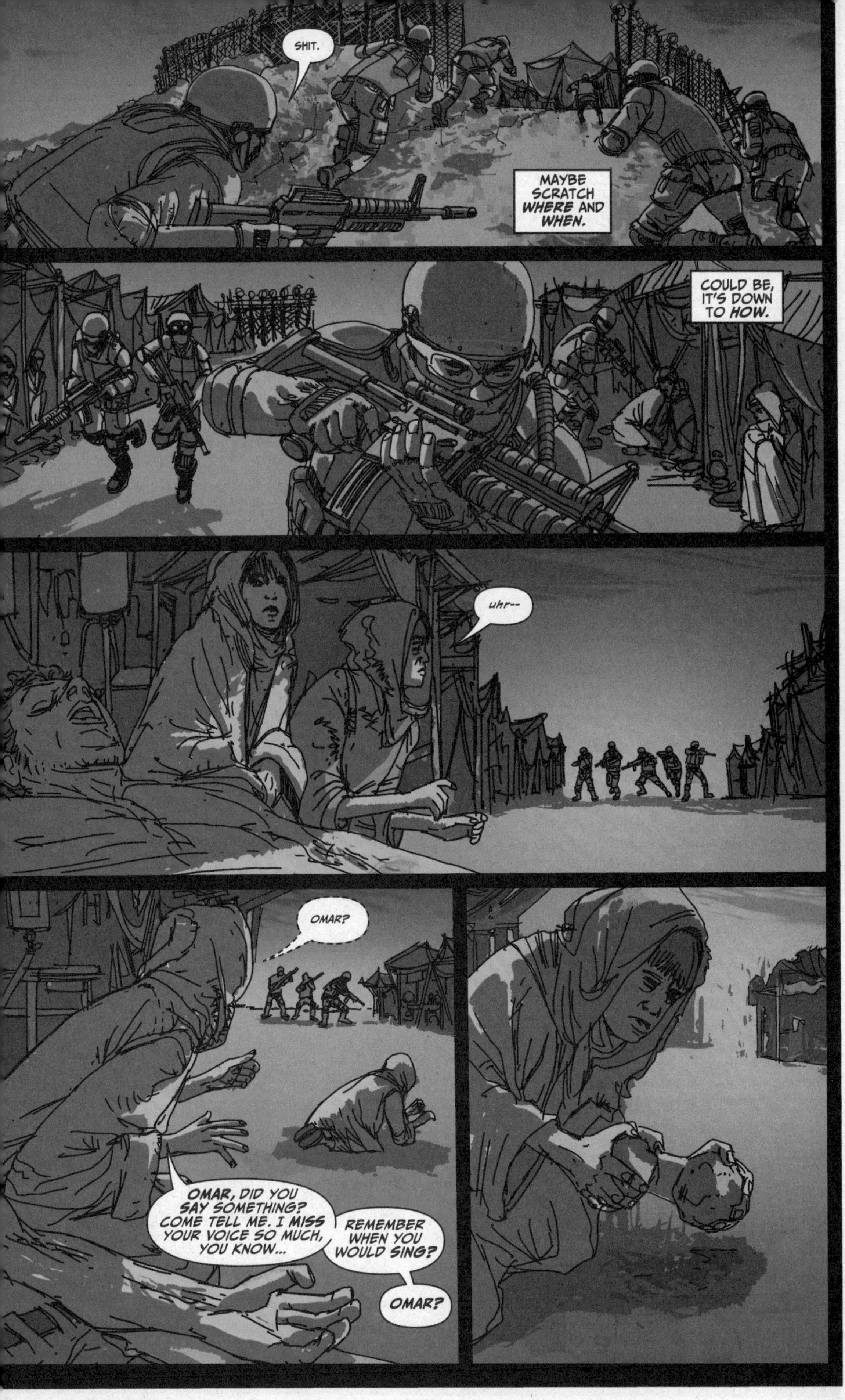
SHIT.
MAYBE SCRATCH WHERE AND WHEN.
COULD BE, IT'S DOWN TO HOW.
uhr--
OMAR?
OMAR, DID YOU SAY SOMETHING? COME TELL ME. I MISS YOUR VOICE SO MUCH, YOU KNOW...
REMEMBER WHEN YOU WOULD SING?
OMAR?

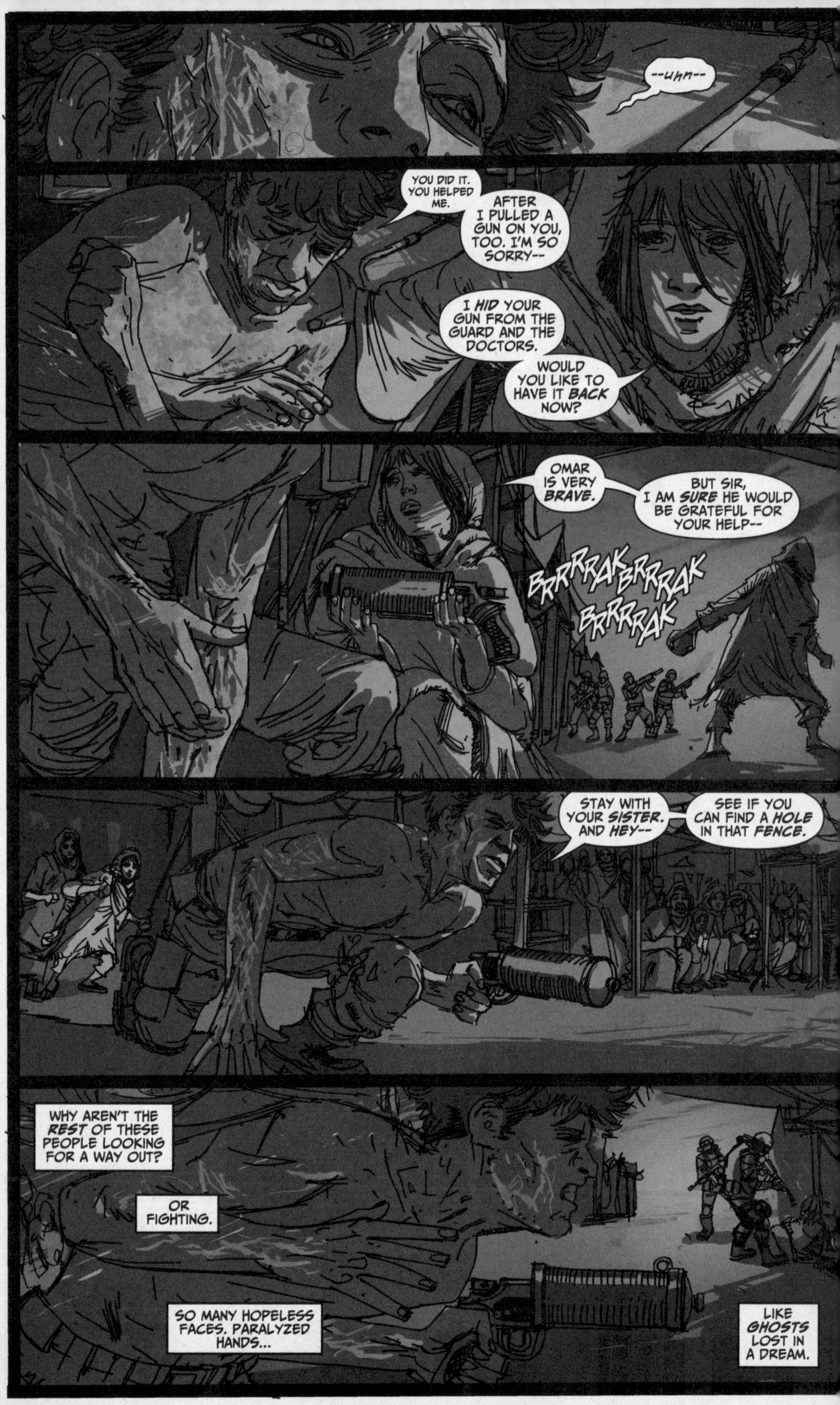
--uhn--
YOU DID IT. YOU HELPED ME.
AFTER I PULLED A GUN ON YOU, TOO. I'M SO SORRY--
I HID YOUR GUN FROM THE GUARD AND THE DOCTORS.
WOULD YOU LIKE TO HAVE IT BACK NOW?
OMAR IS VERY BRAVE.
BUT SIR, I AM SURE HE WOULD BE GRATEFUL FOR YOUR HELP--
BRRRRAK BRRRRAK
BRRRRAK
STAY WITH YOUR SISTER. AND HEY--
SEE IF YOU CAN FIND A HOLE IN THAT FENCE.
WHY AREN'T THE REST OF THESE PEOPLE LOOKING FOR A WAY OUT?
OR FIGHTING.
SO MANY HOPELESS FACES. PARALYZED HANDS...
LIKE GHOSTS LOST IN A DREAM.

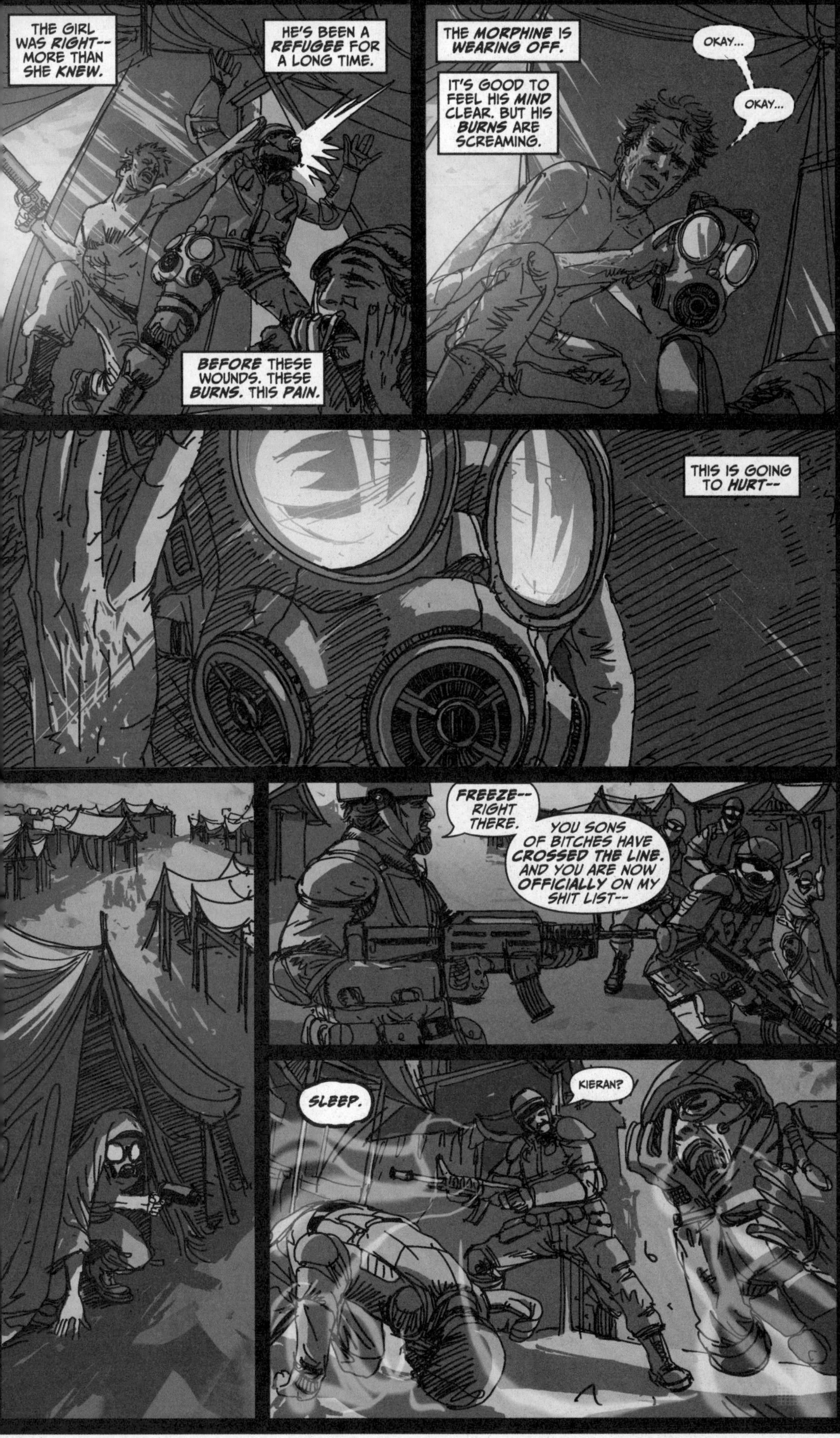
THE GIRL WAS RIGHT-- MORE THAN SHE KNEW.
HE'S BEEN A REFUGEE FOR A LONG TIME.
BEFORE THESE WOUNDS. THESE BURNS. THIS PAIN.
THE MORPHINE IS WEARING OFF.
IT'S GOOD TO FEEL HIS MIND CLEAR. BUT HIS BURNS ARE SCREAMING.
OKAY...
OKAY...
THIS IS GOING TO HURT--
FREEZE-- RIGHT THERE.
YOU SONS OF BITCHES HAVE CROSSED THE LINE. AND YOU ARE NOW OFFICIALLY ON MY SHIT LIST--
SLEEP.
KIERAN?

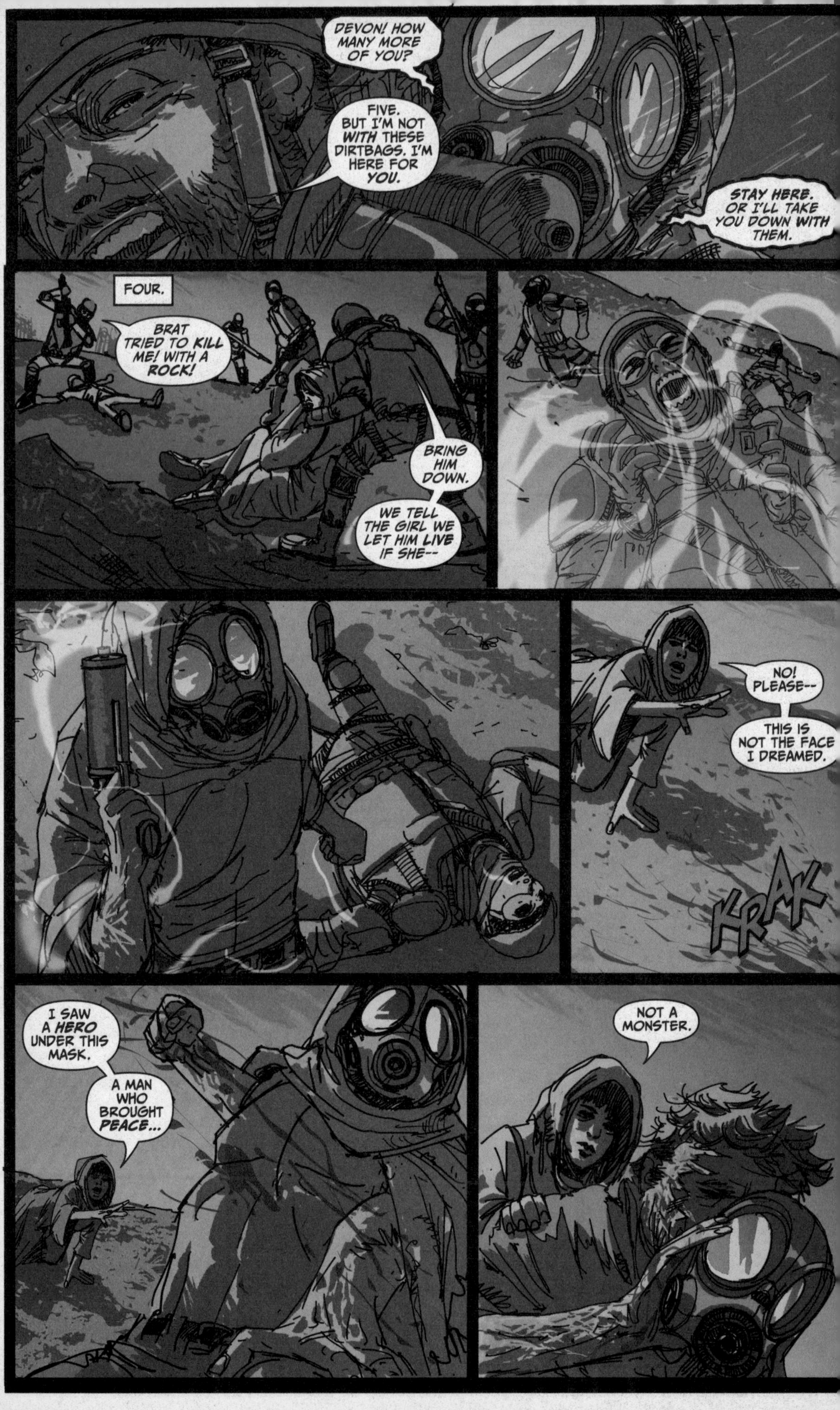
DEVON! HOW MANY MORE OF YOU?
FIVE. BUT I'M NOT WITH THESE DIRTBAGS. I'M HERE FOR YOU.
STAY HERE. OR I'LL TAKE YOU DOWN WITH THEM.
FOUR.
BRAT TRIED TO KILL ME! WITH A ROCK!
BRING HIM DOWN.
WE TELL THE GIRL WE LET HIM LIVE IF SHE--
NO! PLEASE--
THIS IS NOT THE FACE I DREAMED.
KRAK
I SAW A HERO UNDER THIS MASK.
A MAN WHO BROUGHT PEACE...
NOT A MONSTER.

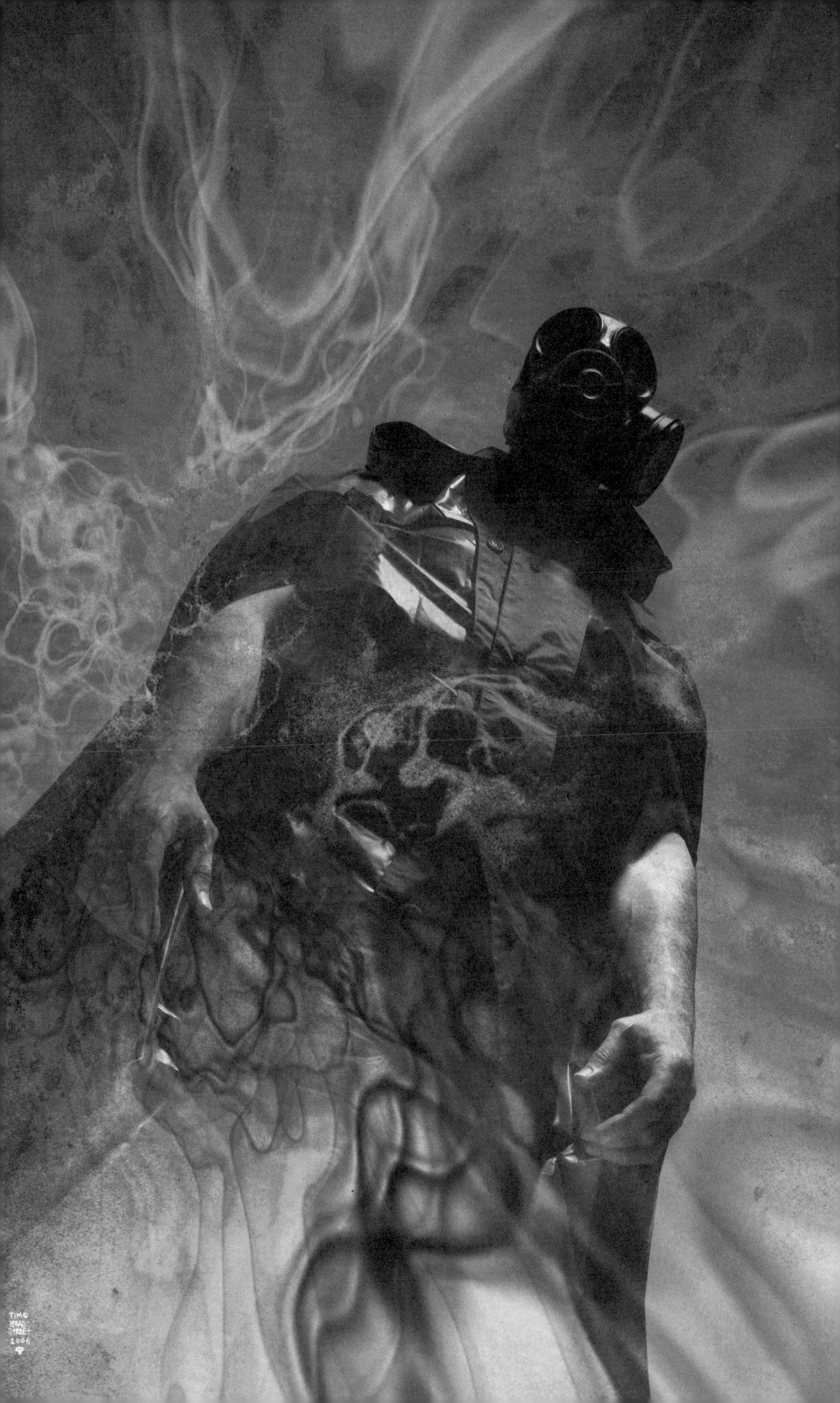
TIMO
BRAD-
STREET
2006

CHAPTER THREE

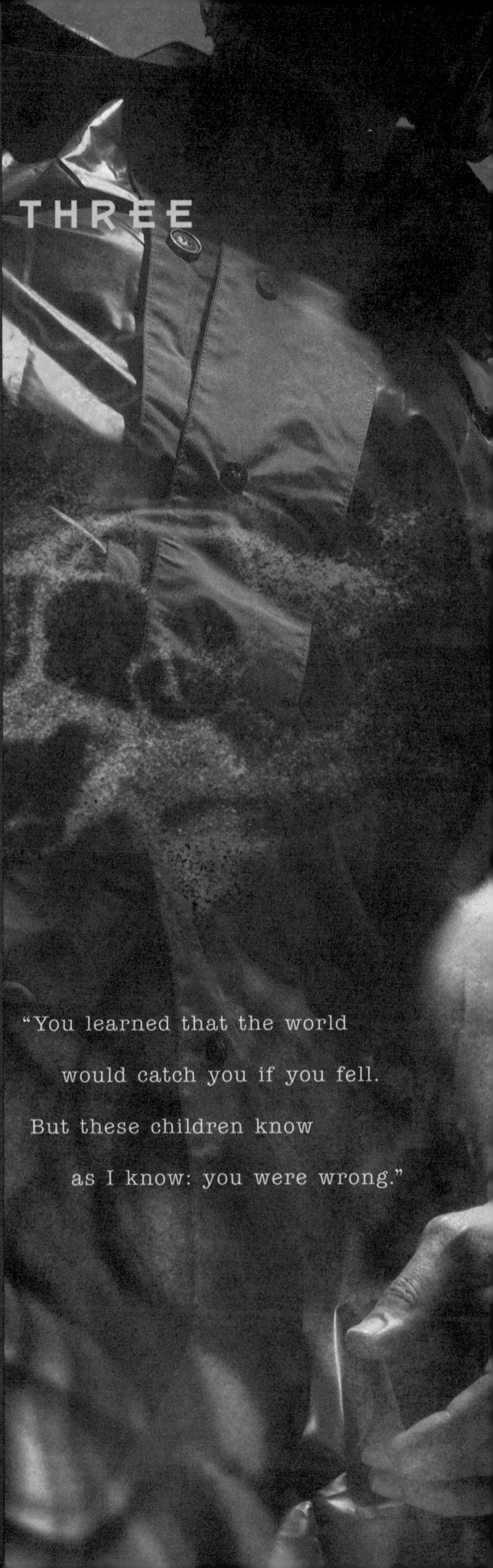

"You learned that the world
would catch you if you fell.
But these children know
as I know: you were wrong."

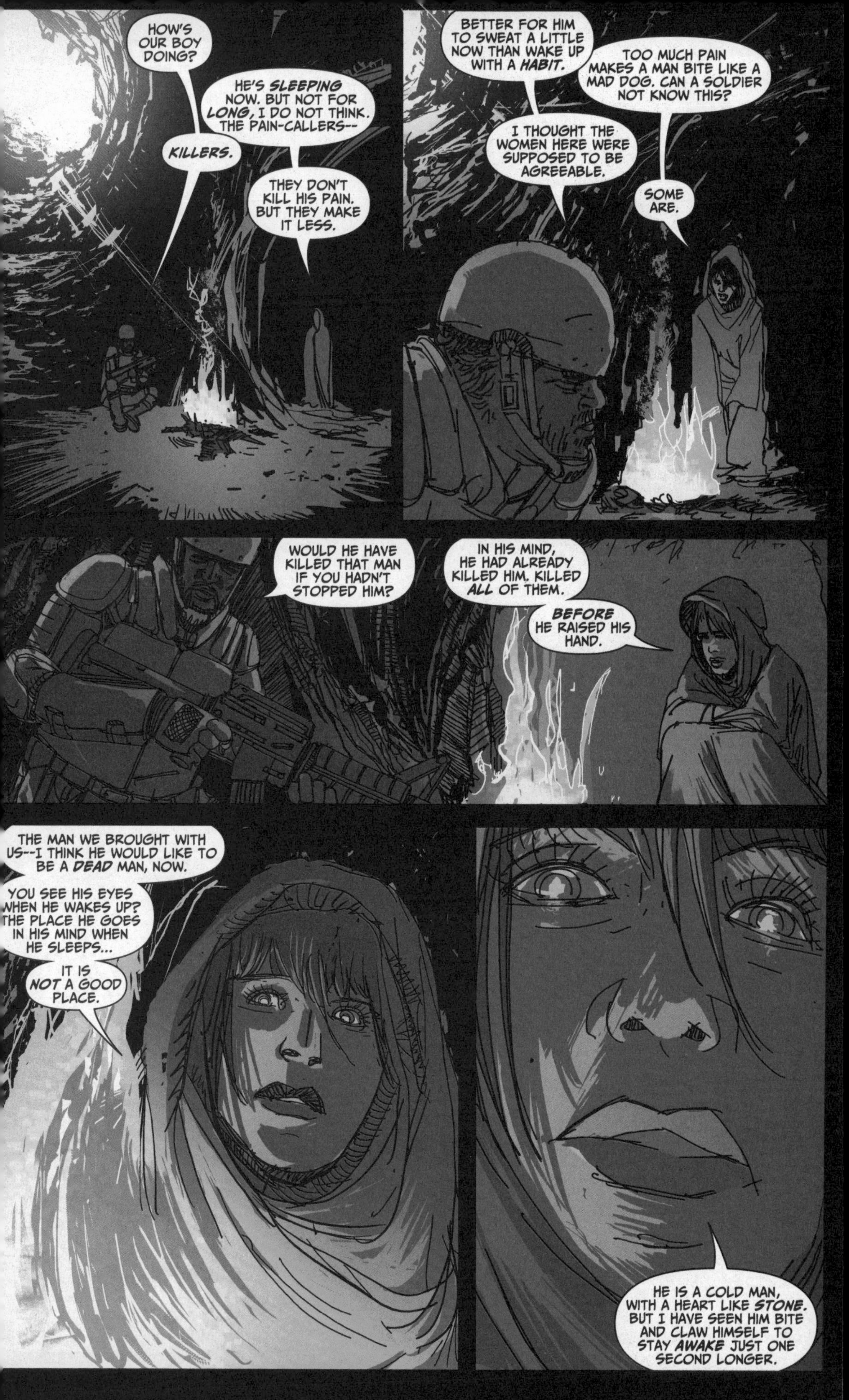
HOW'S OUR BOY DOING?
HE'S SLEEPING NOW. BUT NOT FOR LONG, I DO NOT THINK. THE PAIN-CALLERS--
KILLERS.
THEY DON'T KILL HIS PAIN. BUT THEY MAKE IT LESS.
BETTER FOR HIM TO SWEAT A LITTLE NOW THAN WAKE UP WITH A HABIT.
TOO MUCH PAIN MAKES A MAN BITE LIKE A MAD DOG. CAN A SOLDIER NOT KNOW THIS?
I THOUGHT THE WOMEN HERE WERE SUPPOSED TO BE AGREEABLE.
SOME ARE.
WOULD HE HAVE KILLED THAT MAN IF YOU HADN'T STOPPED HIM?
IN HIS MIND, HE HAD ALREADY KILLED HIM. KILLED ALL OF THEM.
BEFORE HE RAISED HIS HAND.
THE MAN WE BROUGHT WITH US--I THINK HE WOULD LIKE TO BE A DEAD MAN, NOW.
YOU SEE HIS EYES WHEN HE WAKES UP? THE PLACE HE GOES IN HIS MIND WHEN HE SLEEPS...
IT IS NOT A GOOD PLACE.
HE IS A COLD MAN, WITH A HEART LIKE STONE. BUT I HAVE SEEN HIM BITE AND CLAW HIMSELF TO STAY AWAKE JUST ONE SECOND LONGER.

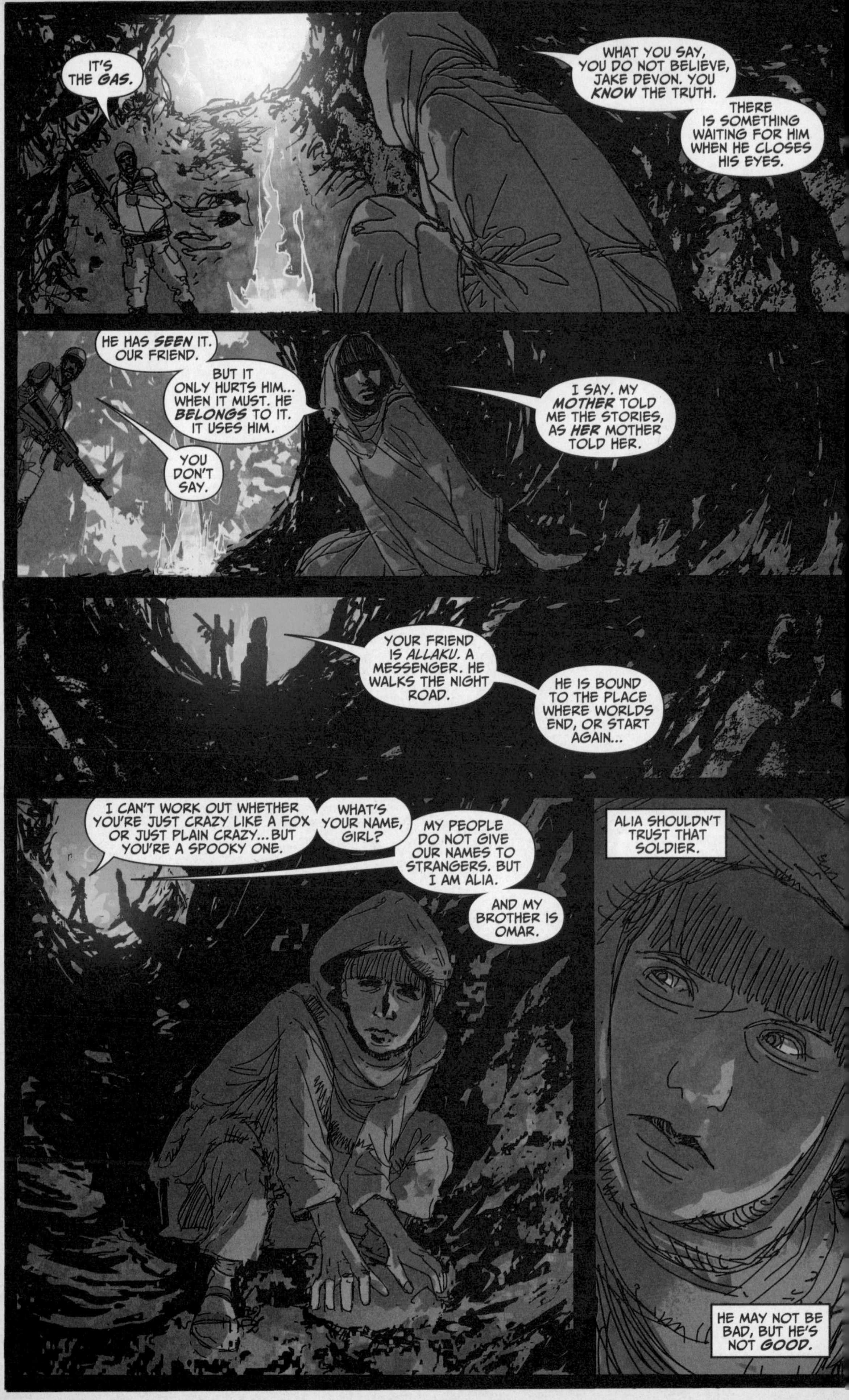
IT'S THE GAS.
WHAT YOU SAY, YOU DO NOT BELIEVE, JAKE DEVON. YOU KNOW THE TRUTH.
THERE IS SOMETHING WAITING FOR HIM WHEN HE CLOSES HIS EYES.
HE HAS SEEN IT. OUR FRIEND.
BUT IT ONLY HURTS HIM... WHEN IT MUST. HE BELONGS TO IT. IT USES HIM.
YOU DON'T SAY.
I SAY. MY MOTHER TOLD ME THE STORIES, AS HER MOTHER TOLD HER.
YOUR FRIEND IS ALLAKU. A MESSENGER. HE WALKS THE NIGHT ROAD.
HE IS BOUND TO THE PLACE WHERE WORLDS END, OR START AGAIN...
I CAN'T WORK OUT WHETHER YOU'RE JUST CRAZY LIKE A FOX OR JUST PLAIN CRAZY...BUT YOU'RE A SPOOKY ONE.
WHAT'S YOUR NAME, GIRL?
MY PEOPLE DO NOT GIVE OUR NAMES TO STRANGERS. BUT I AM ALIA.
AND MY BROTHER IS OMAR.
ALIA SHOULDN'T TRUST THAT SOLDIER.
HE MAY NOT BE BAD, BUT HE'S NOT GOOD.

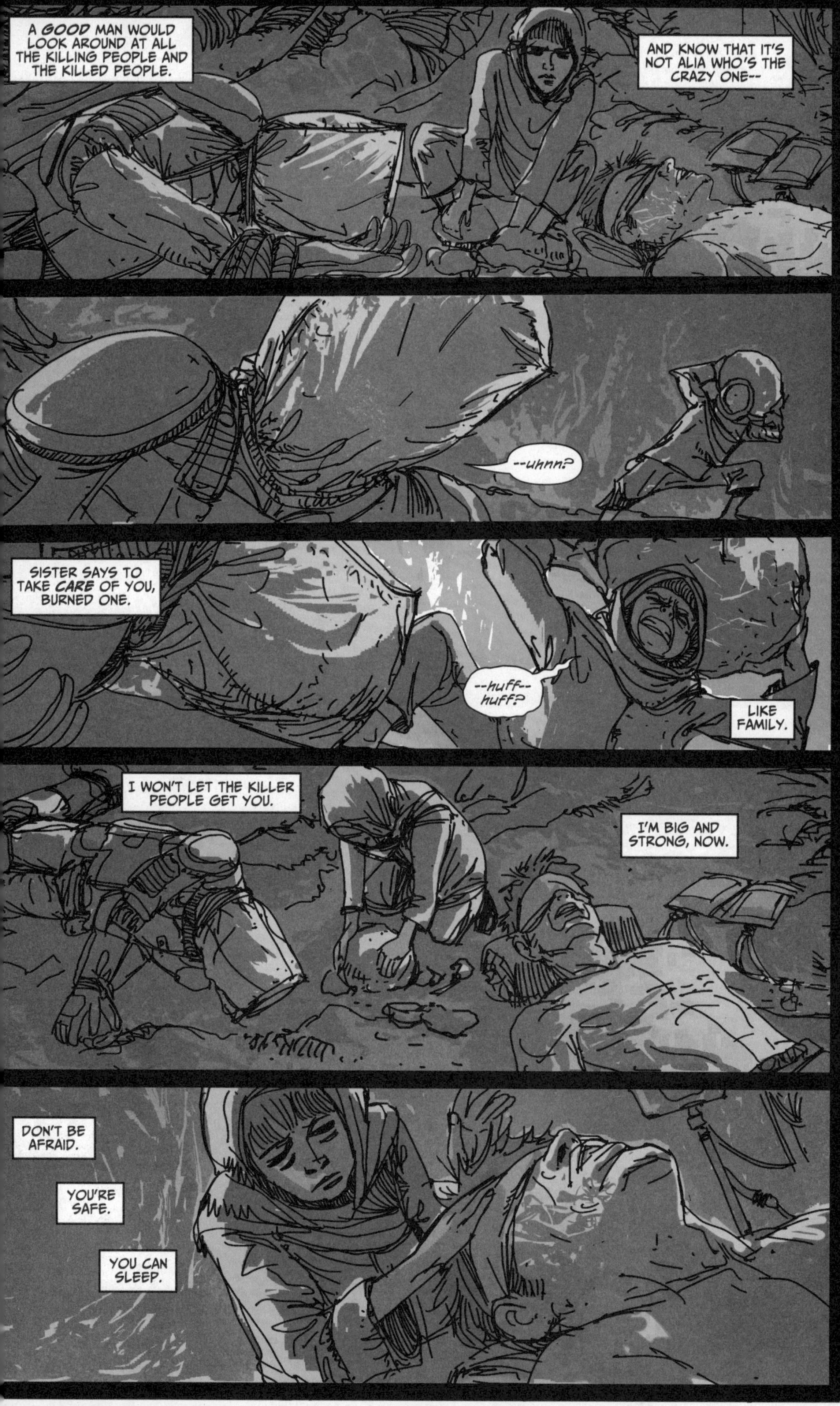
A GOOD MAN WOULD LOOK AROUND AT ALL THE KILLING PEOPLE AND THE KILLED PEOPLE.
AND KNOW THAT IT'S NOT ALIA WHO'S THE CRAZY ONE--
--uhnn?
SISTER SAYS TO TAKE CARE OF YOU, BURNED ONE.
--huff--huff?
LIKE FAMILY.
I WON'T LET THE KILLER PEOPLE GET YOU.
I'M BIG AND STRONG, NOW.
DON'T BE AFRAID.
YOU'RE SAFE.
YOU CAN SLEEP.

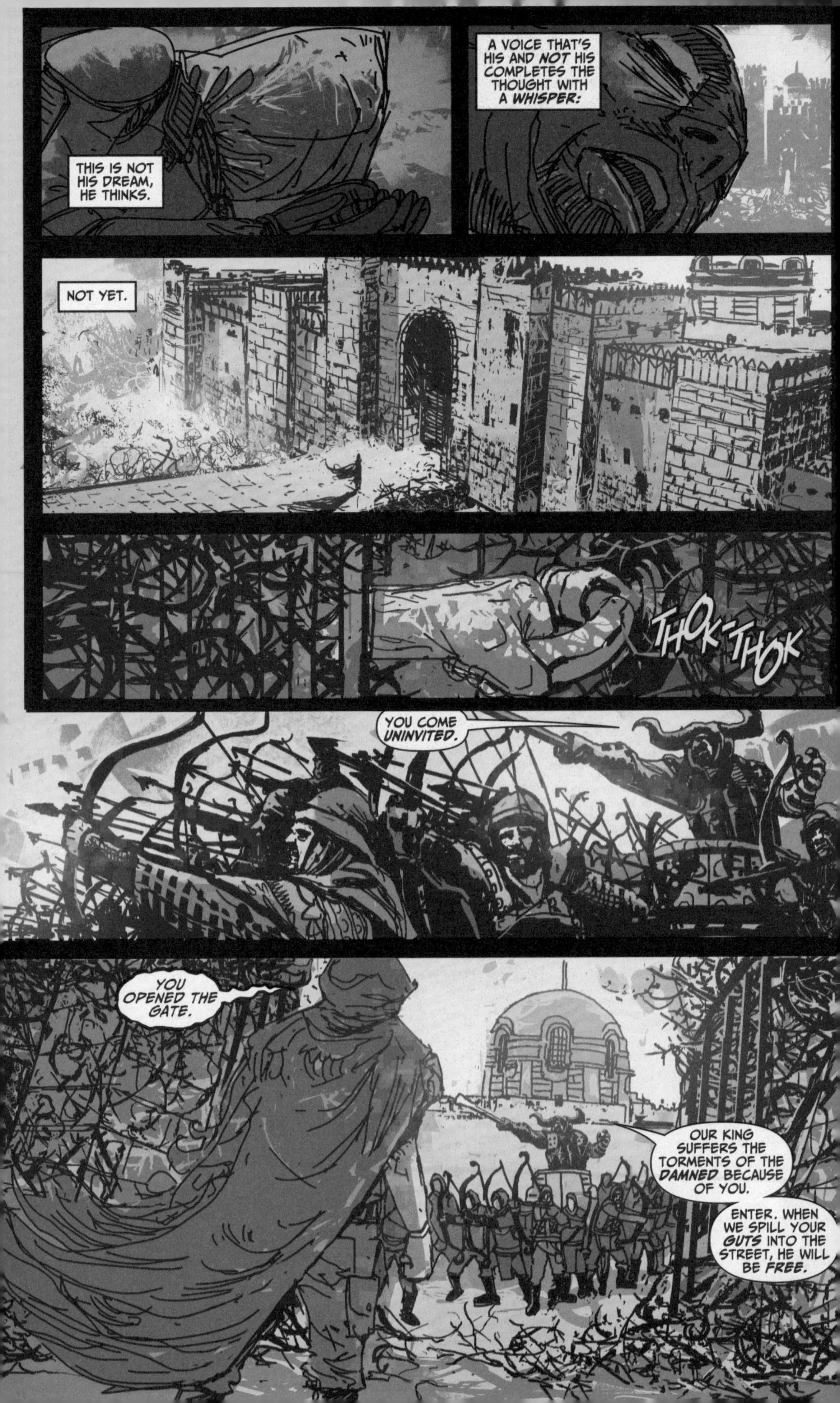
THIS IS NOT HIS DREAM, HE THINKS.
A VOICE THAT'S HIS AND NOT HIS COMPLETES THE THOUGHT WITH A WHISPER:
NOT YET.
THOK-THOK
YOU COME UNINVITED.
YOU OPENED THE GATE.
OUR KING SUFFERS THE TORMENTS OF THE DAMNED BECAUSE OF YOU.
ENTER. WHEN WE SPILL YOUR GUTS INTO THE STREET, HE WILL BE FREE.

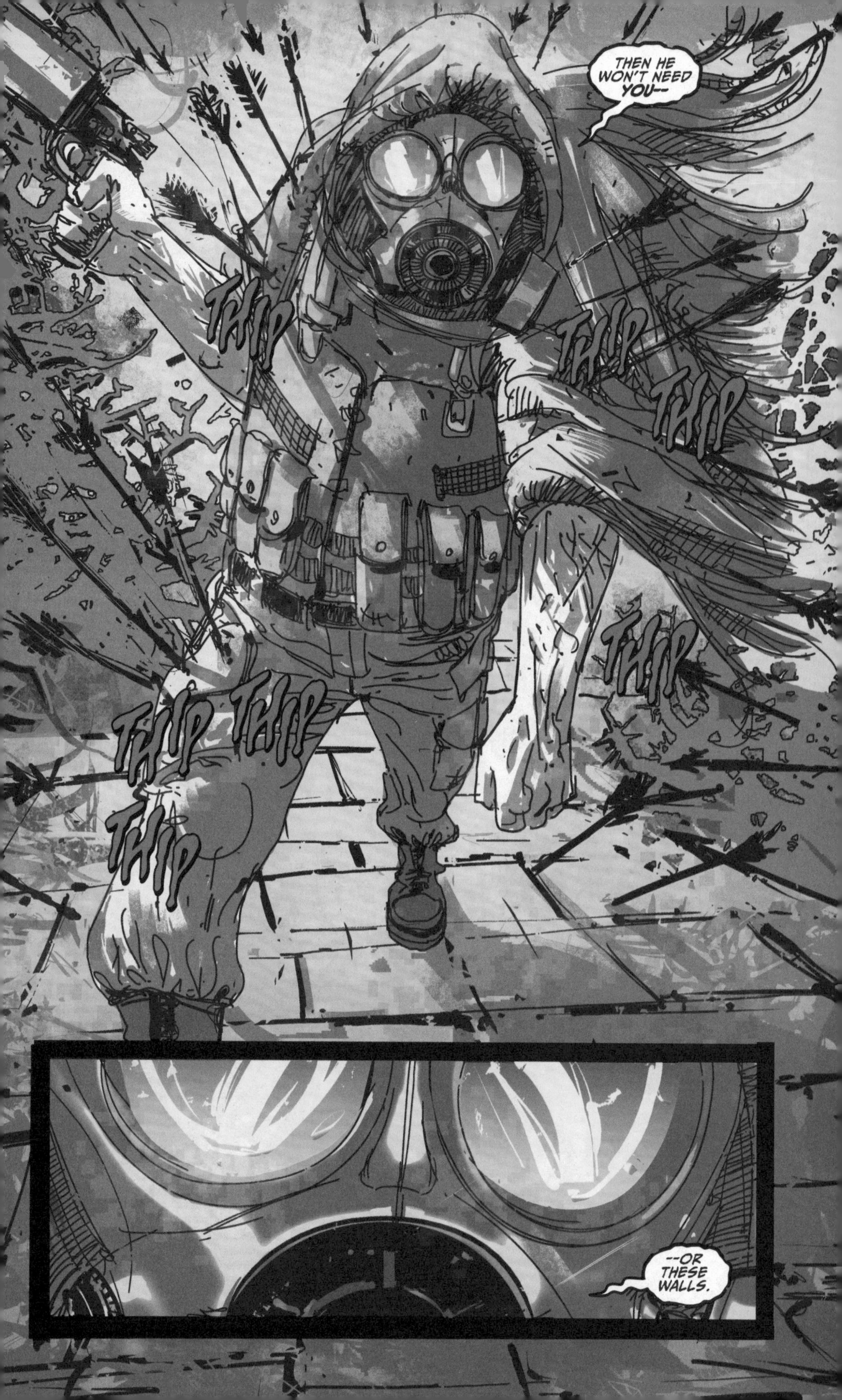

THEN HE WON'T NEED YOU--
THIP
THIP
THIP
THIP
THIP
THIP
THIP
--OR THESE WALLS.

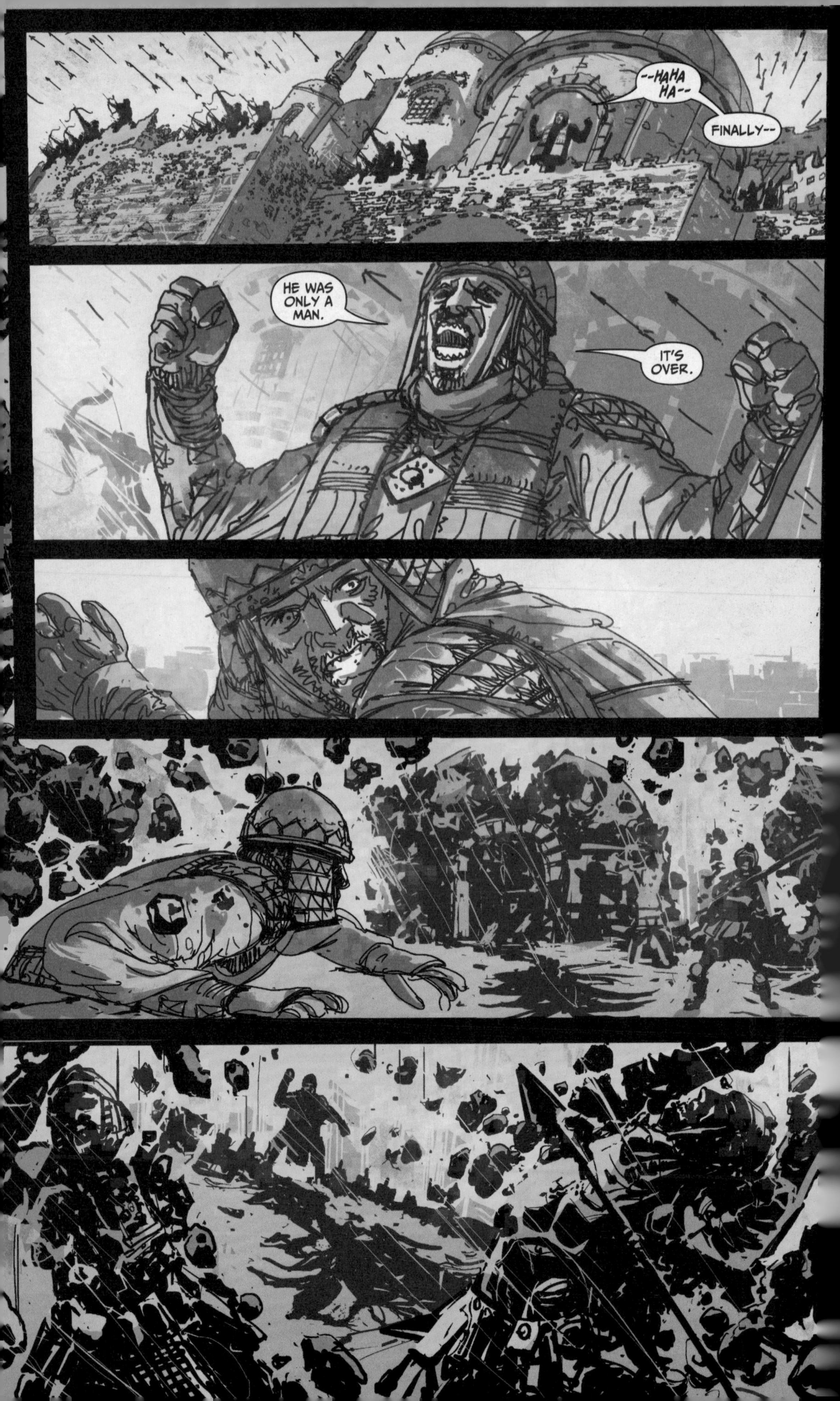

--HAHA HA--
FINALLY--
HE WAS ONLY A MAN.
IT'S OVER.

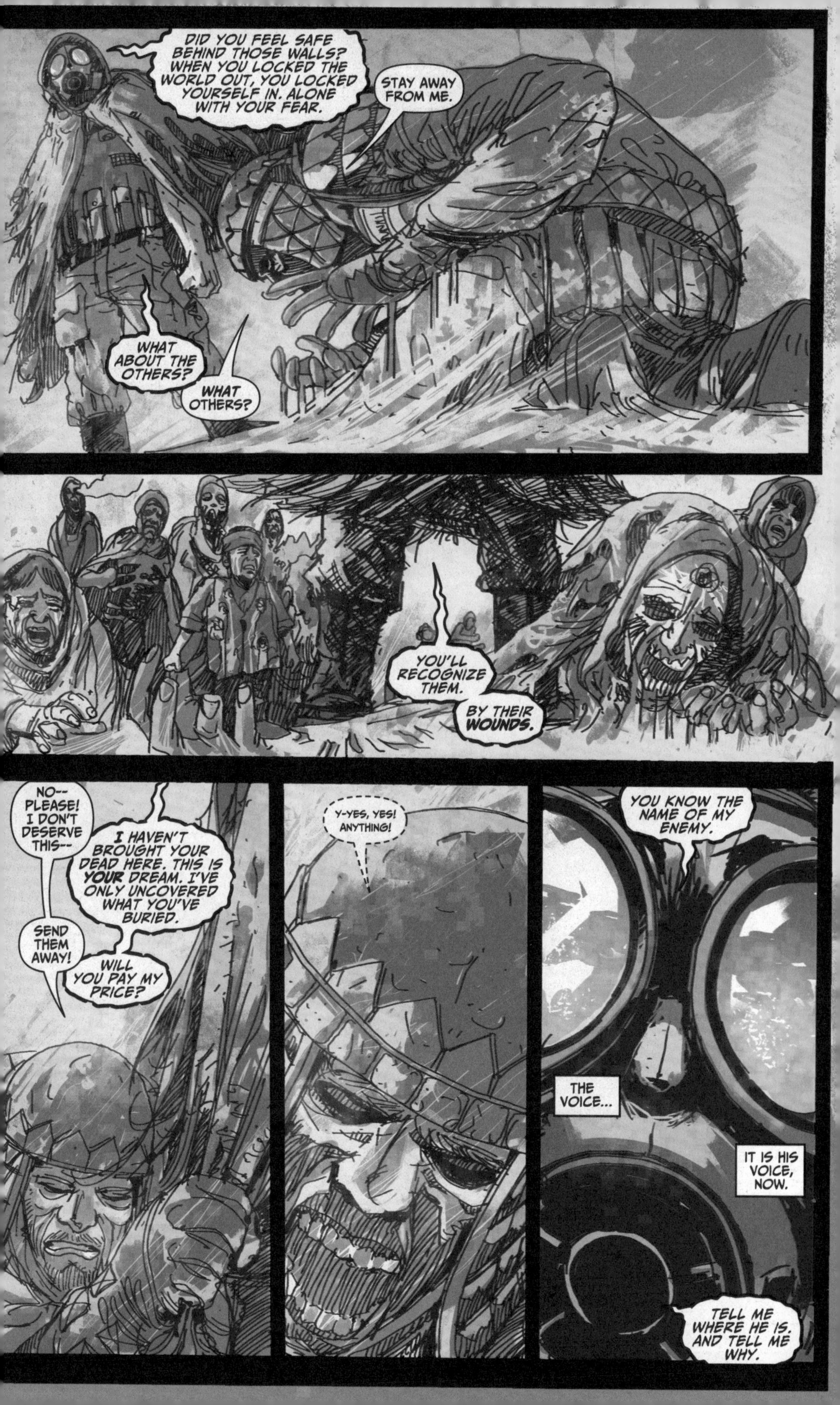

DID YOU FEEL SAFE BEHIND THOSE WALLS? WHEN YOU LOCKED THE WORLD OUT, YOU LOCKED YOURSELF IN. ALONE WITH YOUR FEAR.
STAY AWAY FROM ME.
WHAT ABOUT THE OTHERS?
WHAT OTHERS?
YOU'LL RECOGNIZE THEM.
BY THEIR **WOUNDS.**
NO-- PLEASE! I DON'T DESERVE THIS--
I HAVEN'T BROUGHT YOUR DEAD HERE. THIS IS **YOUR** DREAM. I'VE ONLY UNCOVERED WHAT YOU'VE BURIED.
SEND THEM AWAY!
WILL YOU PAY MY PRICE?
Y-YES, YES! ANYTHING!
YOU KNOW THE NAME OF MY ENEMY.
THE VOICE...
IT IS HIS VOICE, NOW.
TELL ME WHERE HE IS. AND TELL ME WHY.

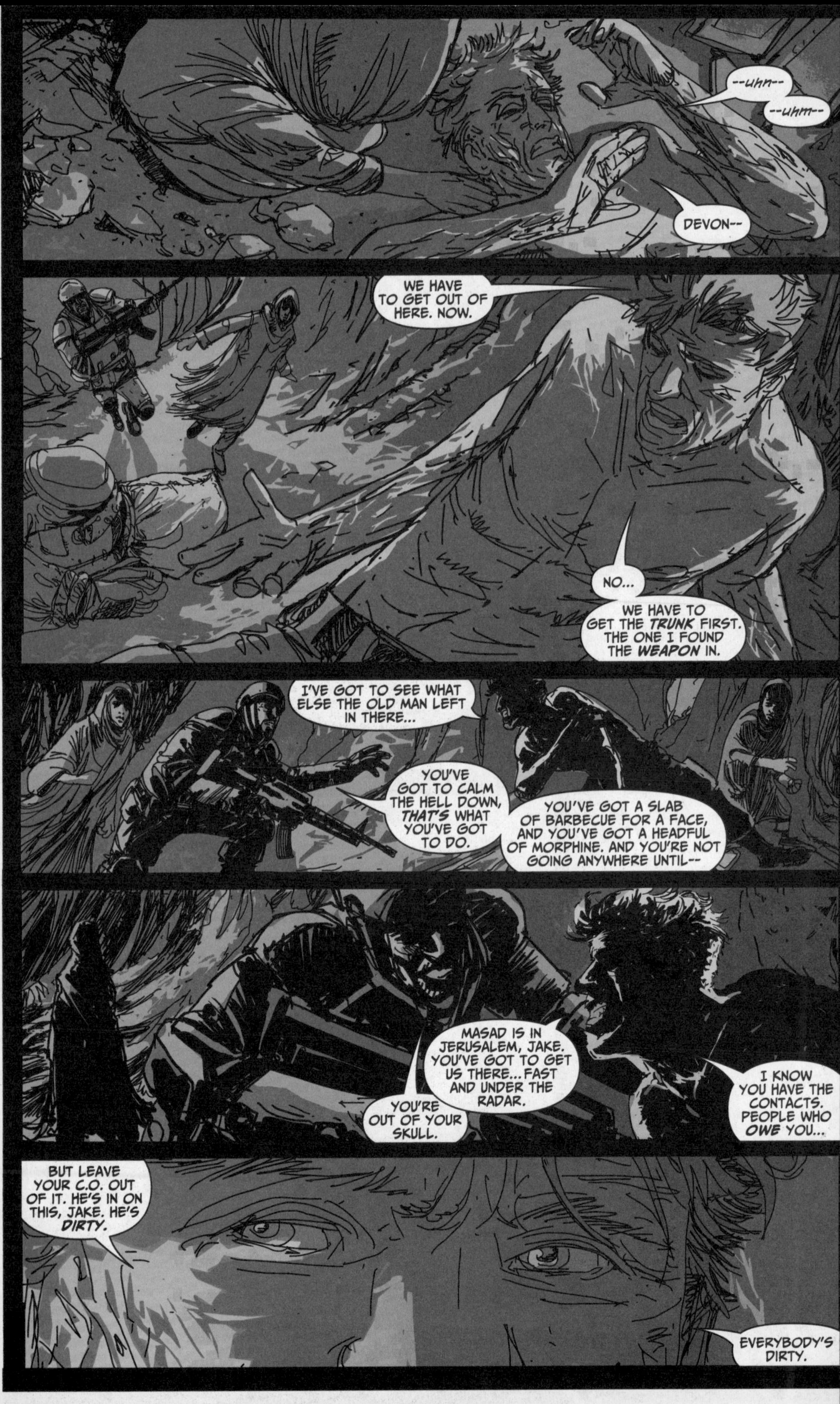
--uhn--
--uhm--
DEVON--
WE HAVE TO GET OUT OF HERE. NOW.
NO...
WE HAVE TO GET THE TRUNK FIRST. THE ONE I FOUND THE WEAPON IN.
I'VE GOT TO SEE WHAT ELSE THE OLD MAN LEFT IN THERE...
YOU'VE GOT TO CALM THE HELL DOWN, THAT'S WHAT YOU'VE GOT TO DO.
YOU'VE GOT A SLAB OF BARBECUE FOR A FACE, AND YOU'VE GOT A HEADFUL OF MORPHINE. AND YOU'RE NOT GOING ANYWHERE UNTIL--
MASAD IS IN JERUSALEM, JAKE. YOU'VE GOT TO GET US THERE... FAST AND UNDER THE RADAR.
YOU'RE OUT OF YOUR SKULL.
I KNOW YOU HAVE THE CONTACTS. PEOPLE WHO OWE YOU...
BUT LEAVE YOUR C.O. OUT OF IT. HE'S IN ON THIS, JAKE. HE'S DIRTY.
EVERYBODY'S DIRTY.

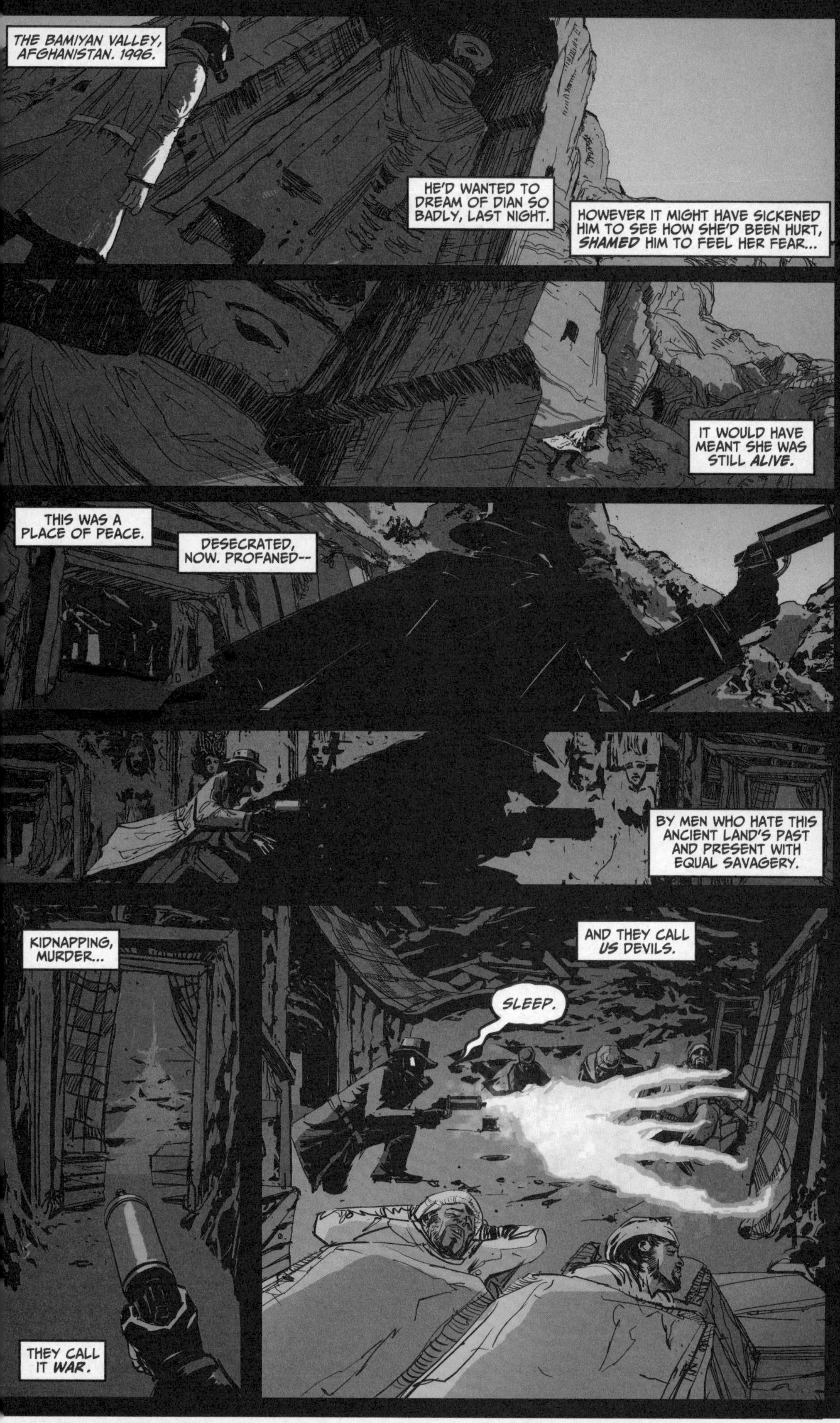

THE BAMIYAN VALLEY, AFGHANISTAN. 1996.
HE'D WANTED TO DREAM OF DIAN SO BADLY, LAST NIGHT.
HOWEVER IT MIGHT HAVE SICKENED HIM TO SEE HOW SHE'D BEEN HURT, SHAMED HIM TO FEEL HER FEAR...
IT WOULD HAVE MEANT SHE WAS STILL ALIVE.
THIS WAS A PLACE OF PEACE.
DESECRATED, NOW. PROFANED--
BY MEN WHO HATE THIS ANCIENT LAND'S PAST AND PRESENT WITH EQUAL SAVAGERY.
KIDNAPPING, MURDER...
THEY CALL IT WAR.
AND THEY CALL US DEVILS.
SLEEP.

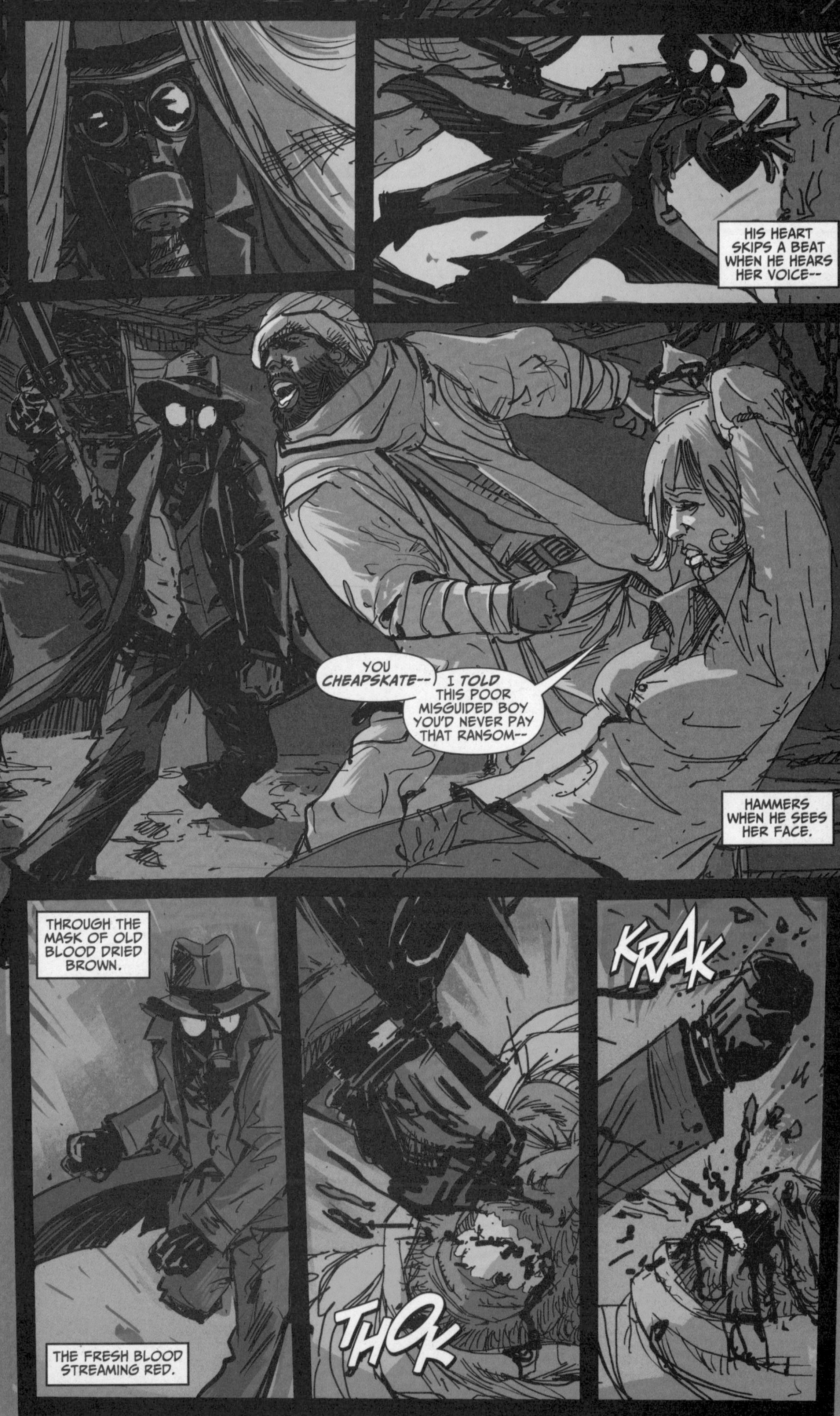
HIS HEART SKIPS A BEAT WHEN HE HEARS HER VOICE--
YOU CHEAPSKATE--
I TOLD THIS POOR MISGUIDED BOY YOU'D NEVER PAY THAT RANSOM--
HAMMERS WHEN HE SEES HER FACE.
THROUGH THE MASK OF OLD BLOOD DRIED BROWN.
THE FRESH BLOOD STREAMING RED.
THOK
KRAK

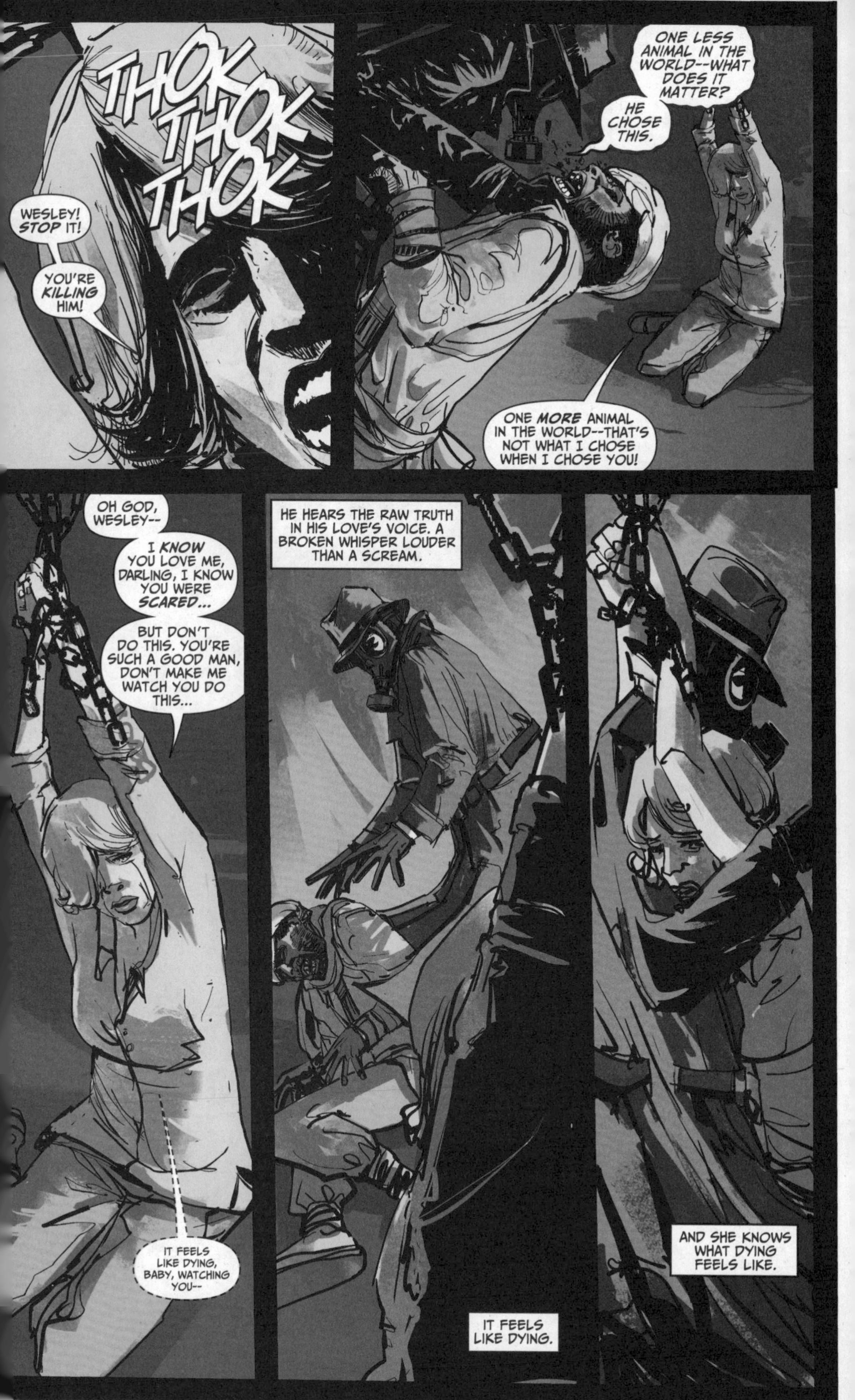
THOK THOK THOK
WESLEY! STOP IT!
YOU'RE KILLING HIM!
ONE LESS ANIMAL IN THE WORLD--WHAT DOES IT MATTER?
HE CHOSE THIS.
ONE MORE ANIMAL IN THE WORLD--THAT'S NOT WHAT I CHOSE WHEN I CHOSE YOU!
OH GOD, WESLEY--
I KNOW YOU LOVE ME, DARLING, I KNOW YOU WERE SCARED...
BUT DON'T DO THIS. YOU'RE SUCH A GOOD MAN, DON'T MAKE ME WATCH YOU DO THIS...
IT FEELS LIKE DYING, BABY, WATCHING YOU--
HE HEARS THE RAW TRUTH IN HIS LOVE'S VOICE. A BROKEN WHISPER LOUDER THAN A SCREAM.
IT FEELS LIKE DYING.
AND SHE KNOWS WHAT DYING FEELS LIKE.

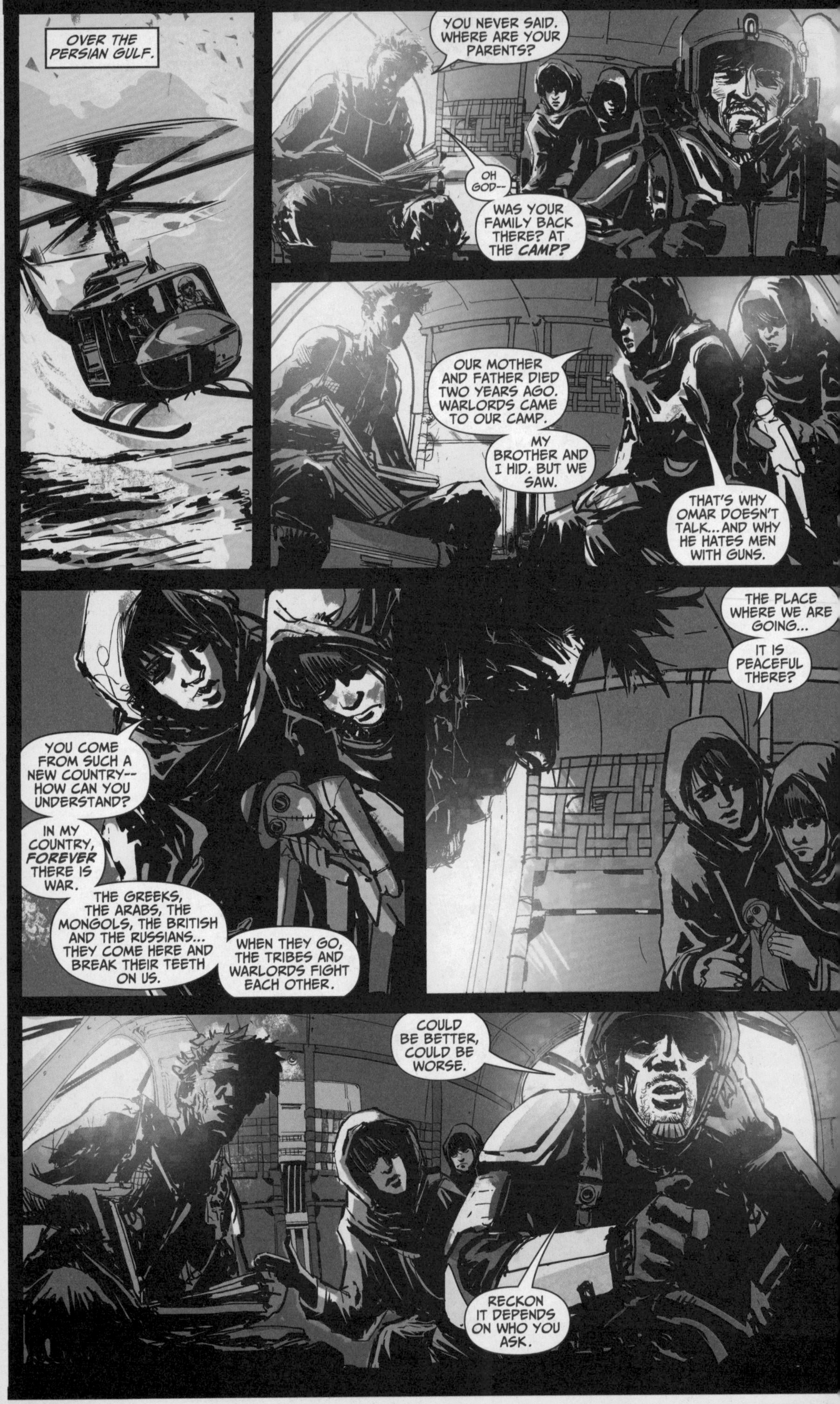
OVER THE PERSIAN GULF.
YOU NEVER SAID. WHERE ARE YOUR PARENTS?
OH GOD--
WAS YOUR FAMILY BACK THERE? AT THE *CAMP?*
OUR MOTHER AND FATHER DIED TWO YEARS AGO. WARLORDS CAME TO OUR CAMP.
MY BROTHER AND I HID. BUT WE SAW.
THAT'S WHY OMAR DOESN'T TALK...AND WHY HE HATES MEN WITH GUNS.
YOU COME FROM SUCH A NEW COUNTRY-- HOW CAN YOU UNDERSTAND?
IN MY COUNTRY, *FOREVER* THERE IS WAR.
THE GREEKS, THE ARABS, THE MONGOLS, THE BRITISH AND THE RUSSIANS... THEY COME HERE AND BREAK THEIR TEETH ON US.
WHEN THEY GO, THE TRIBES AND WARLORDS FIGHT EACH OTHER.
THE PLACE WHERE WE ARE GOING...
IT IS PEACEFUL THERE?
COULD BE BETTER, COULD BE WORSE.
RECKON IT DEPENDS ON WHO YOU ASK.

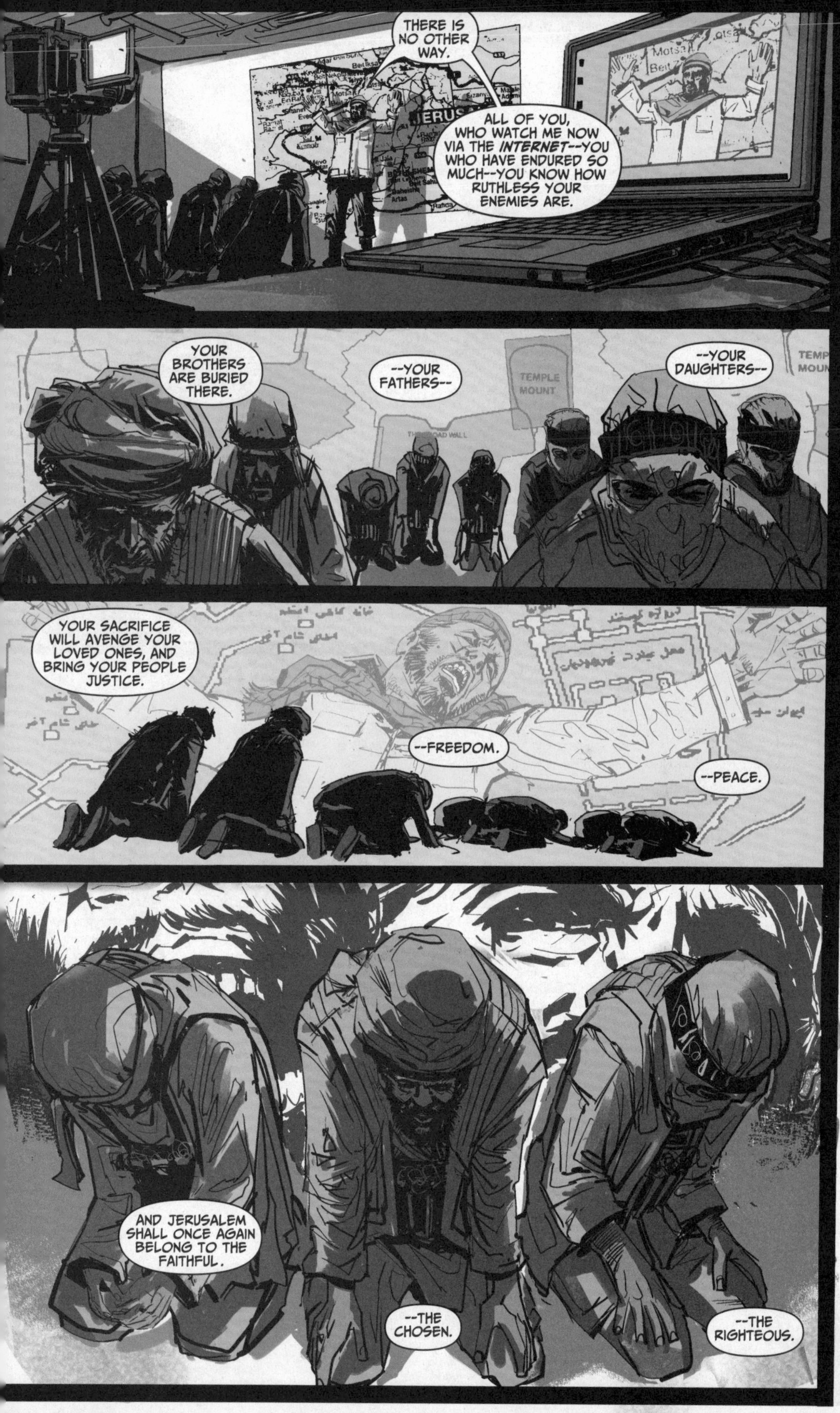

THERE IS NO OTHER WAY.
ALL OF YOU, WHO WATCH ME NOW VIA THE *INTERNET*--YOU WHO HAVE ENDURED SO MUCH--YOU KNOW HOW RUTHLESS YOUR ENEMIES ARE.
YOUR BROTHERS ARE BURIED THERE.
--YOUR FATHERS--
--YOUR DAUGHTERS--
TEMPLE MOUNT
YOUR SACRIFICE WILL AVENGE YOUR LOVED ONES, AND BRING YOUR PEOPLE JUSTICE.
--FREEDOM.
--PEACE.
AND JERUSALEM SHALL ONCE AGAIN BELONG TO THE FAITHFUL.
--THE CHOSEN.
--THE RIGHTEOUS.

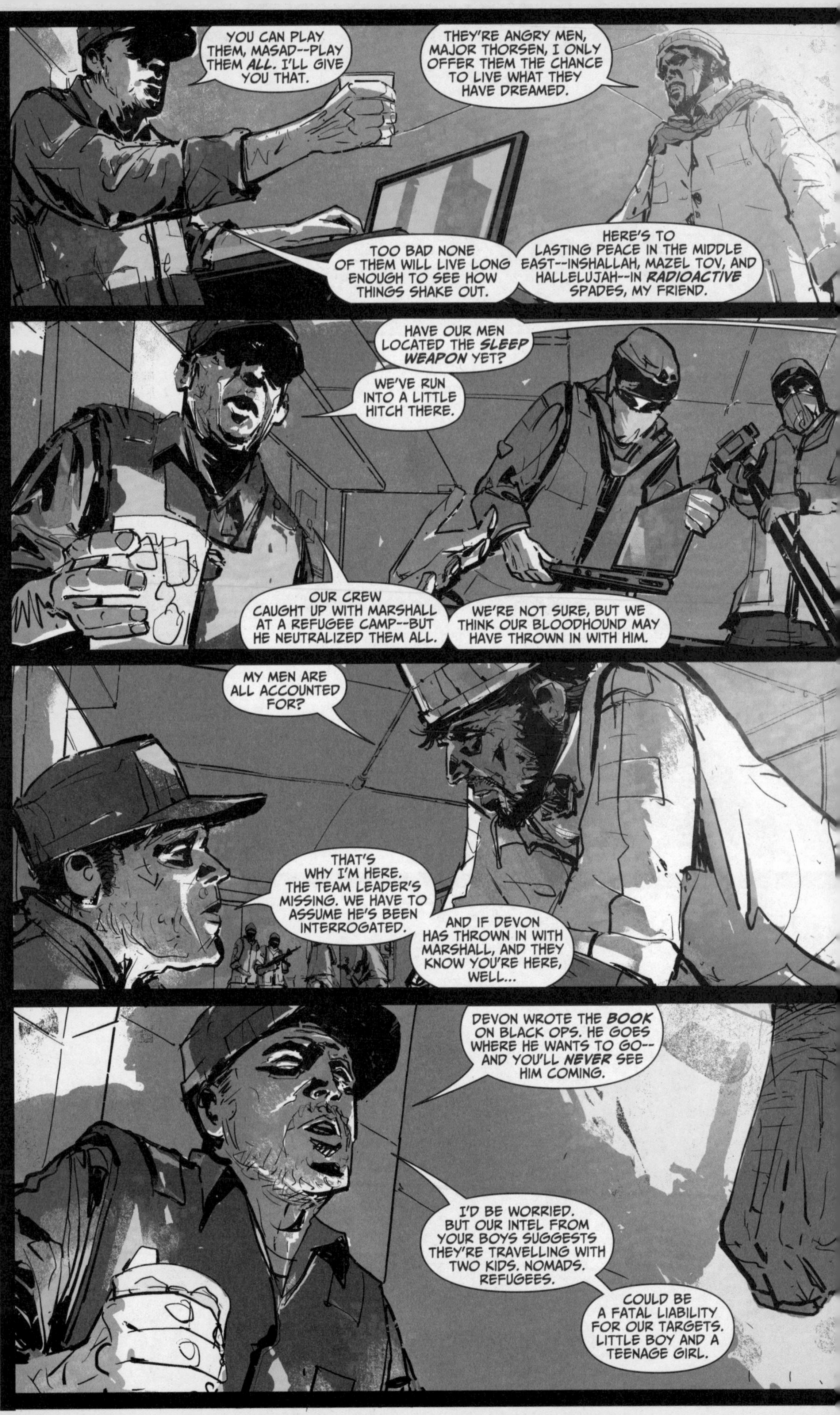

YOU CAN PLAY THEM, MASAD--PLAY THEM *ALL*. I'LL GIVE YOU THAT.
THEY'RE ANGRY MEN, MAJOR THORSEN, I ONLY OFFER THEM THE CHANCE TO LIVE WHAT THEY HAVE DREAMED.
TOO BAD NONE OF THEM WILL LIVE LONG ENOUGH TO SEE HOW THINGS SHAKE OUT.
HERE'S TO LASTING PEACE IN THE MIDDLE EAST--INSHALLAH, MAZEL TOV, AND HALLELUJAH--IN *RADIOACTIVE* SPADES, MY FRIEND.
HAVE OUR MEN LOCATED THE *SLEEP WEAPON* YET?
WE'VE RUN INTO A LITTLE HITCH THERE.
OUR CREW CAUGHT UP WITH MARSHALL AT A REFUGEE CAMP--BUT HE NEUTRALIZED THEM ALL.
WE'RE NOT SURE, BUT WE THINK OUR BLOODHOUND MAY HAVE THROWN IN WITH HIM.
MY MEN ARE ALL ACCOUNTED FOR?
THAT'S WHY I'M HERE. THE TEAM LEADER'S MISSING. WE HAVE TO ASSUME HE'S BEEN INTERROGATED.
AND IF DEVON HAS THROWN IN WITH MARSHALL, AND THEY KNOW YOU'RE HERE, WELL...
DEVON WROTE THE *BOOK* ON BLACK OPS. HE GOES WHERE HE WANTS TO GO--AND YOU'LL *NEVER* SEE HIM COMING.
I'D BE WORRIED. BUT OUR INTEL FROM YOUR BOYS SUGGESTS THEY'RE TRAVELLING WITH TWO KIDS. NOMADS. REFUGEES.
COULD BE A FATAL LIABILITY FOR OUR TARGETS. LITTLE BOY AND A TEENAGE GIRL.

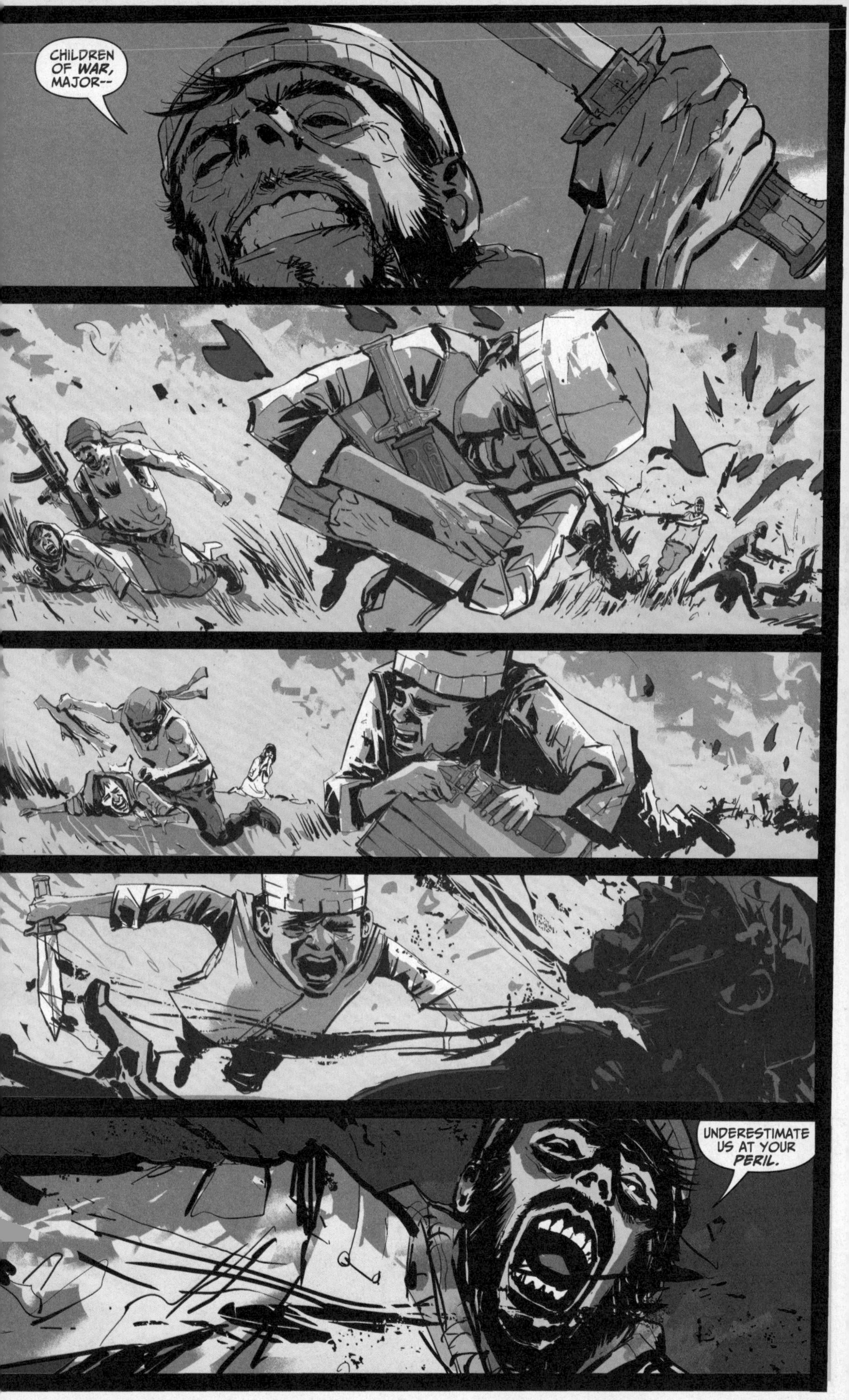
CHILDREN OF WAR, MAJOR--
UNDERESTIMATE US AT YOUR PERIL.

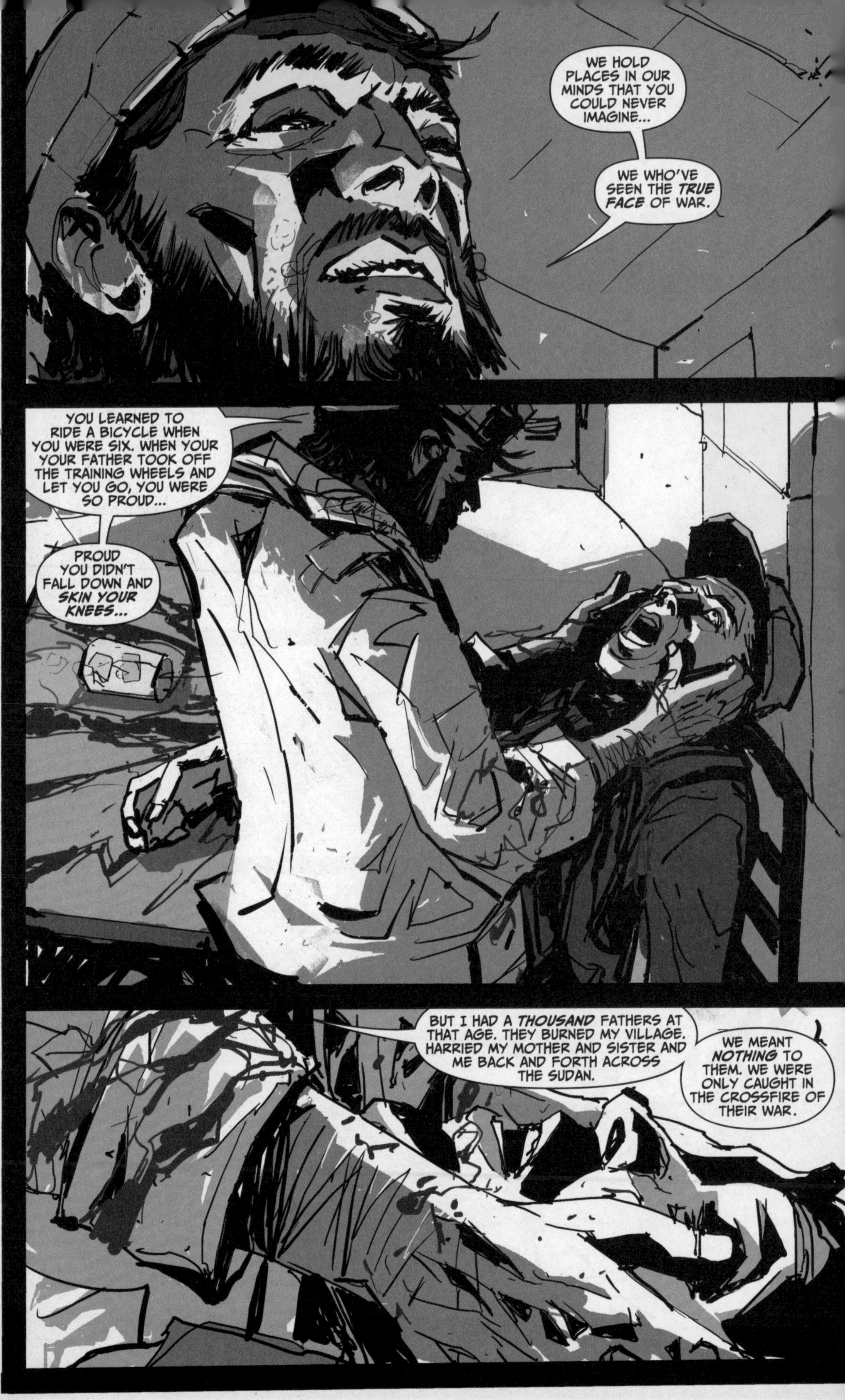
WE HOLD PLACES IN OUR MINDS THAT YOU COULD NEVER IMAGINE...
WE WHO'VE SEEN THE TRUE FACE OF WAR.
YOU LEARNED TO RIDE A BICYCLE WHEN YOU WERE SIX. WHEN YOUR YOUR FATHER TOOK OFF THE TRAINING WHEELS AND LET YOU GO, YOU WERE SO PROUD...
PROUD YOU DIDN'T FALL DOWN AND SKIN YOUR KNEES...
BUT I HAD A THOUSAND FATHERS AT THAT AGE. THEY BURNED MY VILLAGE. HARRIED MY MOTHER AND SISTER AND ME BACK AND FORTH ACROSS THE SUDAN.
WE MEANT NOTHING TO THEM. WE WERE ONLY CAUGHT IN THE CROSSFIRE OF THEIR WAR.

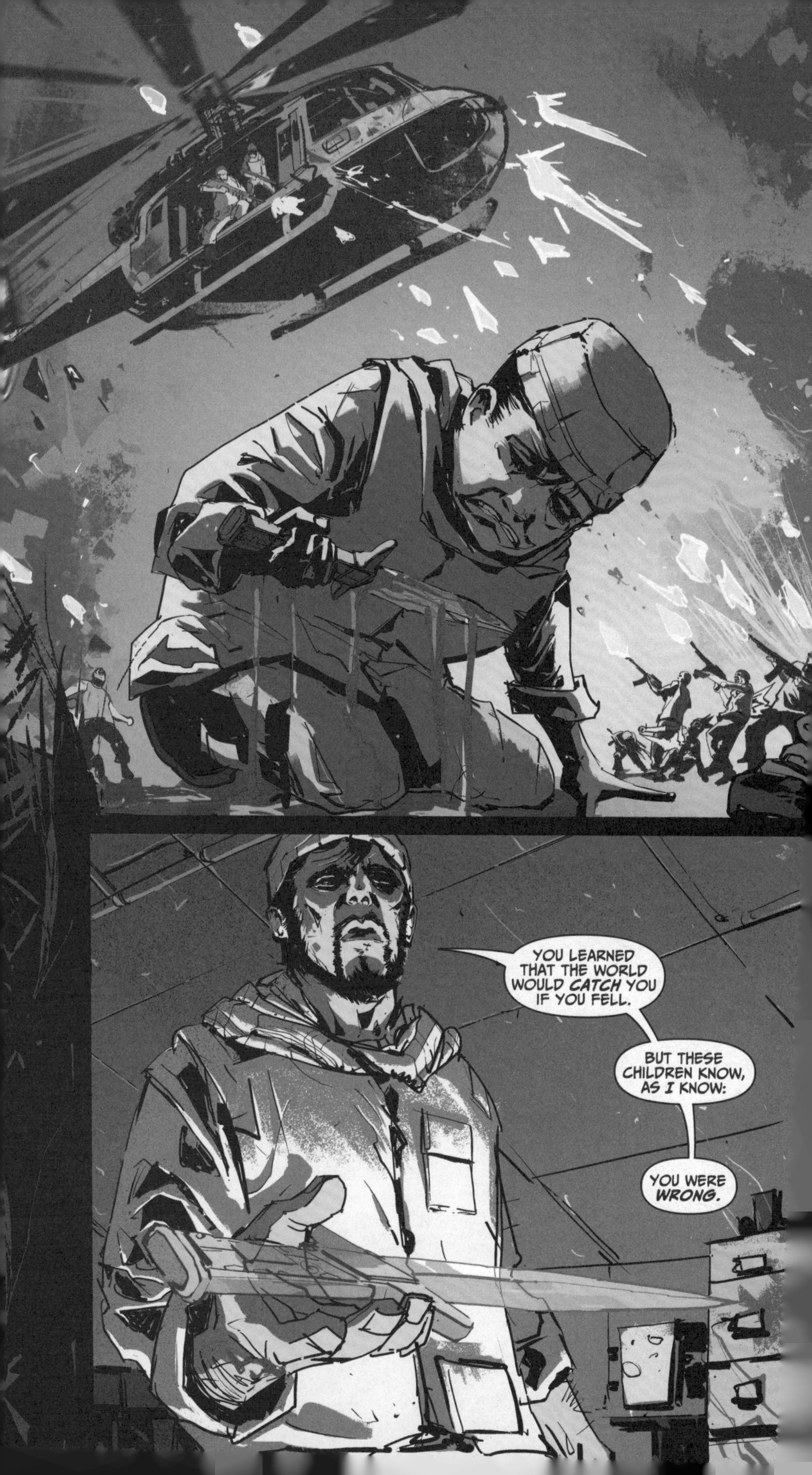
YOU LEARNED THAT THE WORLD WOULD CATCH YOU IF YOU FELL.
BUT THESE CHILDREN KNOW, AS I KNOW:
YOU WERE WRONG.

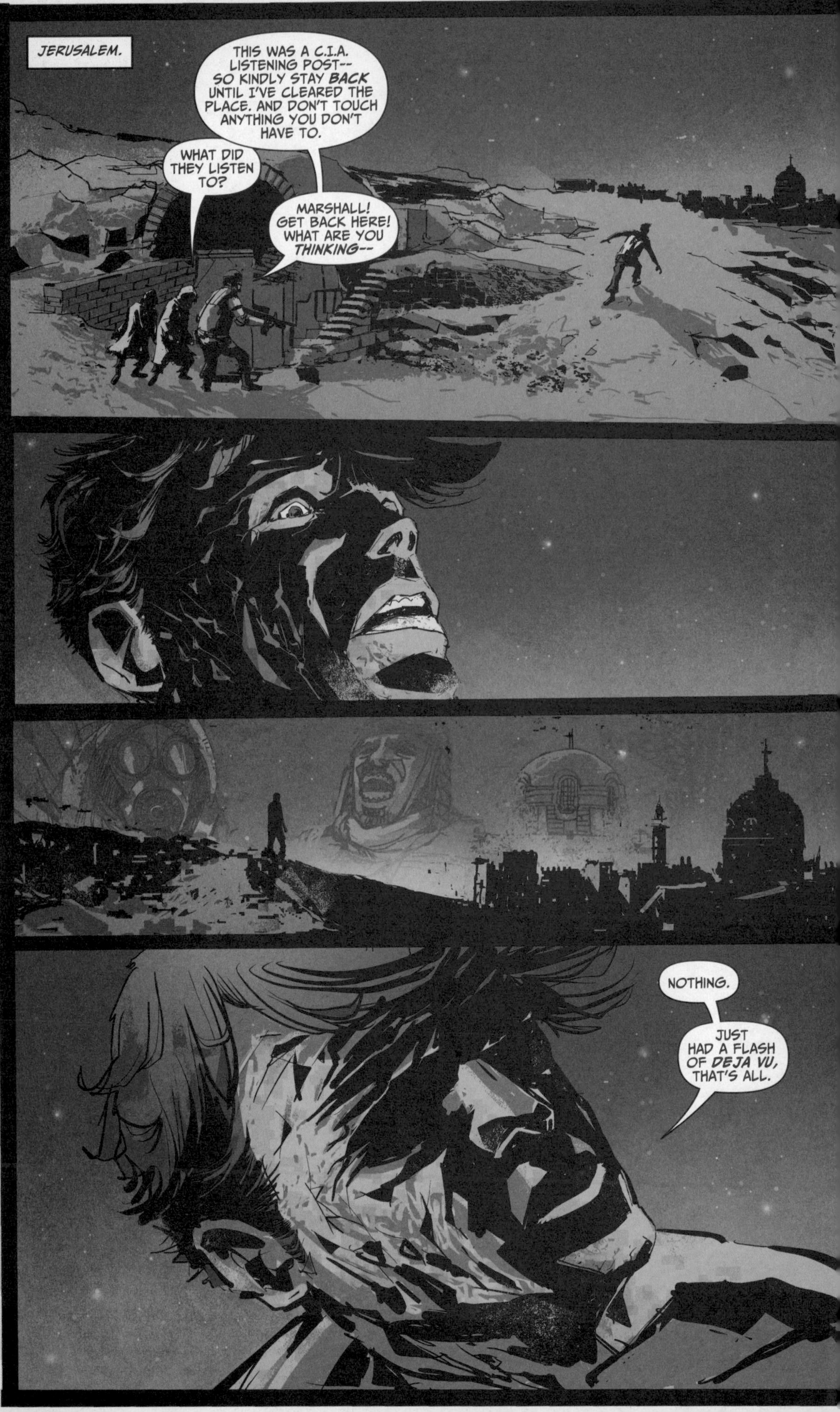
JERUSALEM.
THIS WAS A C.I.A. LISTENING POST-- SO KINDLY STAY BACK UNTIL I'VE CLEARED THE PLACE. AND DON'T TOUCH ANYTHING YOU DON'T HAVE TO.
WHAT DID THEY LISTEN TO?
MARSHALL! GET BACK HERE! WHAT ARE YOU THINKING--
NOTHING.
JUST HAD A FLASH OF DEJA VU, THAT'S ALL.

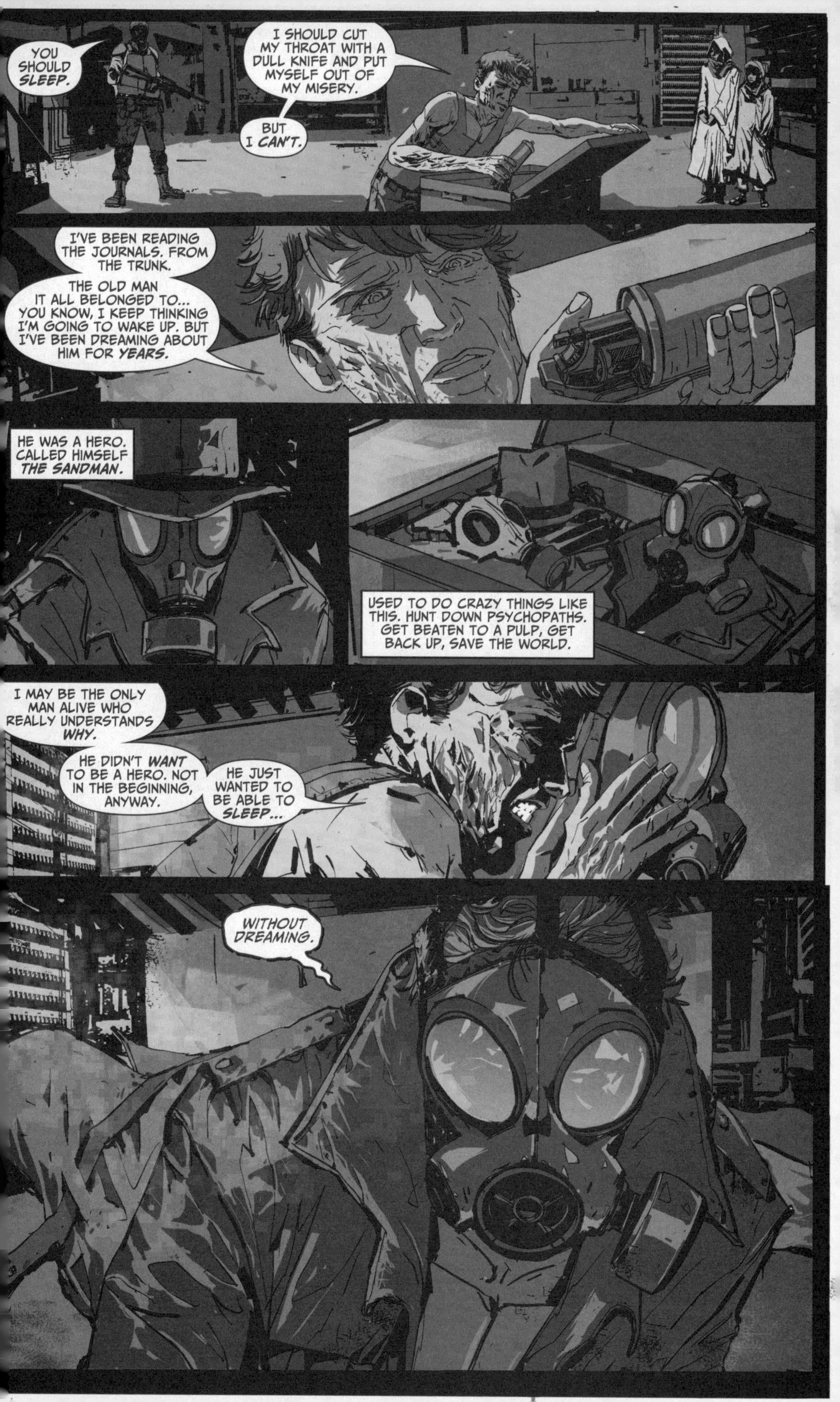

YOU SHOULD SLEEP.
I SHOULD CUT MY THROAT WITH A DULL KNIFE AND PUT MYSELF OUT OF MY MISERY.
BUT I CAN'T.
I'VE BEEN READING THE JOURNALS. FROM THE TRUNK.
THE OLD MAN IT ALL BELONGED TO... YOU KNOW, I KEEP THINKING I'M GOING TO WAKE UP. BUT I'VE BEEN DREAMING ABOUT HIM FOR YEARS.
HE WAS A HERO. CALLED HIMSELF THE SANDMAN.
USED TO DO CRAZY THINGS LIKE THIS. HUNT DOWN PSYCHOPATHS. GET BEATEN TO A PULP, GET BACK UP, SAVE THE WORLD.
I MAY BE THE ONLY MAN ALIVE WHO REALLY UNDERSTANDS WHY.
HE DIDN'T WANT TO BE A HERO. NOT IN THE BEGINNING, ANYWAY.
HE JUST WANTED TO BE ABLE TO SLEEP...
WITHOUT DREAMING.

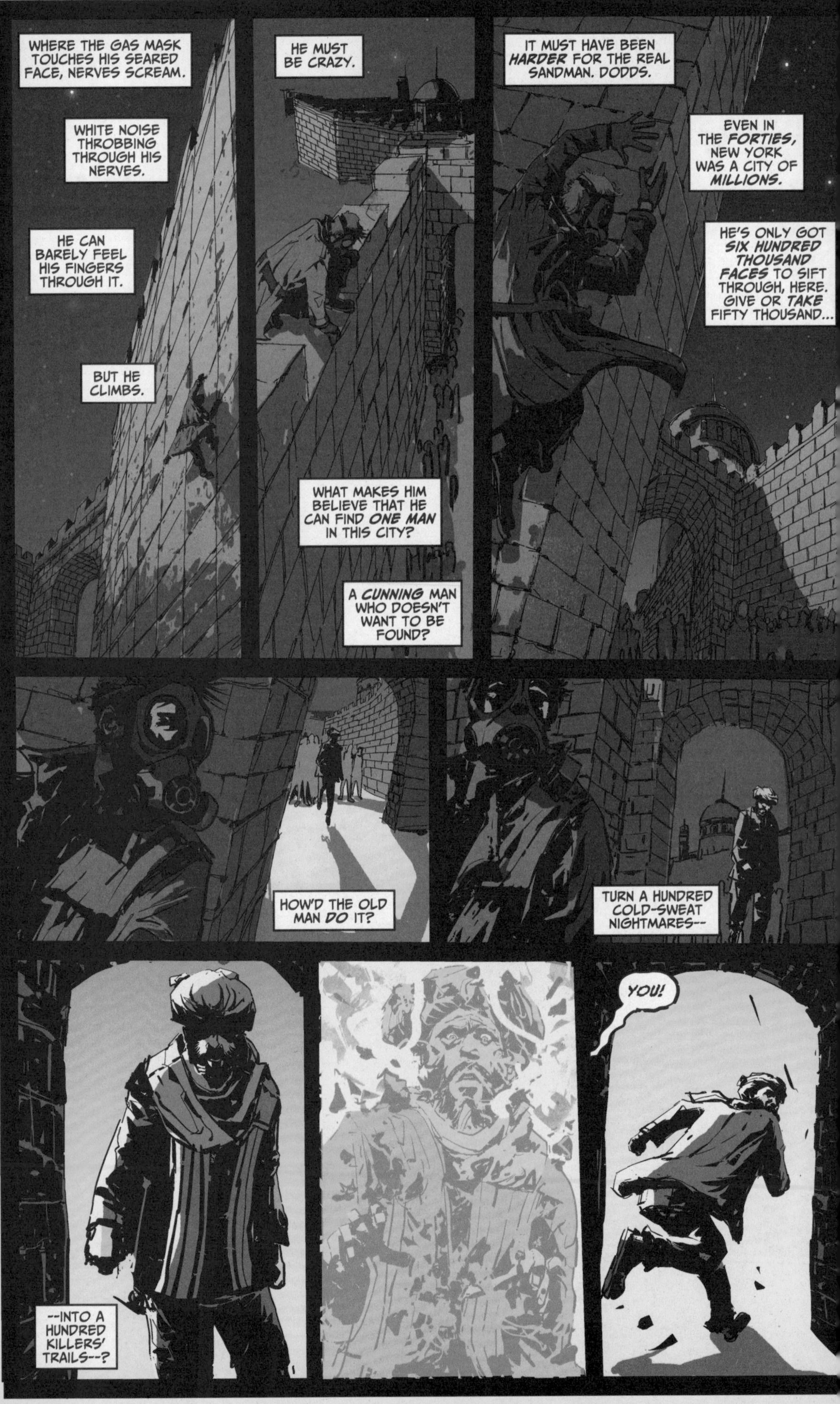
WHERE THE GAS MASK TOUCHES HIS SEARED FACE, NERVES SCREAM.
WHITE NOISE THROBBING THROUGH HIS NERVES.
HE CAN BARELY FEEL HIS FINGERS THROUGH IT.
BUT HE CLIMBS.
HE MUST BE CRAZY.
WHAT MAKES HIM BELIEVE THAT HE CAN FIND *ONE MAN* IN THIS CITY?
A *CUNNING* MAN WHO DOESN'T WANT TO BE FOUND?
IT MUST HAVE BEEN *HARDER* FOR THE REAL SANDMAN. DODDS.
EVEN IN THE *FORTIES*, NEW YORK WAS A CITY OF *MILLIONS*.
HE'S ONLY GOT *SIX HUNDRED THOUSAND FACES* TO SIFT THROUGH, HERE. GIVE OR *TAKE* FIFTY THOUSAND...
HOW'D THE OLD MAN *DO* IT?
TURN A HUNDRED COLD-SWEAT NIGHTMARES--
--INTO A HUNDRED KILLERS' TRAILS--?
YOU!

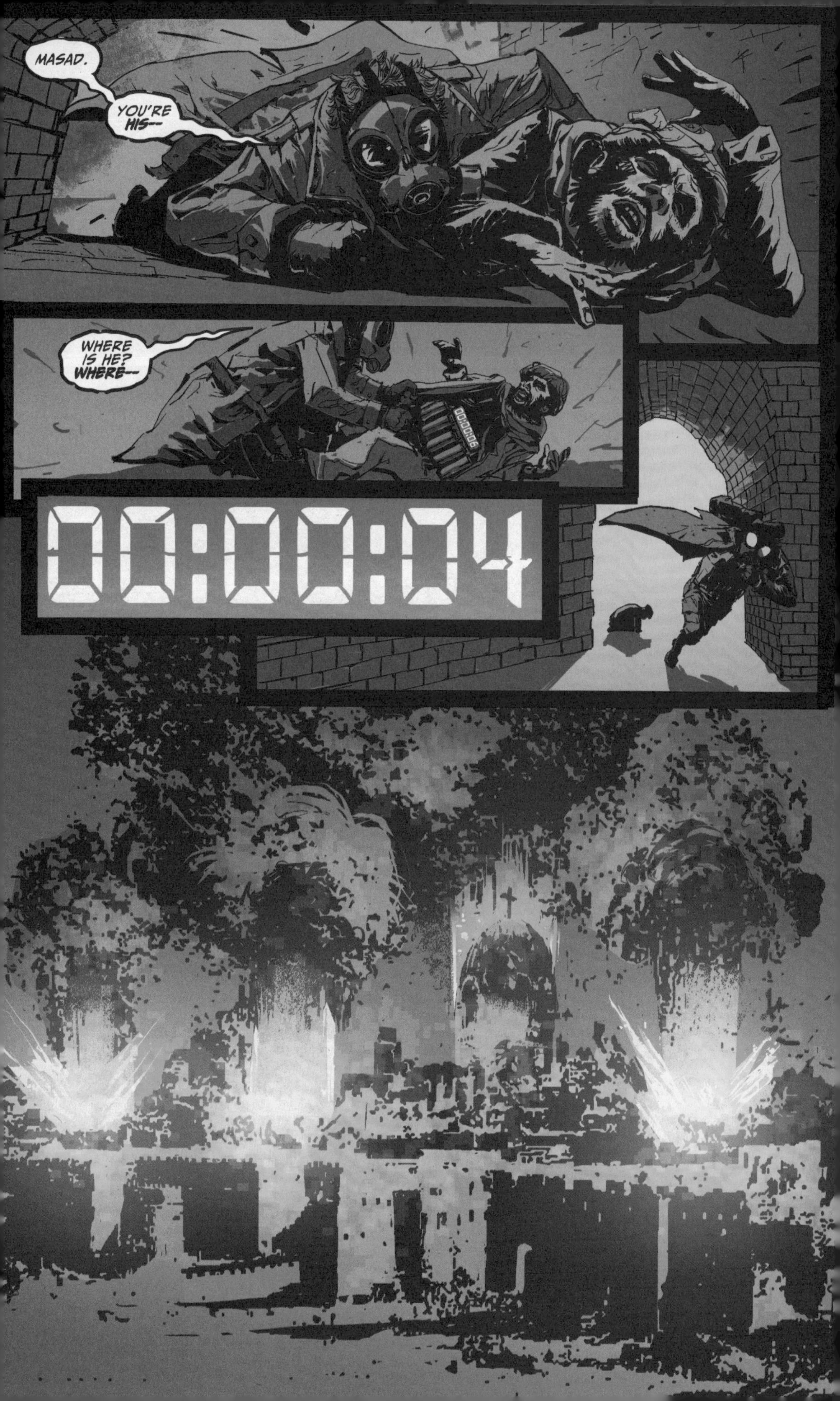
MASAD.
YOU'RE HIS--
WHERE IS HE? WHERE--
00:00:06
00:00:04

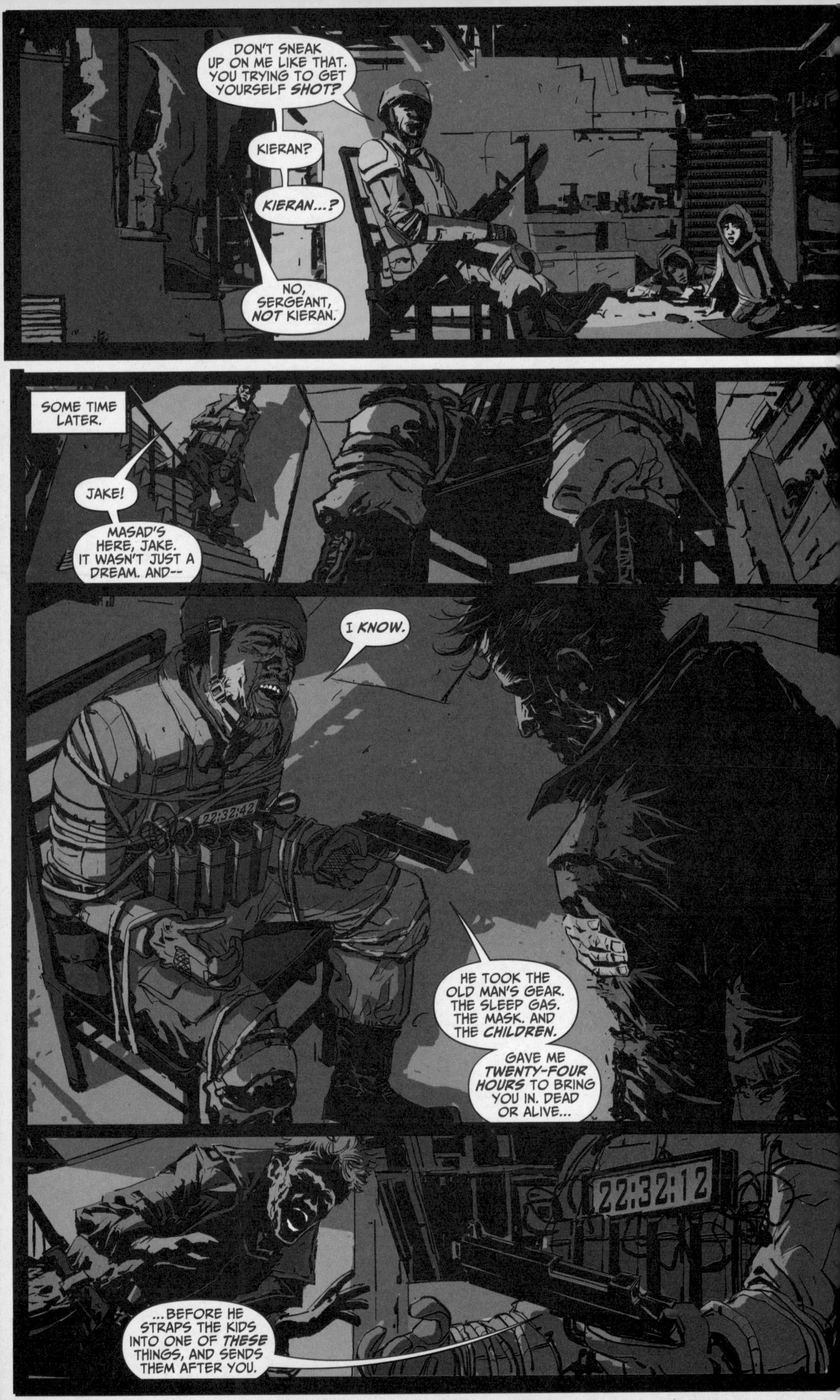

DON'T SNEAK UP ON ME LIKE THAT. YOU TRYING TO GET YOURSELF SHOT?
KIERAN?
KIERAN...?
NO, SERGEANT, NOT KIERAN.
SOME TIME LATER.
JAKE!
MASAD'S HERE, JAKE. IT WASN'T JUST A DREAM. AND--
I KNOW.
22:32:42
HE TOOK THE OLD MAN'S GEAR. THE SLEEP GAS. THE MASK. AND THE CHILDREN.
GAVE ME TWENTY-FOUR HOURS TO BRING YOU IN. DEAD OR ALIVE...
22:32:12
...BEFORE HE STRAPS THE KIDS INTO ONE OF THESE THINGS, AND SENDS THEM AFTER YOU.

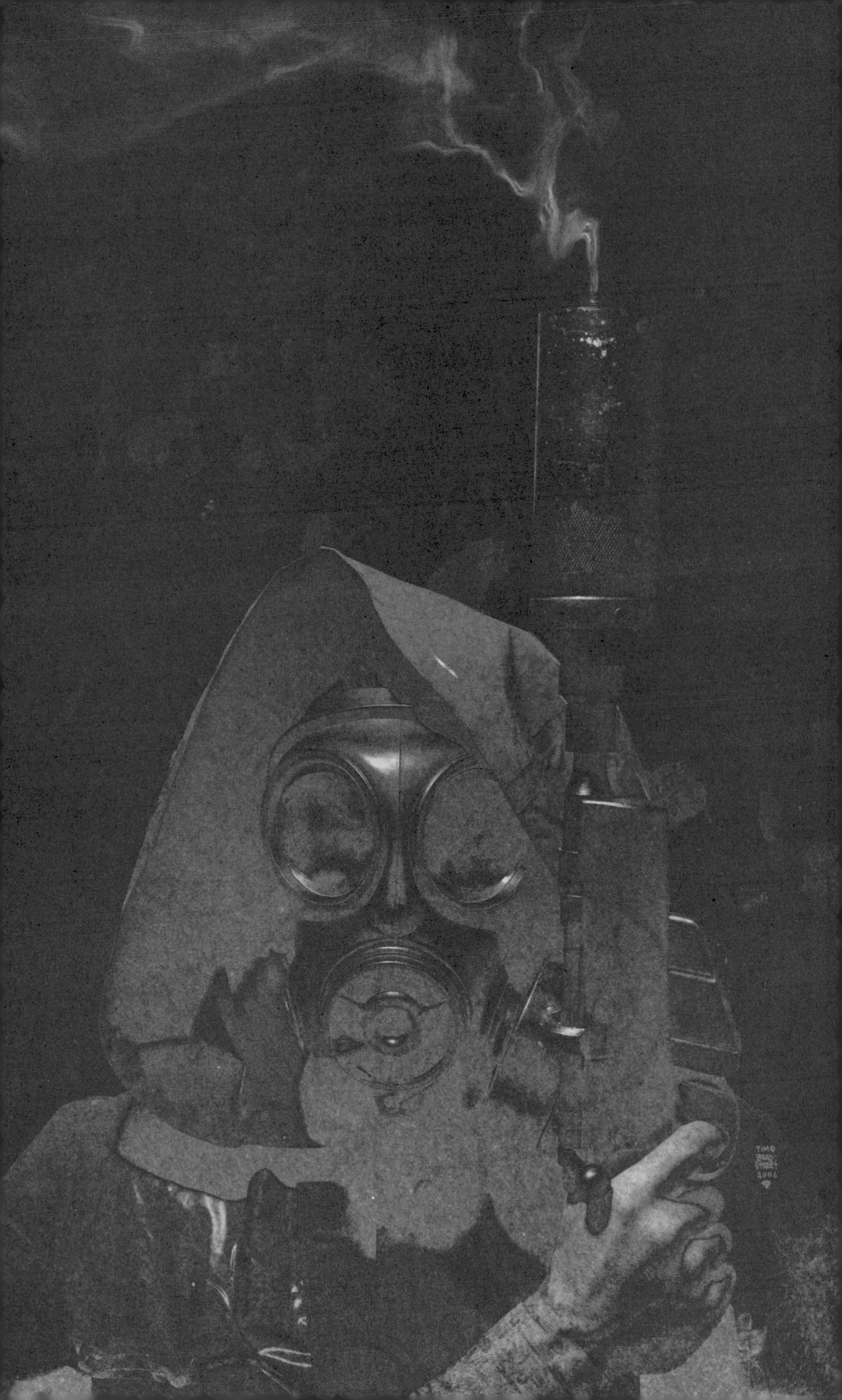
2006

CHAPTER FOUR

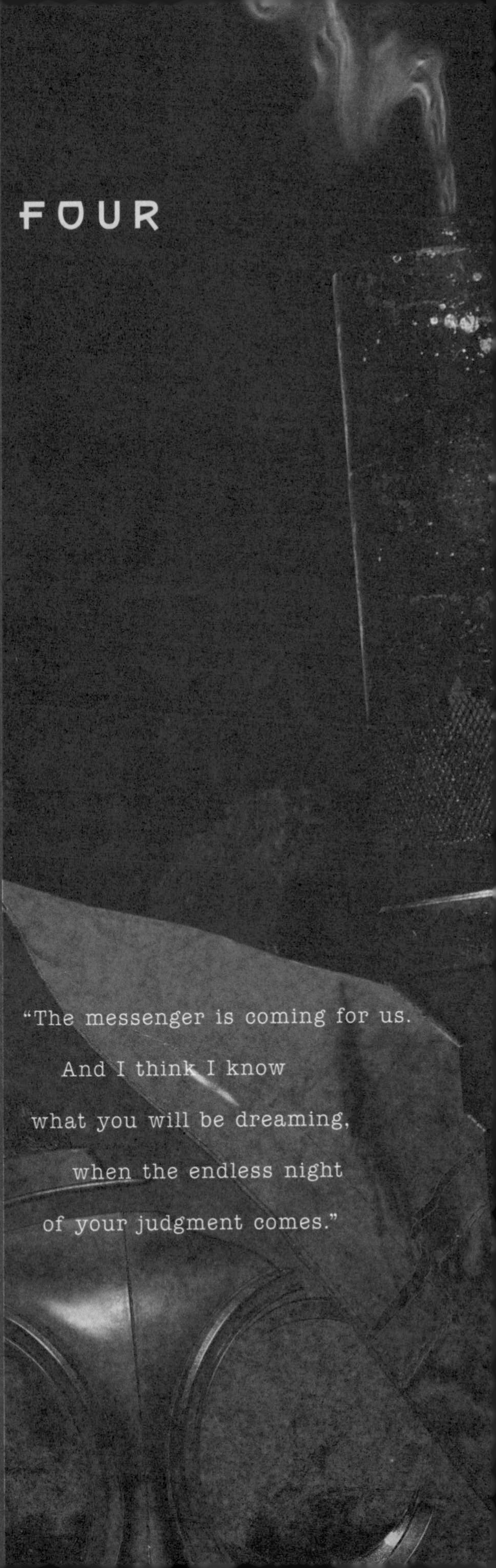

"The messenger is coming for us.
And I think I know
what you will be dreaming,
when the endless night
of your judgment comes."

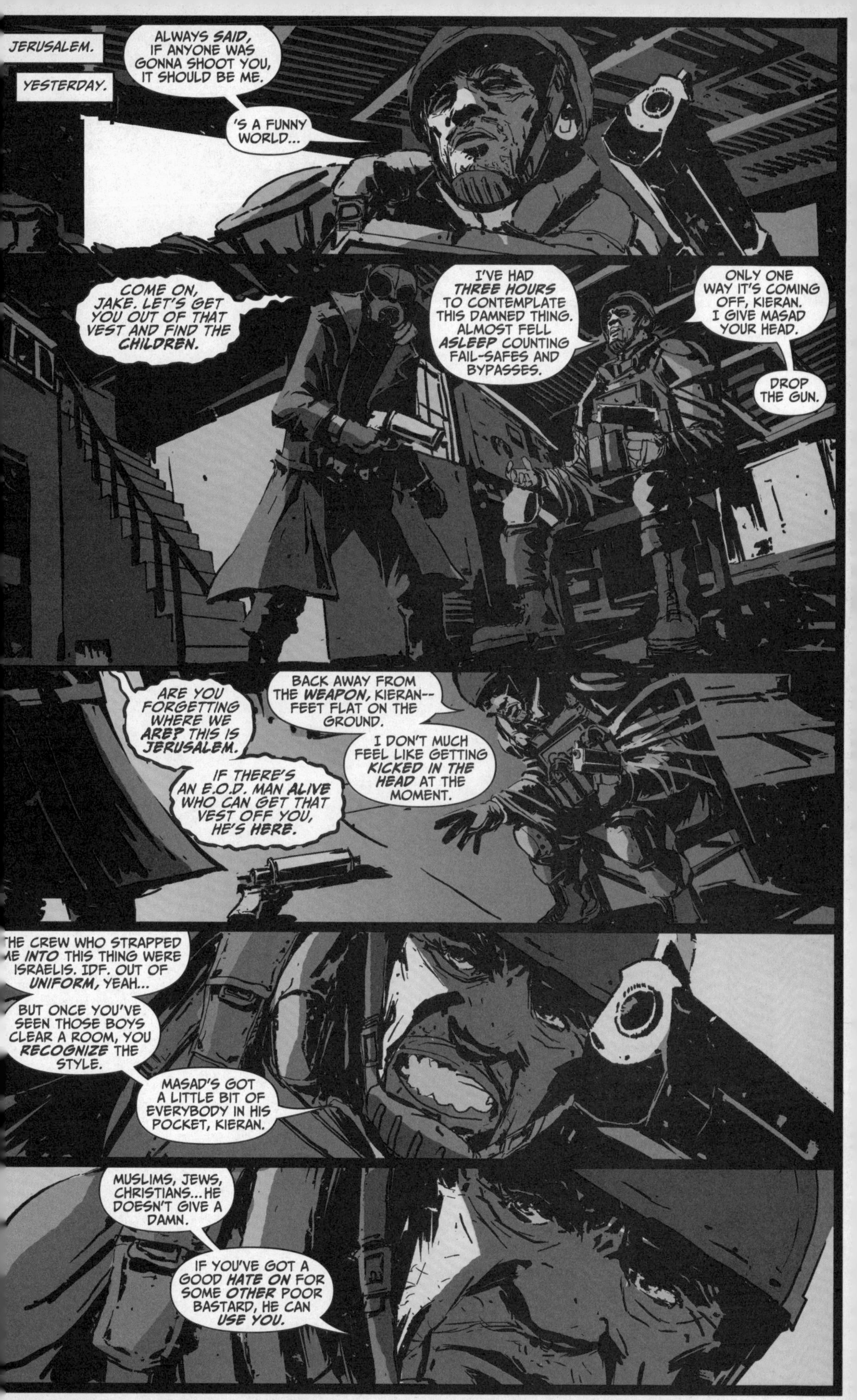

JERUSALEM.
YESTERDAY.
ALWAYS SAID, IF ANYONE WAS GONNA SHOOT YOU, IT SHOULD BE ME.
'S A FUNNY WORLD...
COME ON, JAKE. LET'S GET YOU OUT OF THAT VEST AND FIND THE CHILDREN.
I'VE HAD THREE HOURS TO CONTEMPLATE THIS DAMNED THING. ALMOST FELL ASLEEP COUNTING FAIL-SAFES AND BYPASSES.
ONLY ONE WAY IT'S COMING OFF, KIERAN. I GIVE MASAD YOUR HEAD.
DROP THE GUN.
ARE YOU FORGETTING WHERE WE ARE? THIS IS JERUSALEM.
IF THERE'S AN E.O.D. MAN ALIVE WHO CAN GET THAT VEST OFF YOU, HE'S HERE.
BACK AWAY FROM THE WEAPON, KIERAN-- FEET FLAT ON THE GROUND.
I DON'T MUCH FEEL LIKE GETTING KICKED IN THE HEAD AT THE MOMENT.
THE CREW WHO STRAPPED ME INTO THIS THING WERE ISRAELIS. IDF. OUT OF UNIFORM, YEAH...
BUT ONCE YOU'VE SEEN THOSE BOYS CLEAR A ROOM, YOU RECOGNIZE THE STYLE.
MASAD'S GOT A LITTLE BIT OF EVERYBODY IN HIS POCKET, KIERAN.
MUSLIMS, JEWS, CHRISTIANS...HE DOESN'T GIVE A DAMN.
IF YOU'VE GOT A GOOD HATE ON FOR SOME OTHER POOR BASTARD, HE CAN USE YOU.

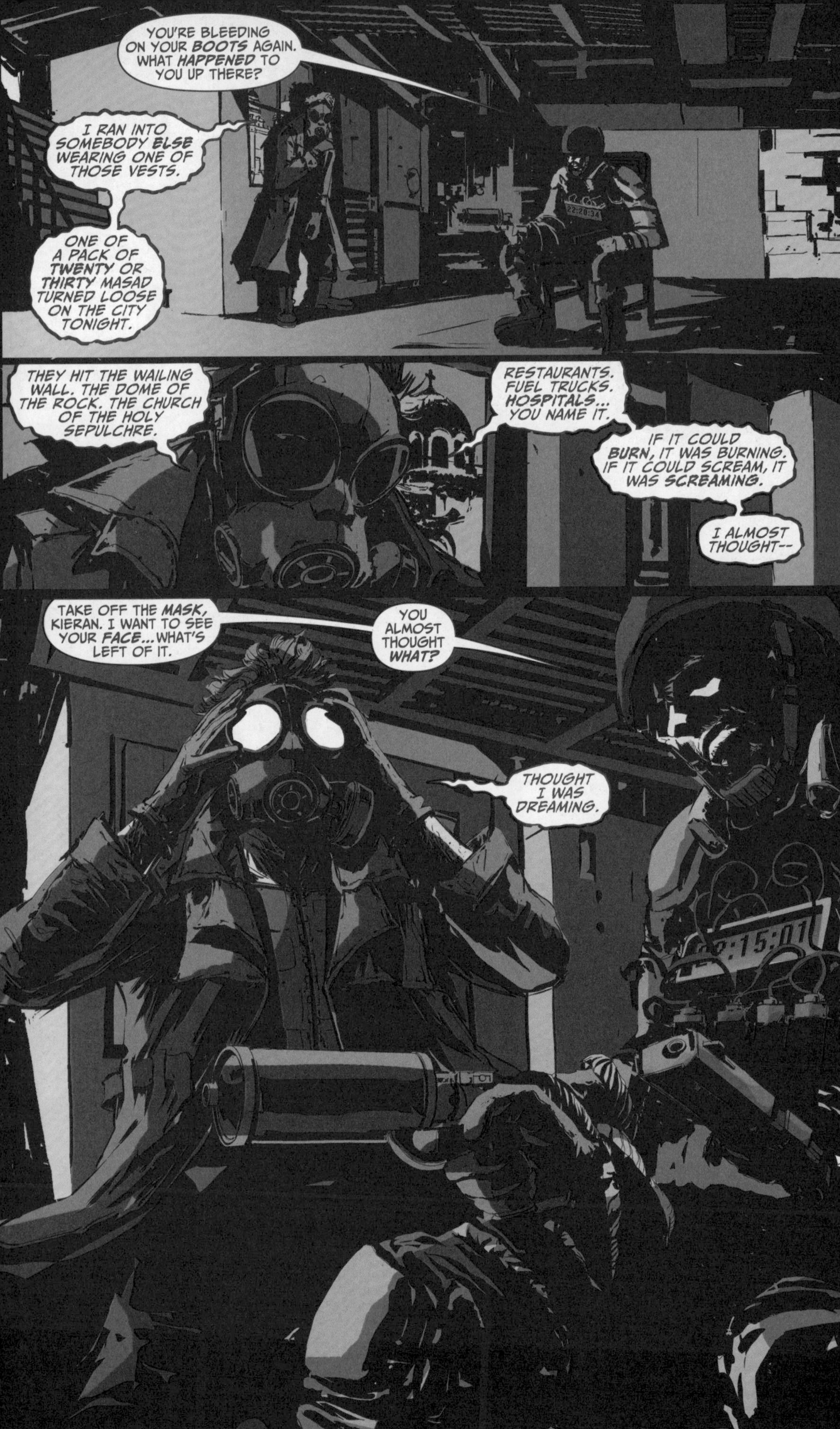
YOU'RE BLEEDING ON YOUR BOOTS AGAIN. WHAT HAPPENED TO YOU UP THERE?
I RAN INTO SOMEBODY ELSE WEARING ONE OF THOSE VESTS.
ONE OF A PACK OF TWENTY OR THIRTY MASAD TURNED LOOSE ON THE CITY TONIGHT.
22:20:34
THEY HIT THE WAILING WALL. THE DOME OF THE ROCK. THE CHURCH OF THE HOLY SEPULCHRE.
RESTAURANTS. FUEL TRUCKS. HOSPITALS... YOU NAME IT.
IF IT COULD BURN, IT WAS BURNING. IF IT COULD SCREAM, IT WAS SCREAMING.
I ALMOST THOUGHT--
TAKE OFF THE MASK, KIERAN. I WANT TO SEE YOUR FACE... WHAT'S LEFT OF IT.
YOU ALMOST THOUGHT WHAT?
THOUGHT I WAS DREAMING.

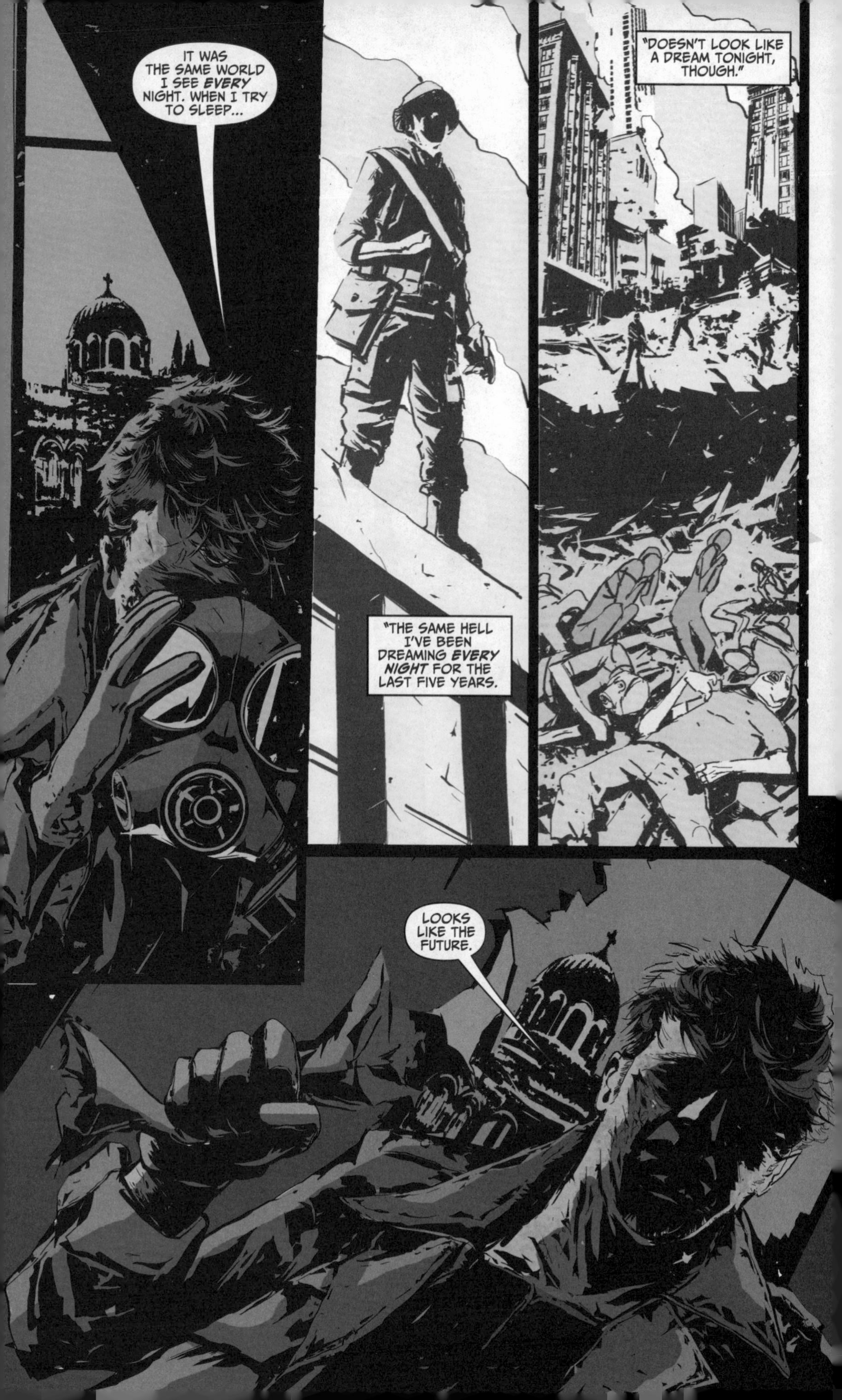
IT WAS THE SAME WORLD I SEE *EVERY* NIGHT. WHEN I TRY TO SLEEP...
"THE SAME HELL I'VE BEEN DREAMING *EVERY NIGHT* FOR THE LAST FIVE YEARS.
"DOESN'T LOOK LIKE A DREAM TONIGHT, THOUGH."
LOOKS LIKE THE FUTURE.

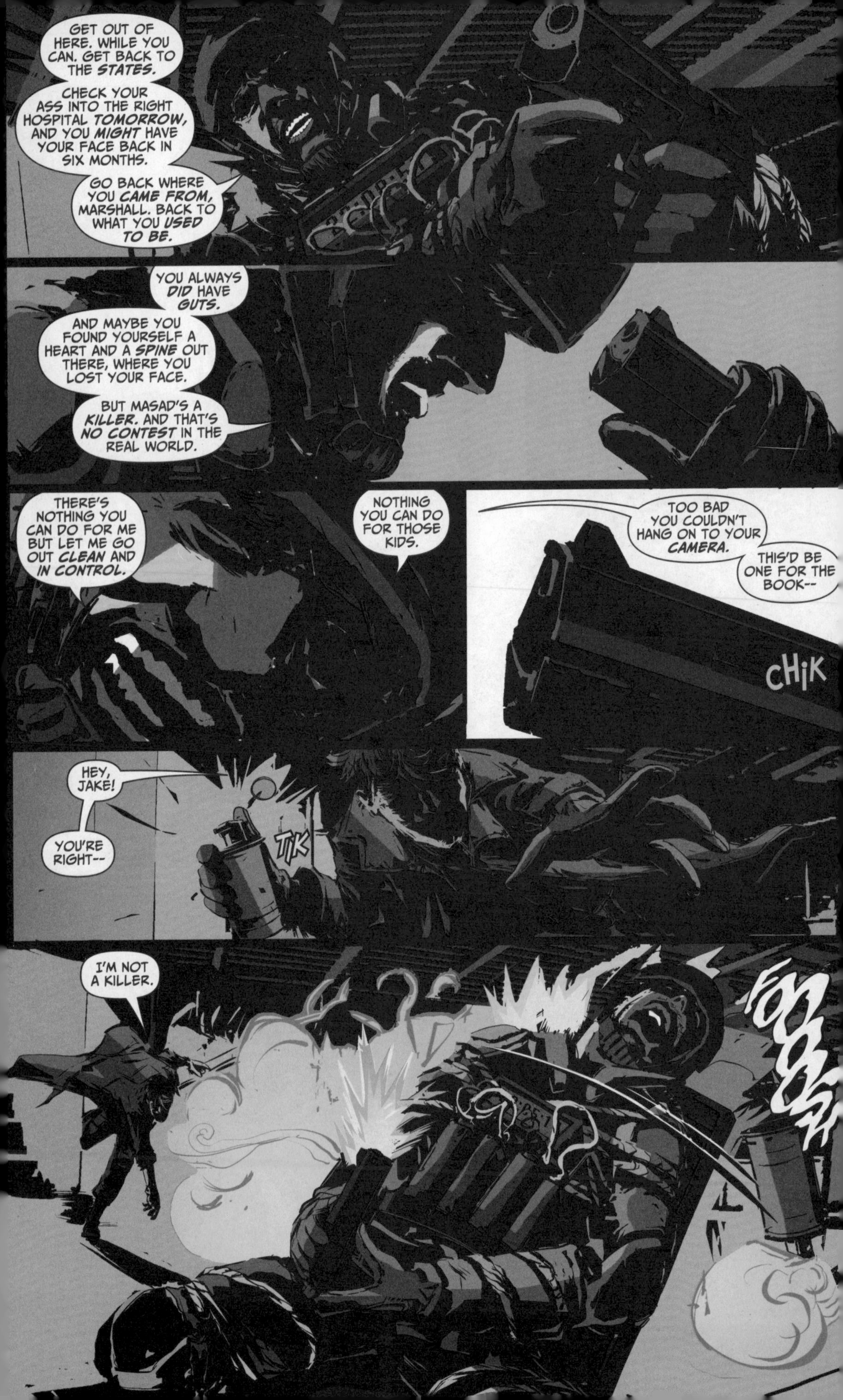
GET OUT OF HERE. WHILE YOU CAN. GET BACK TO THE STATES.
CHECK YOUR ASS INTO THE RIGHT HOSPITAL TOMORROW, AND YOU MIGHT HAVE YOUR FACE BACK IN SIX MONTHS.
GO BACK WHERE YOU CAME FROM, MARSHALL. BACK TO WHAT YOU USED TO BE.
YOU ALWAYS DID HAVE GUTS.
AND MAYBE YOU FOUND YOURSELF A HEART AND A SPINE OUT THERE, WHERE YOU LOST YOUR FACE.
BUT MASAD'S A KILLER. AND THAT'S NO CONTEST IN THE REAL WORLD.
THERE'S NOTHING YOU CAN DO FOR ME BUT LET ME GO OUT CLEAN AND IN CONTROL.
NOTHING YOU CAN DO FOR THOSE KIDS.
TOO BAD YOU COULDN'T HANG ON TO YOUR CAMERA.
THIS'D BE ONE FOR THE BOOK--
CHIK
HEY, JAKE!
YOU'RE RIGHT--
TIK
I'M NOT A KILLER.

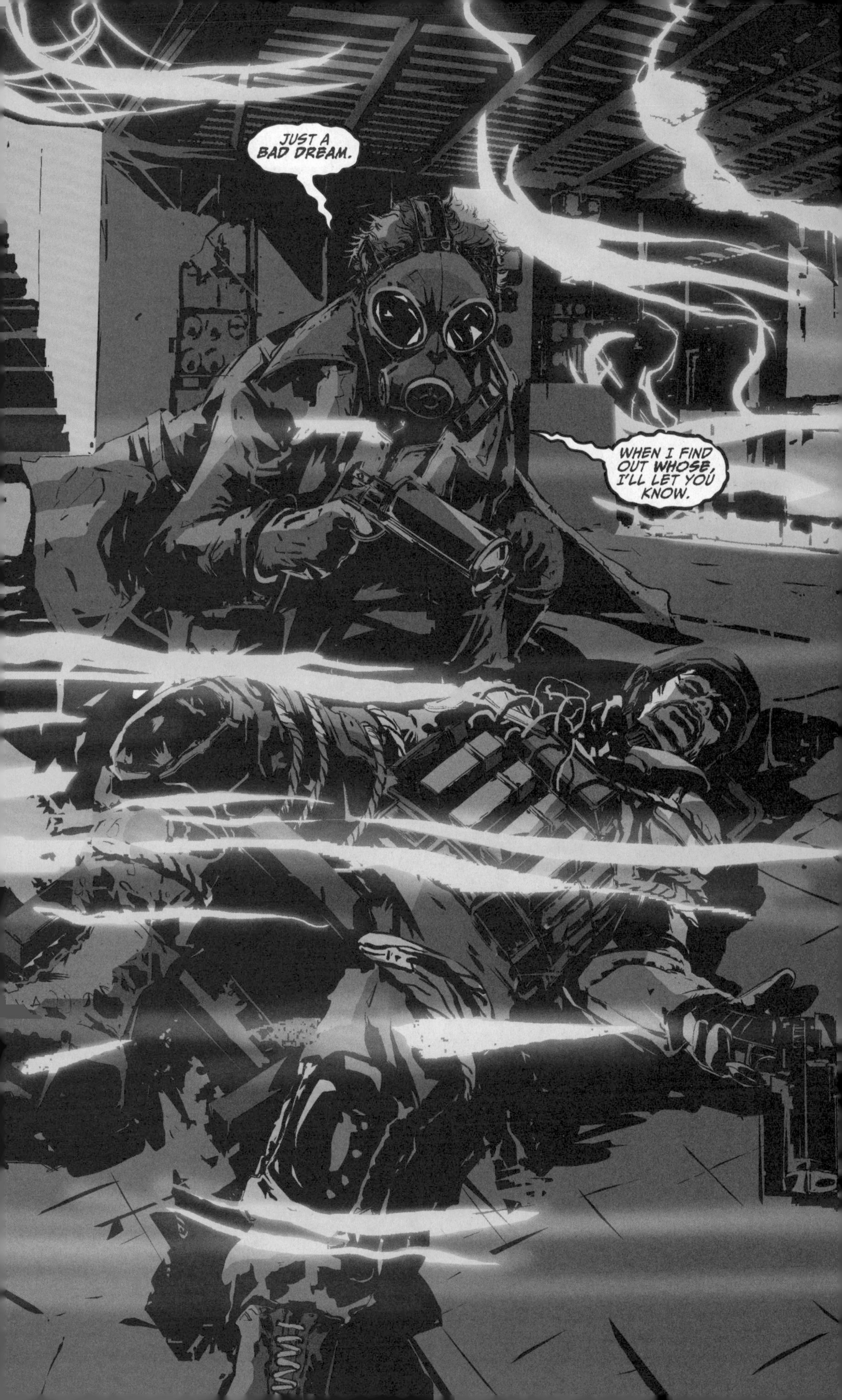
JUST A BAD DREAM.
WHEN I FIND OUT WHOSE, I'LL LET YOU KNOW.

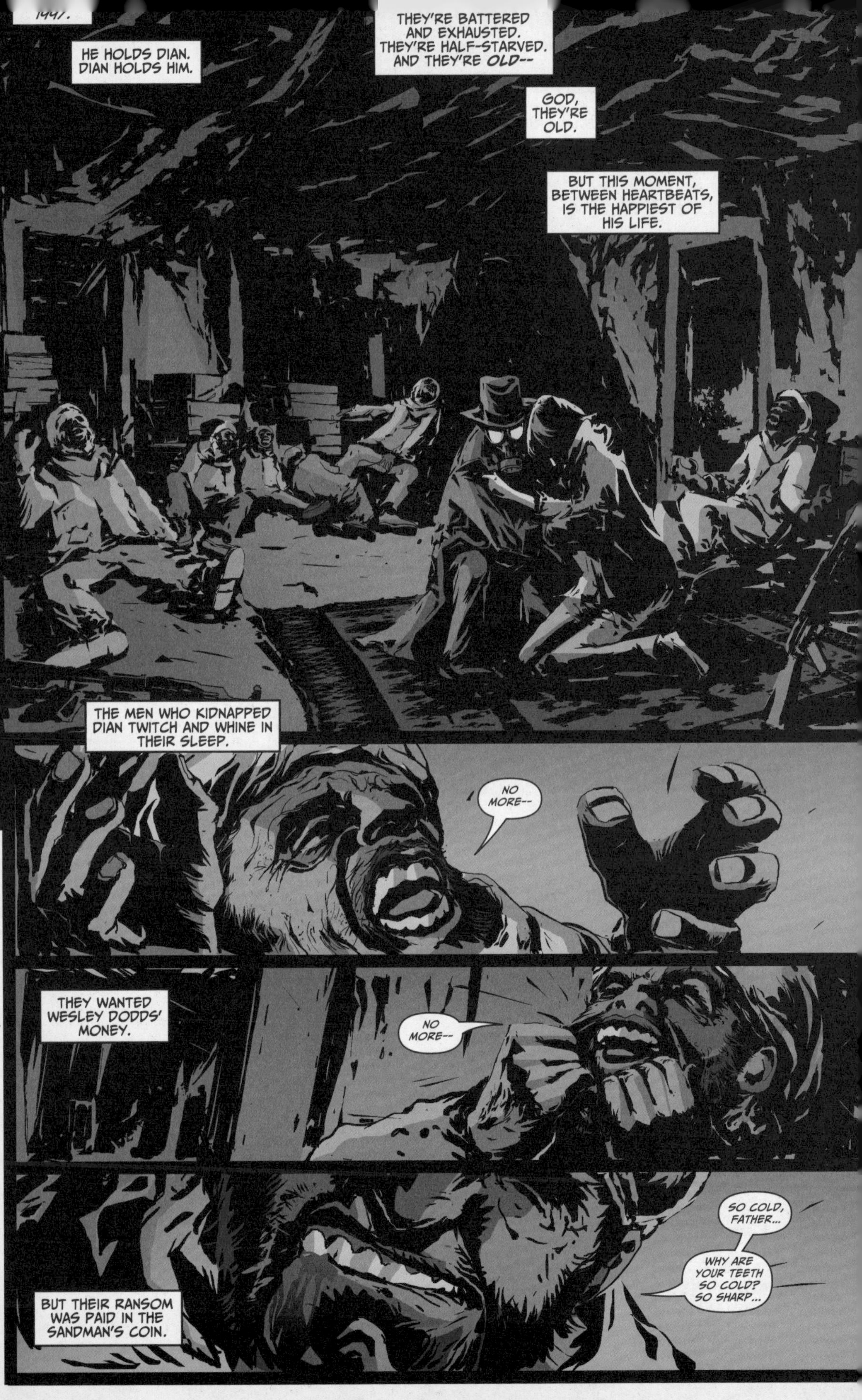
1947.
HE HOLDS DIAN. DIAN HOLDS HIM.
THEY'RE BATTERED AND EXHAUSTED. THEY'RE HALF-STARVED. AND THEY'RE *OLD*--
GOD, THEY'RE OLD.
BUT THIS MOMENT, BETWEEN HEARTBEATS, IS THE HAPPIEST OF HIS LIFE.
THE MEN WHO KIDNAPPED DIAN TWITCH AND WHINE IN THEIR SLEEP.
NO MORE--
THEY WANTED WESLEY DODDS' MONEY.
NO MORE--
BUT THEIR RANSOM WAS PAID IN THE SANDMAN'S COIN.
SO COLD, FATHER...
WHY ARE YOUR TEETH SO COLD? SO SHARP...

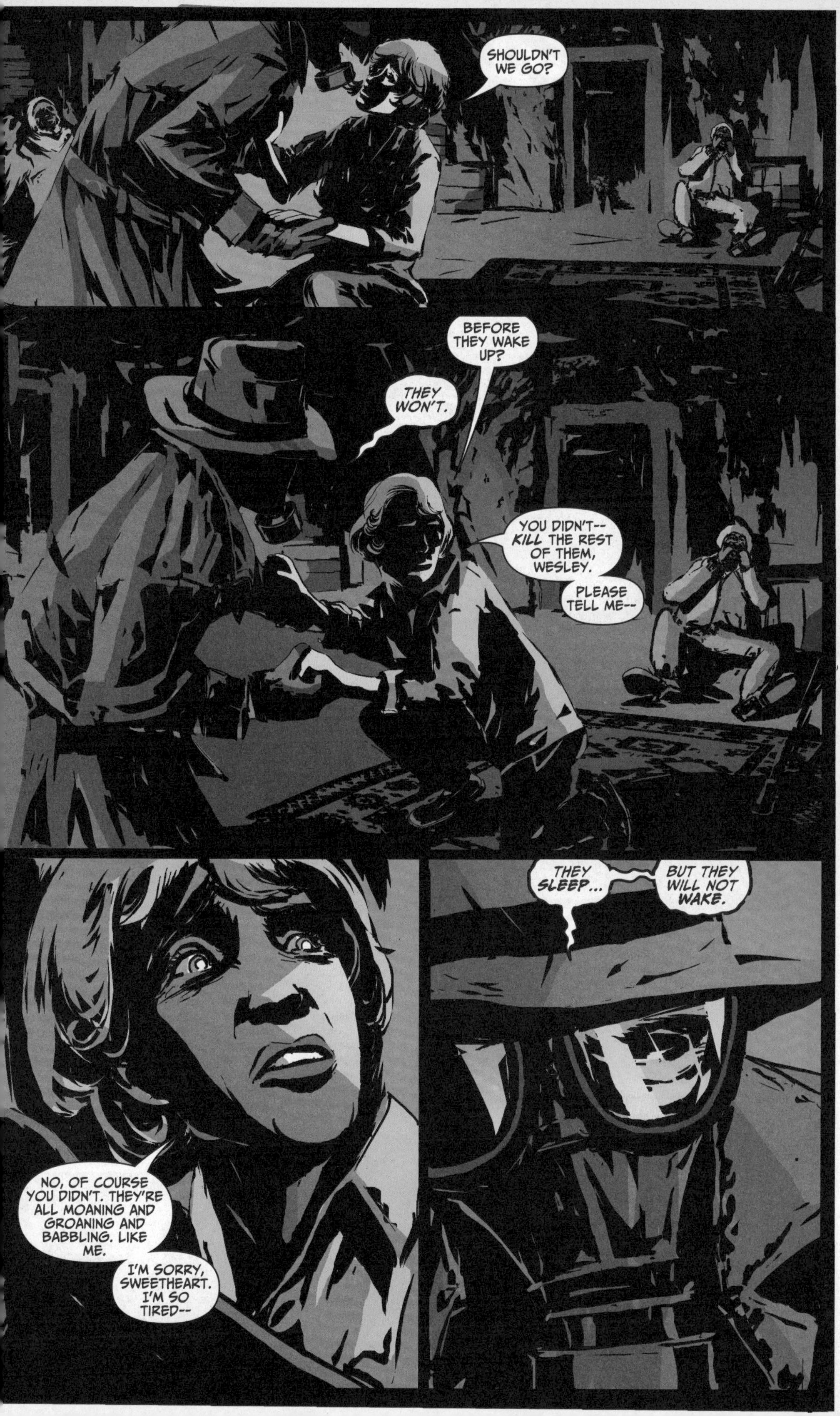
SHOULDN'T WE GO?
BEFORE THEY WAKE UP?
THEY WON'T.
YOU DIDN'T-- KILL THE REST OF THEM, WESLEY.
PLEASE TELL ME--
NO, OF COURSE YOU DIDN'T. THEY'RE ALL MOANING AND GROANING AND BABBLING. LIKE ME.
I'M SORRY, SWEETHEART. I'M SO TIRED--
THEY SLEEP...
BUT THEY WILL NOT WAKE.

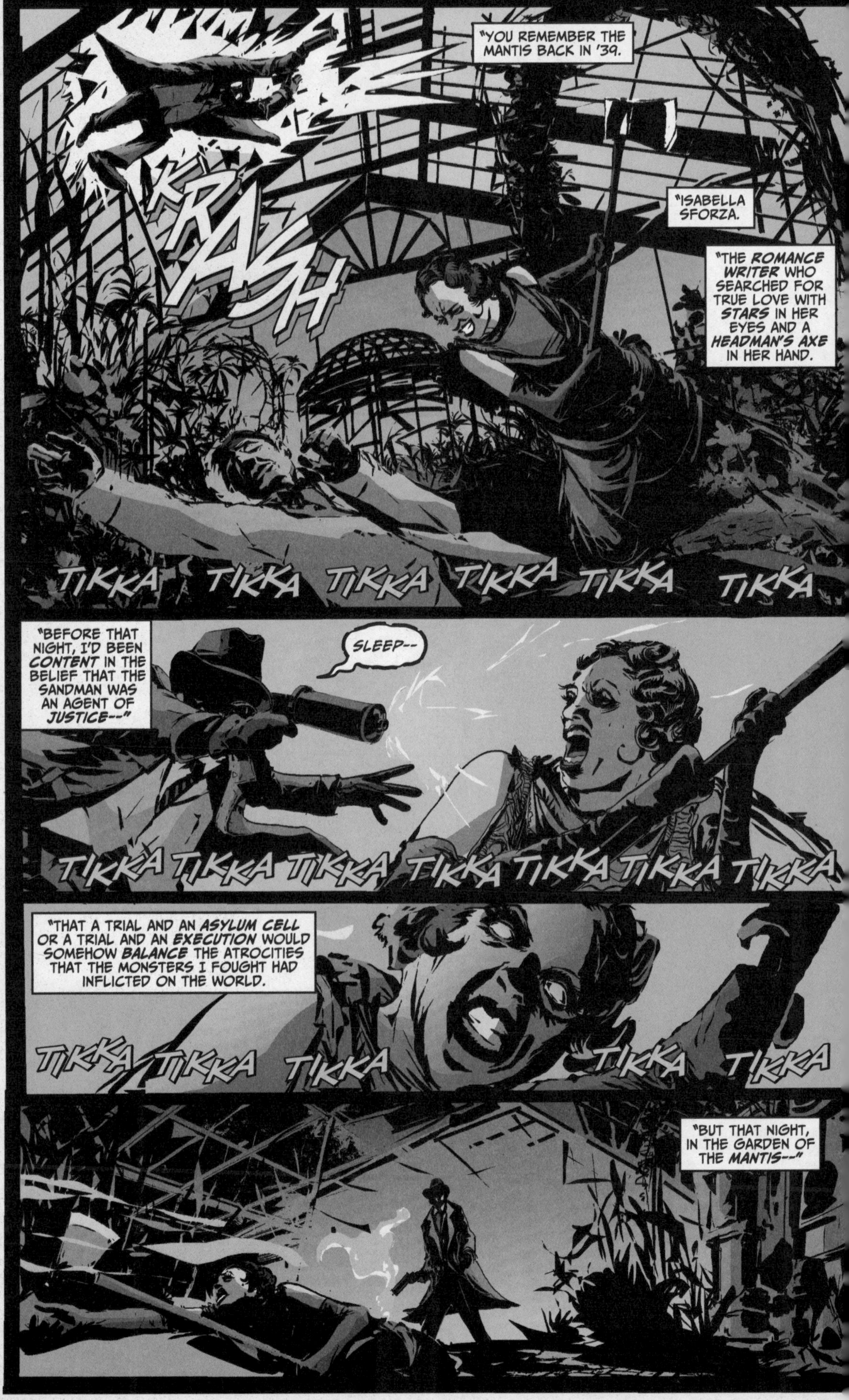

KRASH
"YOU REMEMBER THE MANTIS BACK IN '39.
"ISABELLA SFORZA.
"THE ROMANCE WRITER WHO SEARCHED FOR TRUE LOVE WITH STARS IN HER EYES AND A HEADMAN'S AXE IN HER HAND.
TIKKA TIKKA TIKKA TIKKA TIKKA TIKKA
"BEFORE THAT NIGHT, I'D BEEN CONTENT IN THE BELIEF THAT THE SANDMAN WAS AN AGENT OF JUSTICE--"
SLEEP--
TIKKA TIKKA TIKKA TIKKA TIKKA TIKKA TIKKA
"THAT A TRIAL AND AN ASYLUM CELL OR A TRIAL AND AN EXECUTION WOULD SOMEHOW BALANCE THE ATROCITIES THAT THE MONSTERS I FOUGHT HAD INFLICTED ON THE WORLD.
TIKKA TIKKA TIKKA TIKKA TIKKA
"BUT THAT NIGHT, IN THE GARDEN OF THE MANTIS--"

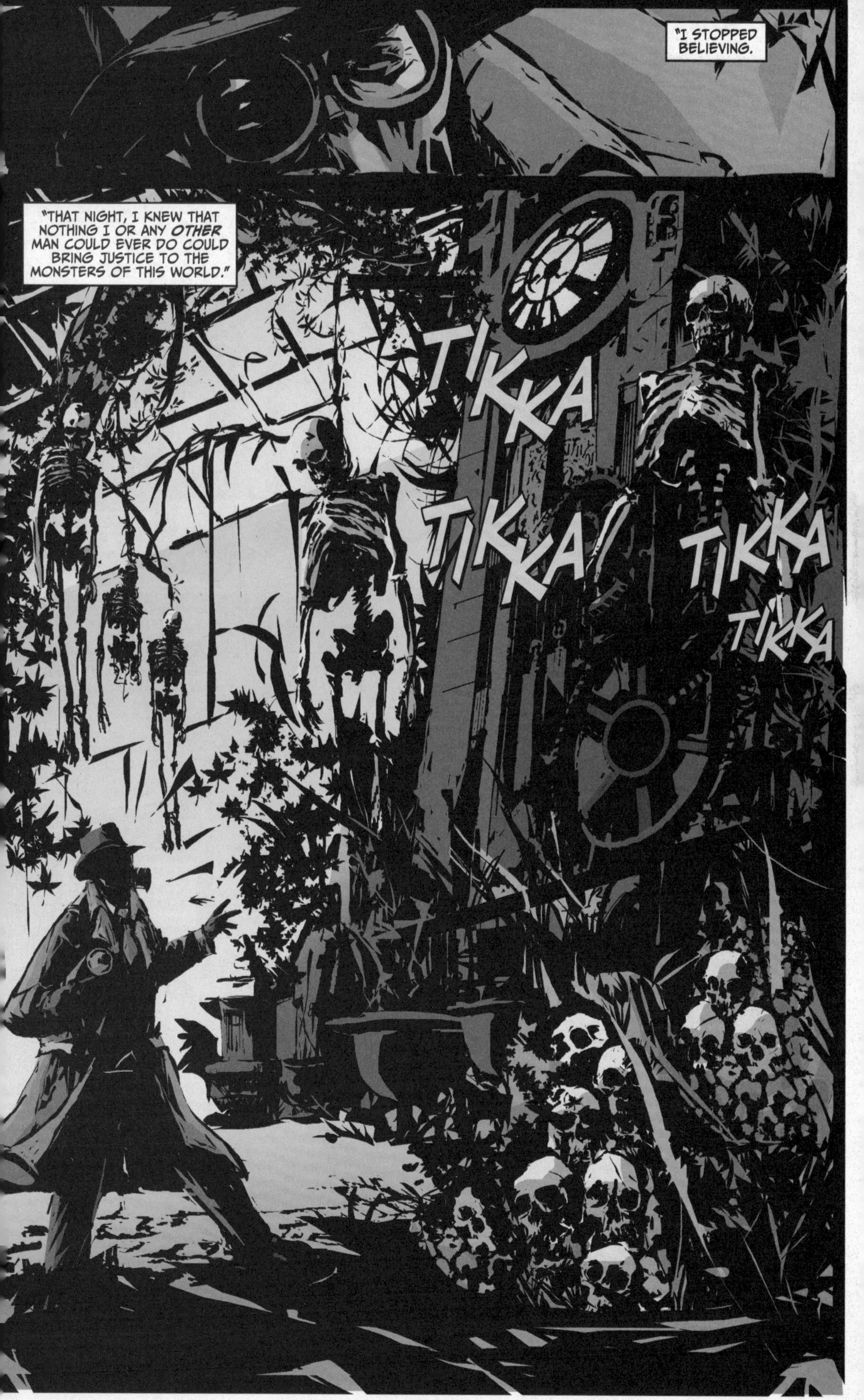
"I STOPPED BELIEVING.
"THAT NIGHT, I KNEW THAT NOTHING I OR ANY OTHER MAN COULD EVER DO COULD BRING JUSTICE TO THE MONSTERS OF THIS WORLD."
TIKKA
TIKKA
TIKKA
TIKKA

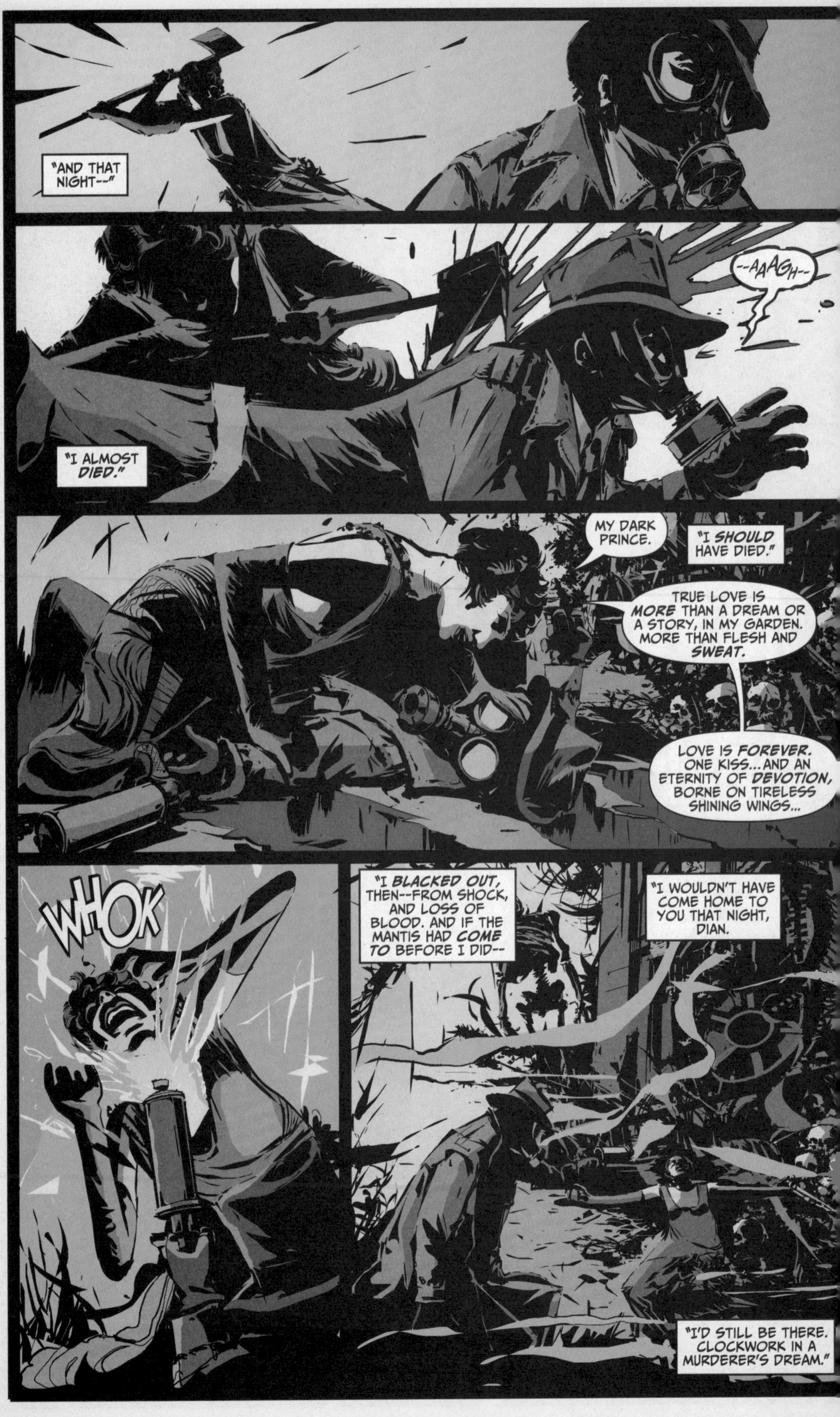
"AND THAT NIGHT--"
--AAAGH--
"I ALMOST DIED."
MY DARK PRINCE.
"I SHOULD HAVE DIED."
TRUE LOVE IS MORE THAN A DREAM OR A STORY, IN MY GARDEN. MORE THAN FLESH AND SWEAT.
LOVE IS FOREVER. ONE KISS... AND AN ETERNITY OF DEVOTION, BORNE ON TIRELESS SHINING WINGS...
WHOK
"I BLACKED OUT, THEN--FROM SHOCK, AND LOSS OF BLOOD. AND IF THE MANTIS HAD COME TO BEFORE I DID--
"I WOULDN'T HAVE COME HOME TO YOU THAT NIGHT, DIAN.
"I'D STILL BE THERE. CLOCKWORK IN A MURDERER'S DREAM."

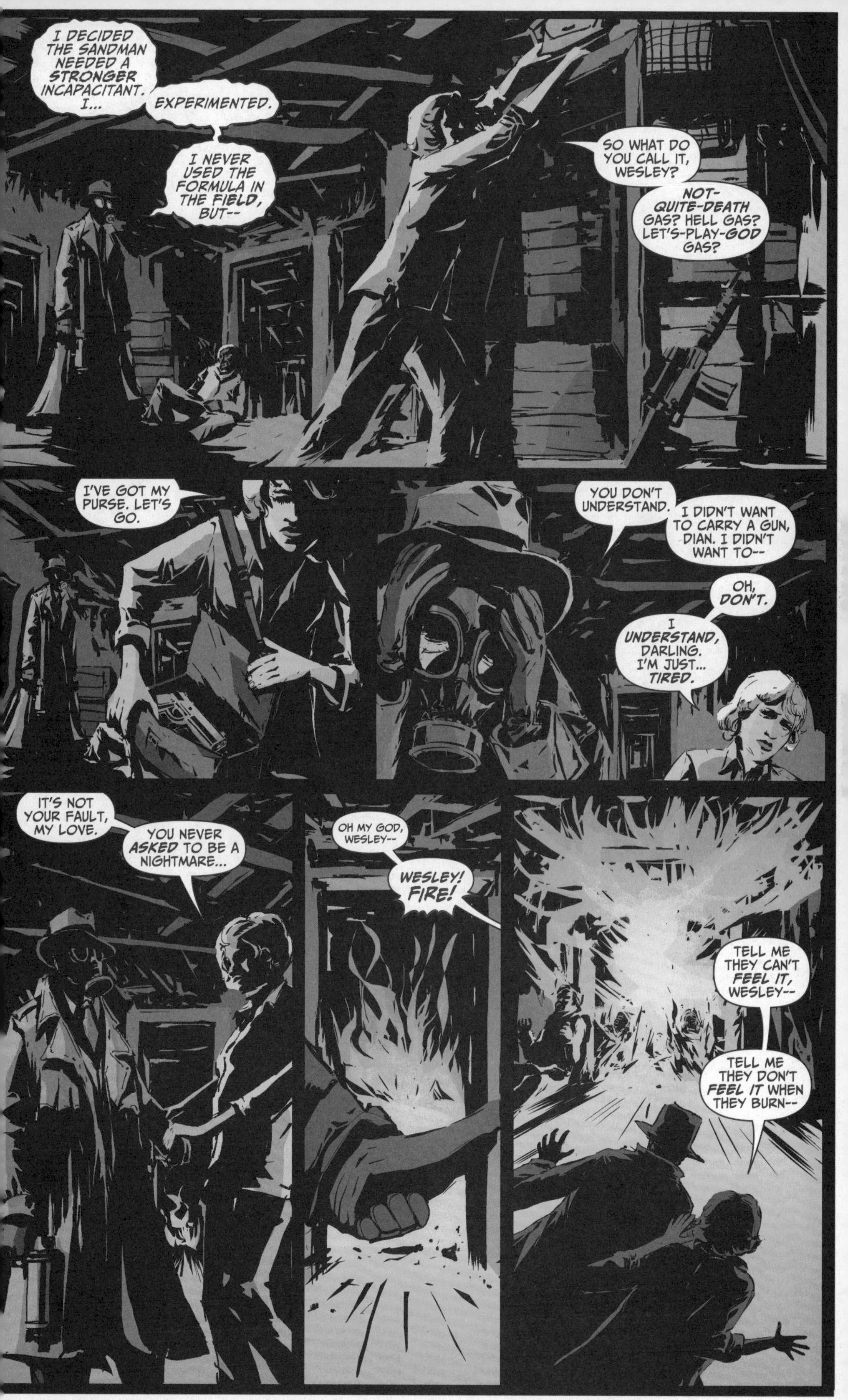
I DECIDED THE SANDMAN NEEDED A STRONGER INCAPACITANT. I...
EXPERIMENTED.
I NEVER USED THE FORMULA IN THE FIELD, BUT--
SO WHAT DO YOU CALL IT, WESLEY?
NOT-QUITE-DEATH GAS? HELL GAS? LET'S-PLAY-GOD GAS?
I'VE GOT MY PURSE. LET'S GO.
YOU DON'T UNDERSTAND.
I DIDN'T WANT TO CARRY A GUN, DIAN. I DIDN'T WANT TO--
OH, DON'T.
I UNDERSTAND, DARLING. I'M JUST... TIRED.
IT'S NOT YOUR FAULT, MY LOVE.
YOU NEVER ASKED TO BE A NIGHTMARE...
OH MY GOD, WESLEY--
WESLEY! FIRE!
TELL ME THEY CAN'T FEEL IT, WESLEY--
TELL ME THEY DON'T FEEL IT WHEN THEY BURN--

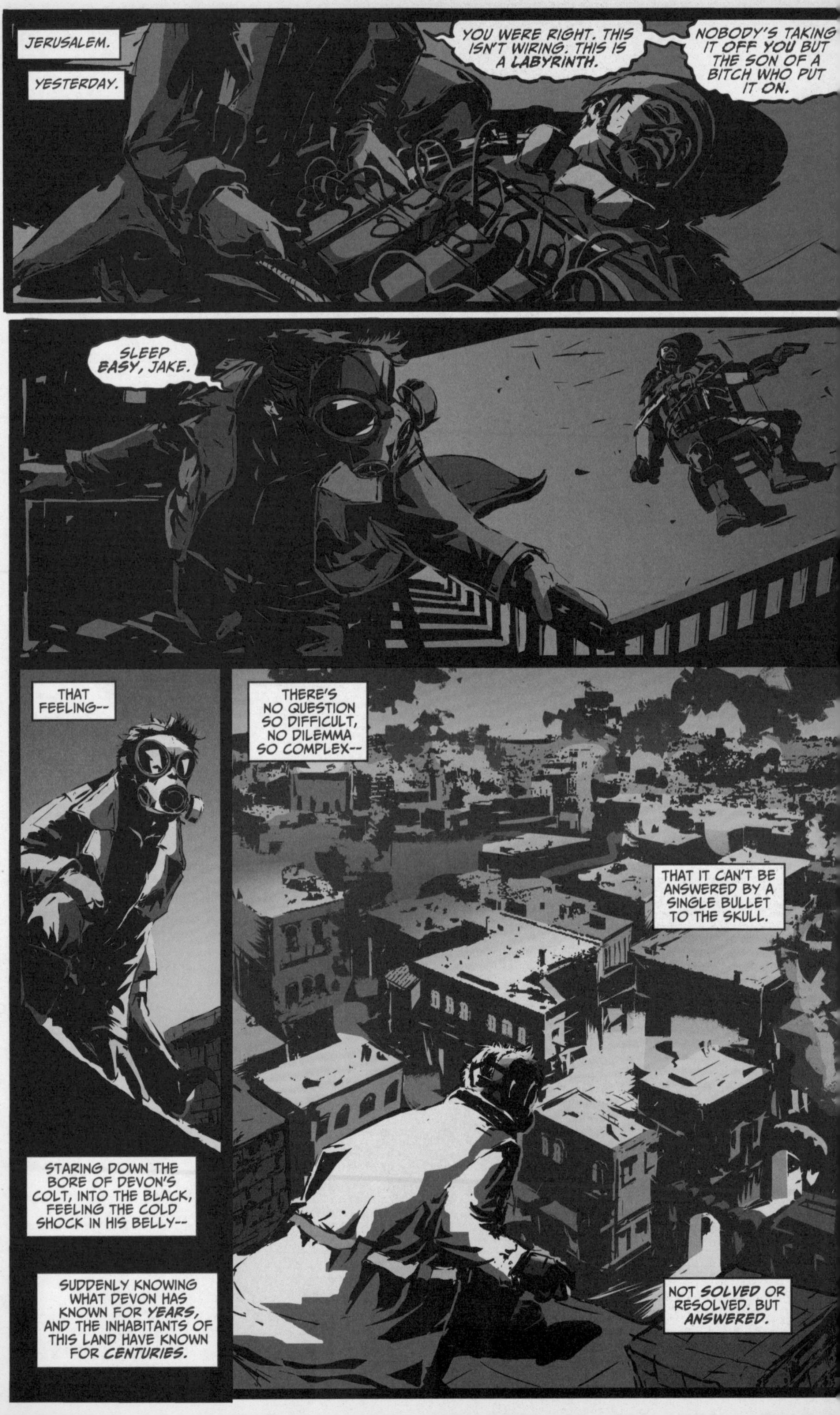
JERUSALEM.
YESTERDAY.
YOU WERE RIGHT. THIS ISN'T WIRING. THIS IS A LABYRINTH.
NOBODY'S TAKING IT OFF YOU BUT THE SON OF A BITCH WHO PUT IT ON.
SLEEP EASY, JAKE.
THAT FEELING--
STARING DOWN THE BORE OF DEVON'S COLT, INTO THE BLACK, FEELING THE COLD SHOCK IN HIS BELLY--
SUDDENLY KNOWING WHAT DEVON HAS KNOWN FOR YEARS, AND THE INHABITANTS OF THIS LAND HAVE KNOWN FOR CENTURIES.
THERE'S NO QUESTION SO DIFFICULT, NO DILEMMA SO COMPLEX--
THAT IT CAN'T BE ANSWERED BY A SINGLE BULLET TO THE SKULL.
NOT SOLVED OR RESOLVED. BUT ANSWERED.

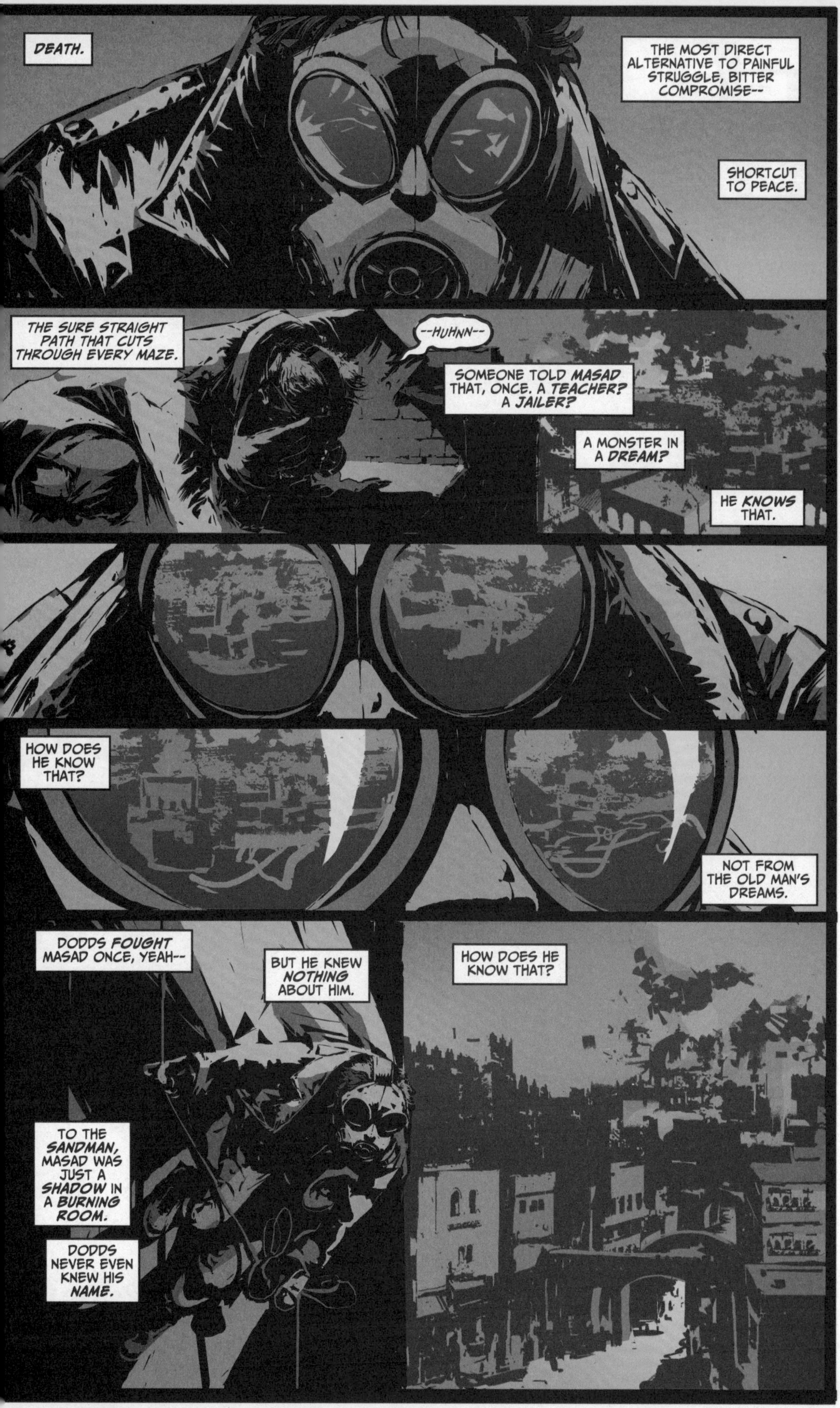
DEATH.
THE MOST DIRECT ALTERNATIVE TO PAINFUL STRUGGLE, BITTER COMPROMISE--
SHORTCUT TO PEACE.
THE SURE STRAIGHT PATH THAT CUTS THROUGH EVERY MAZE.
--HUHNN--
SOMEONE TOLD MASAD THAT, ONCE. A TEACHER? A JAILER?
A MONSTER IN A DREAM?
HE KNOWS THAT.
HOW DOES HE KNOW THAT?
NOT FROM THE OLD MAN'S DREAMS.
DODDS FOUGHT MASAD ONCE, YEAH--
BUT HE KNEW NOTHING ABOUT HIM.
TO THE SANDMAN, MASAD WAS JUST A SHADOW IN A BURNING ROOM.
DODDS NEVER EVEN KNEW HIS NAME.
HOW DOES HE KNOW THAT?

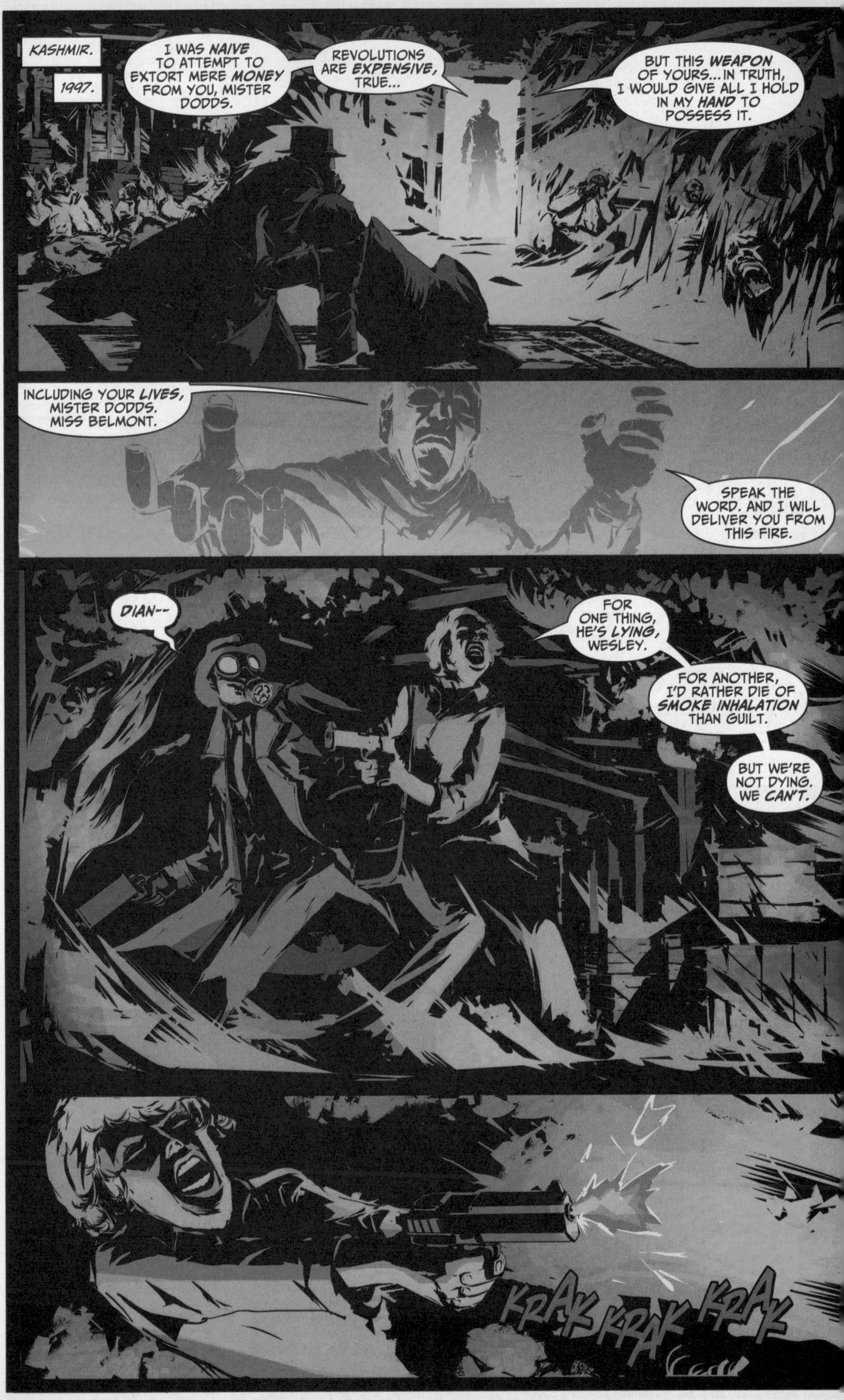
KASHMIR.
1997.
I WAS NAIVE TO ATTEMPT TO EXTORT MERE MONEY FROM YOU, MISTER DODDS.
REVOLUTIONS ARE EXPENSIVE, TRUE...
BUT THIS WEAPON OF YOURS... IN TRUTH, I WOULD GIVE ALL I HOLD IN MY HAND TO POSSESS IT.
INCLUDING YOUR LIVES, MISTER DODDS. MISS BELMONT.
SPEAK THE WORD. AND I WILL DELIVER YOU FROM THIS FIRE.
DIAN--
FOR ONE THING, HE'S LYING, WESLEY.
FOR ANOTHER, I'D RATHER DIE OF SMOKE INHALATION THAN GUILT.
BUT WE'RE NOT DYING. WE CAN'T.
KRAK KRAK KRAK

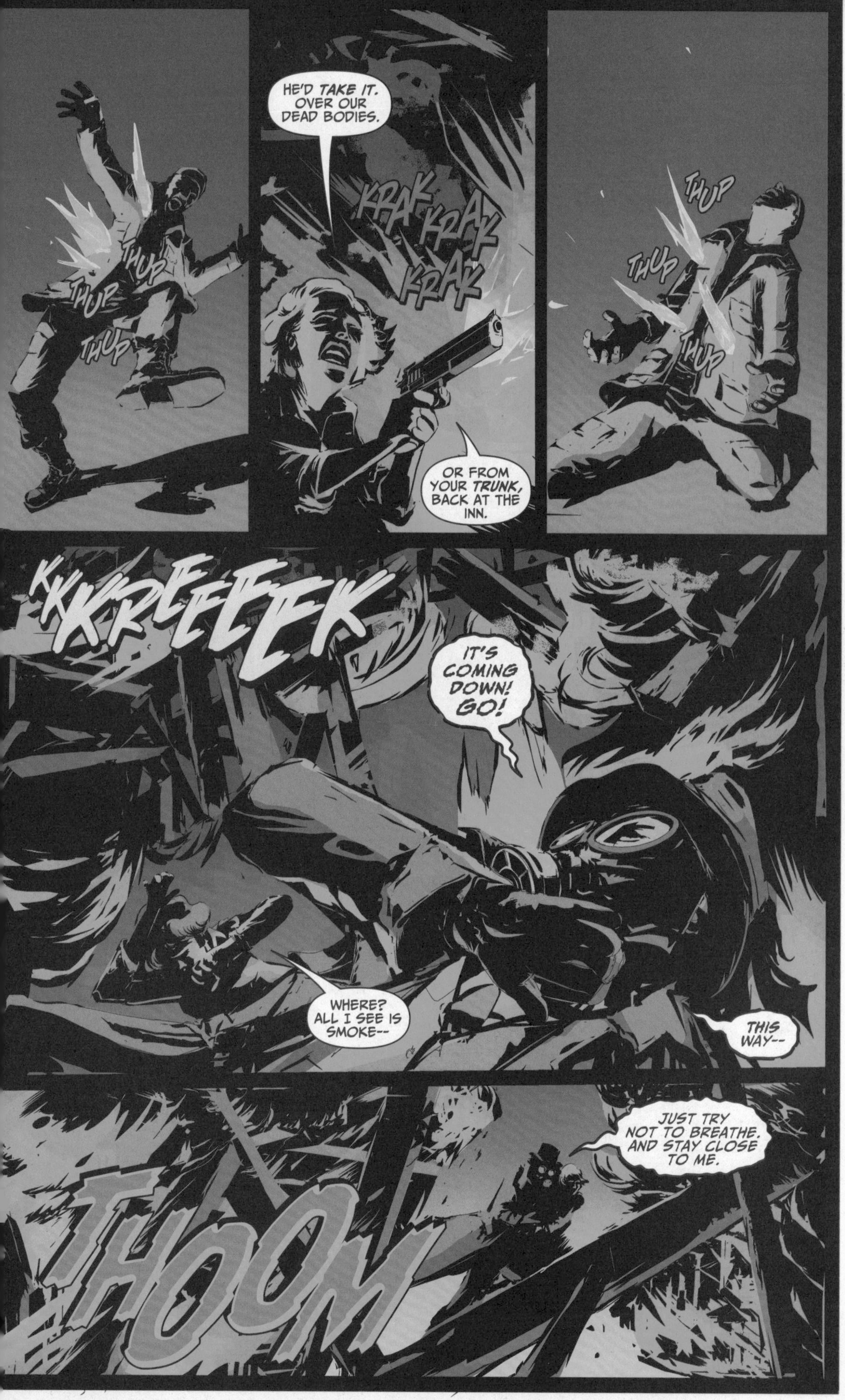
THUP
THUP
THUP
HE'D TAKE IT. OVER OUR DEAD BODIES.
KRAK KRAK KRAK
OR FROM YOUR TRUNK, BACK AT THE INN.
THUP
THUP
THUP
KKKREEEEK
IT'S COMING DOWN! GO!
WHERE? ALL I SEE IS SMOKE--
THIS WAY--
JUST TRY NOT TO BREATHE. AND STAY CLOSE TO ME.
THOOM

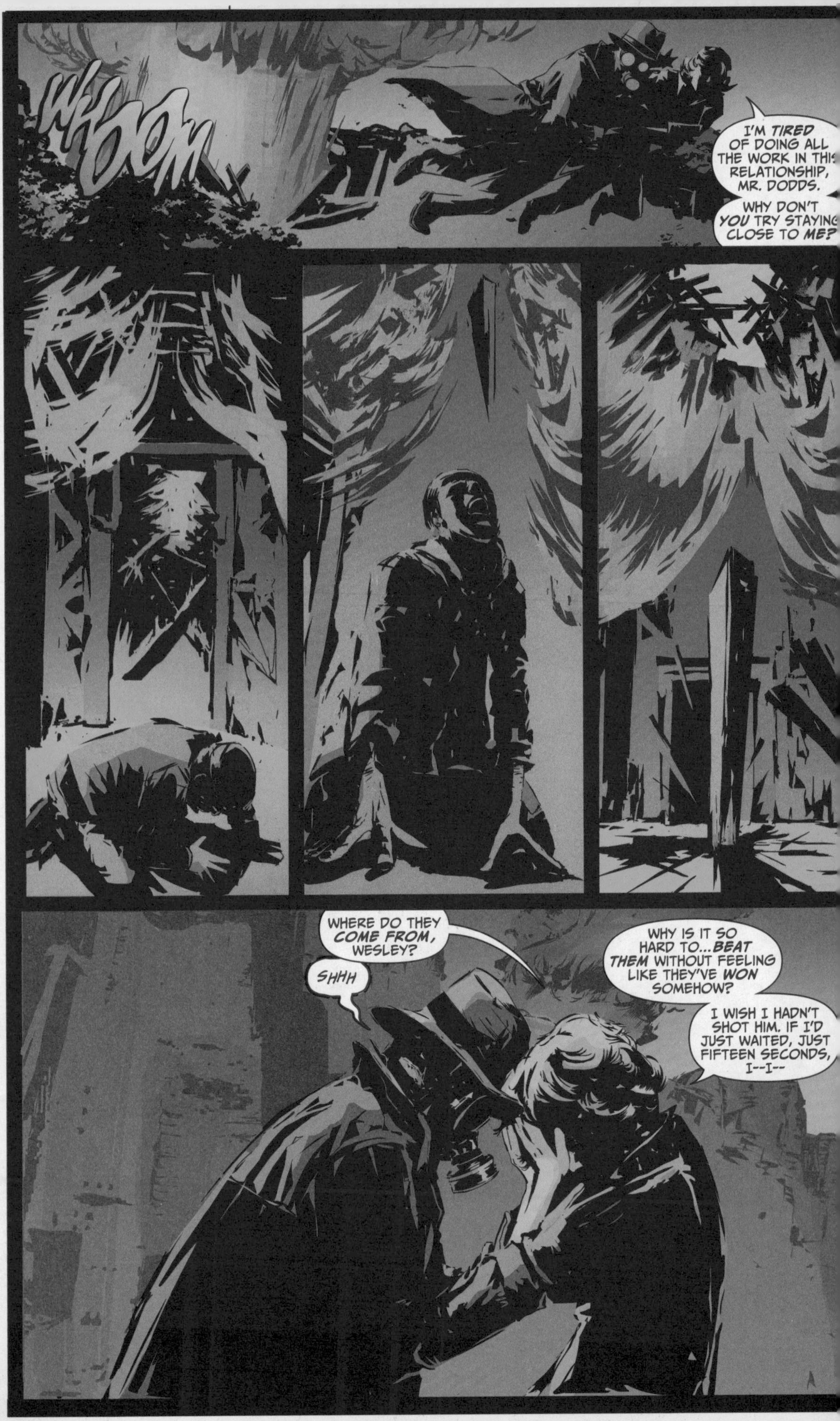

WHOOM
I'M *TIRED* OF DOING ALL THE WORK IN THIS RELATIONSHIP, MR. DODDS.
WHY DON'T *YOU* TRY STAYING CLOSE TO *ME?*
WHERE DO THEY *COME FROM,* WESLEY?
SHHH
WHY IS IT SO HARD TO...*BEAT THEM* WITHOUT FEELING LIKE THEY'VE *WON* SOMEHOW?
I WISH I HADN'T SHOT HIM. IF I'D JUST WAITED, JUST FIFTEEN SECONDS, I--I--

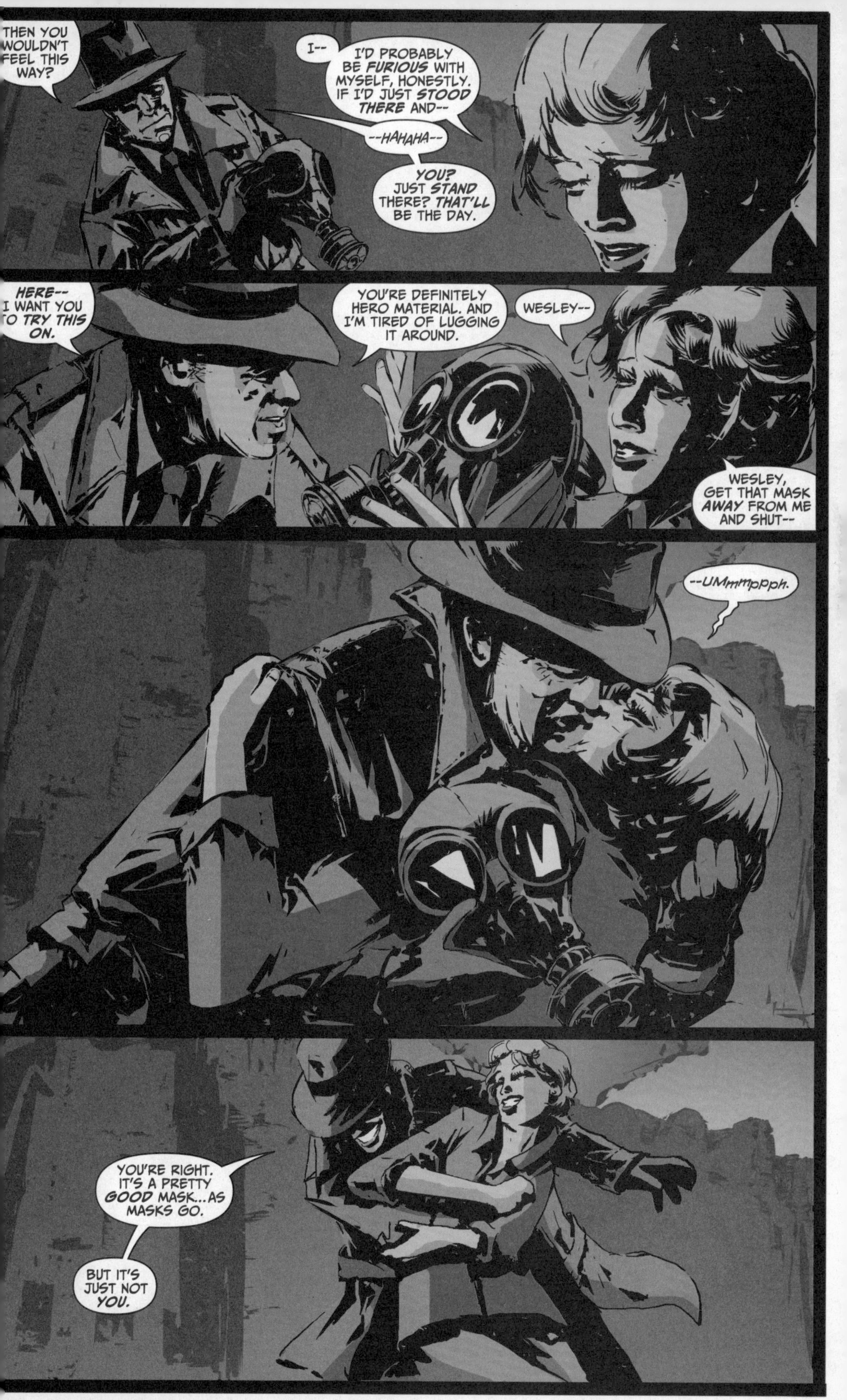
THEN YOU WOULDN'T FEEL THIS WAY?
I--
I'D PROBABLY BE FURIOUS WITH MYSELF, HONESTLY. IF I'D JUST STOOD THERE AND--
--HAHAHA--
YOU? JUST STAND THERE? THAT'LL BE THE DAY.
HERE-- I WANT YOU TO TRY THIS ON.
YOU'RE DEFINITELY HERO MATERIAL. AND I'M TIRED OF LUGGING IT AROUND.
WESLEY--
WESLEY, GET THAT MASK AWAY FROM ME AND SHUT--
--UMmmppph.
YOU'RE RIGHT. IT'S A PRETTY GOOD MASK...AS MASKS GO.
BUT IT'S JUST NOT YOU.

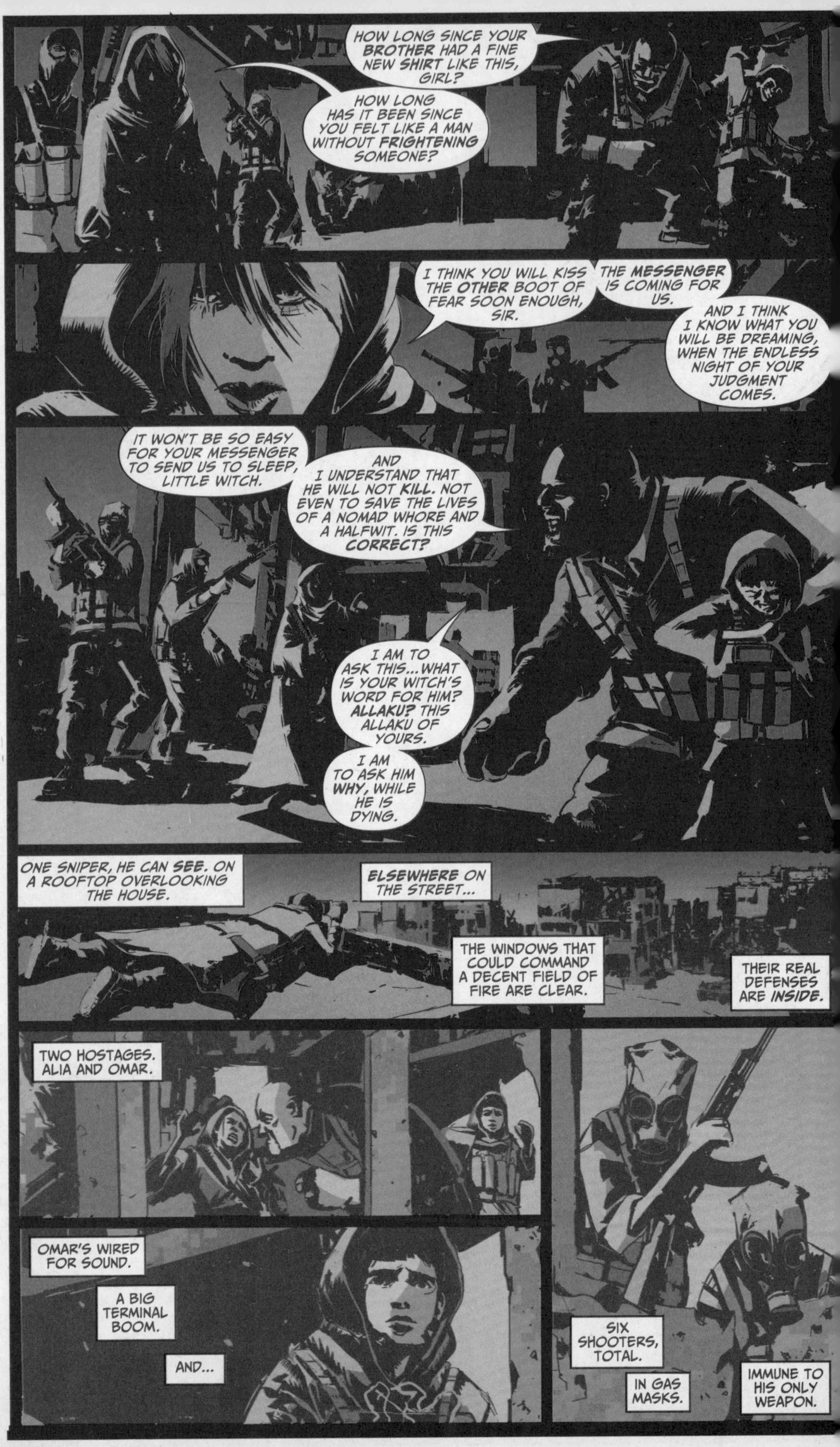
HOW LONG SINCE YOUR BROTHER HAD A FINE NEW SHIRT LIKE THIS, GIRL?
HOW LONG HAS IT BEEN SINCE YOU FELT LIKE A MAN WITHOUT FRIGHTENING SOMEONE?
I THINK YOU WILL KISS THE OTHER BOOT OF FEAR SOON ENOUGH, SIR.
THE MESSENGER IS COMING FOR US.
AND I THINK I KNOW WHAT YOU WILL BE DREAMING, WHEN THE ENDLESS NIGHT OF YOUR JUDGMENT COMES.
IT WON'T BE SO EASY FOR YOUR MESSENGER TO SEND US TO SLEEP, LITTLE WITCH.
AND I UNDERSTAND THAT HE WILL NOT KILL. NOT EVEN TO SAVE THE LIVES OF A NOMAD WHORE AND A HALFWIT. IS THIS CORRECT?
I AM TO ASK THIS...WHAT IS YOUR WITCH'S WORD FOR HIM? ALLAKU? THIS ALLAKU OF YOURS.
I AM TO ASK HIM WHY, WHILE HE IS DYING.
ONE SNIPER, HE CAN SEE. ON A ROOFTOP OVERLOOKING THE HOUSE.
ELSEWHERE ON THE STREET...
THE WINDOWS THAT COULD COMMAND A DECENT FIELD OF FIRE ARE CLEAR.
THEIR REAL DEFENSES ARE INSIDE.
TWO HOSTAGES. ALIA AND OMAR.
OMAR'S WIRED FOR SOUND.
A BIG TERMINAL BOOM.
AND...
SIX SHOOTERS, TOTAL.
IN GAS MASKS.
IMMUNE TO HIS ONLY WEAPON.

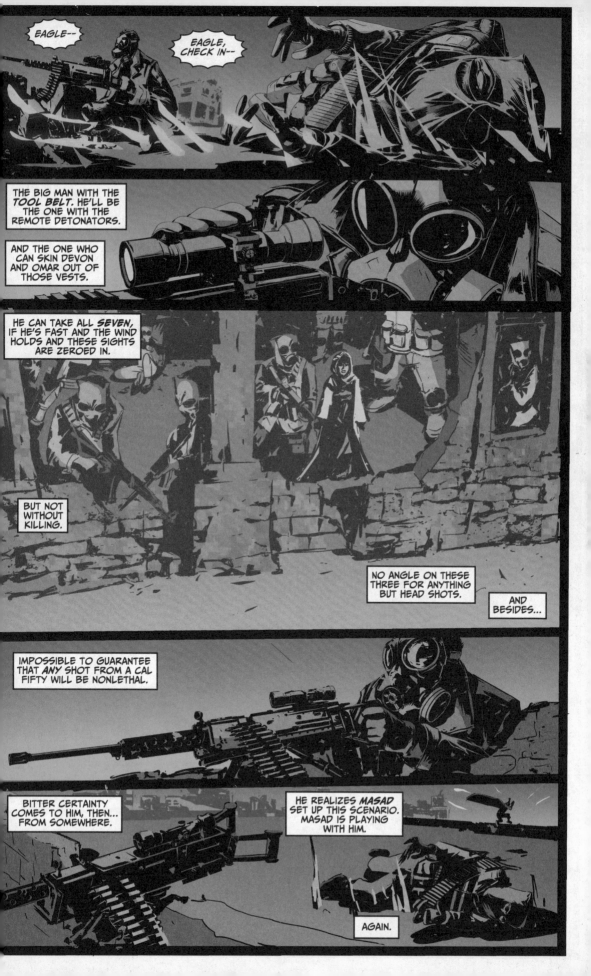

EAGLE--

EAGLE, CHECK IN--

THE BIG MAN WITH THE *TOOL BELT*. HE'LL BE THE ONE WITH THE REMOTE DETONATORS.

AND THE ONE WHO CAN SKIN DEVON AND OMAR OUT OF THOSE VESTS.

HE CAN TAKE ALL *SEVEN*, IF HE'S FAST AND THE WIND HOLDS AND THESE SIGHTS ARE ZEROED IN.

BUT NOT WITHOUT KILLING.

NO ANGLE ON THESE THREE FOR ANYTHING BUT HEAD SHOTS.

AND BESIDES...

IMPOSSIBLE TO GUARANTEE THAT *ANY* SHOT FROM A CAL FIFTY WILL BE NONLETHAL.

BITTER CERTAINTY COMES TO HIM, THEN... FROM SOMEWHERE.

HE REALIZES MASAD SET UP THIS SCENARIO. MASAD IS PLAYING WITH HIM.

AGAIN.

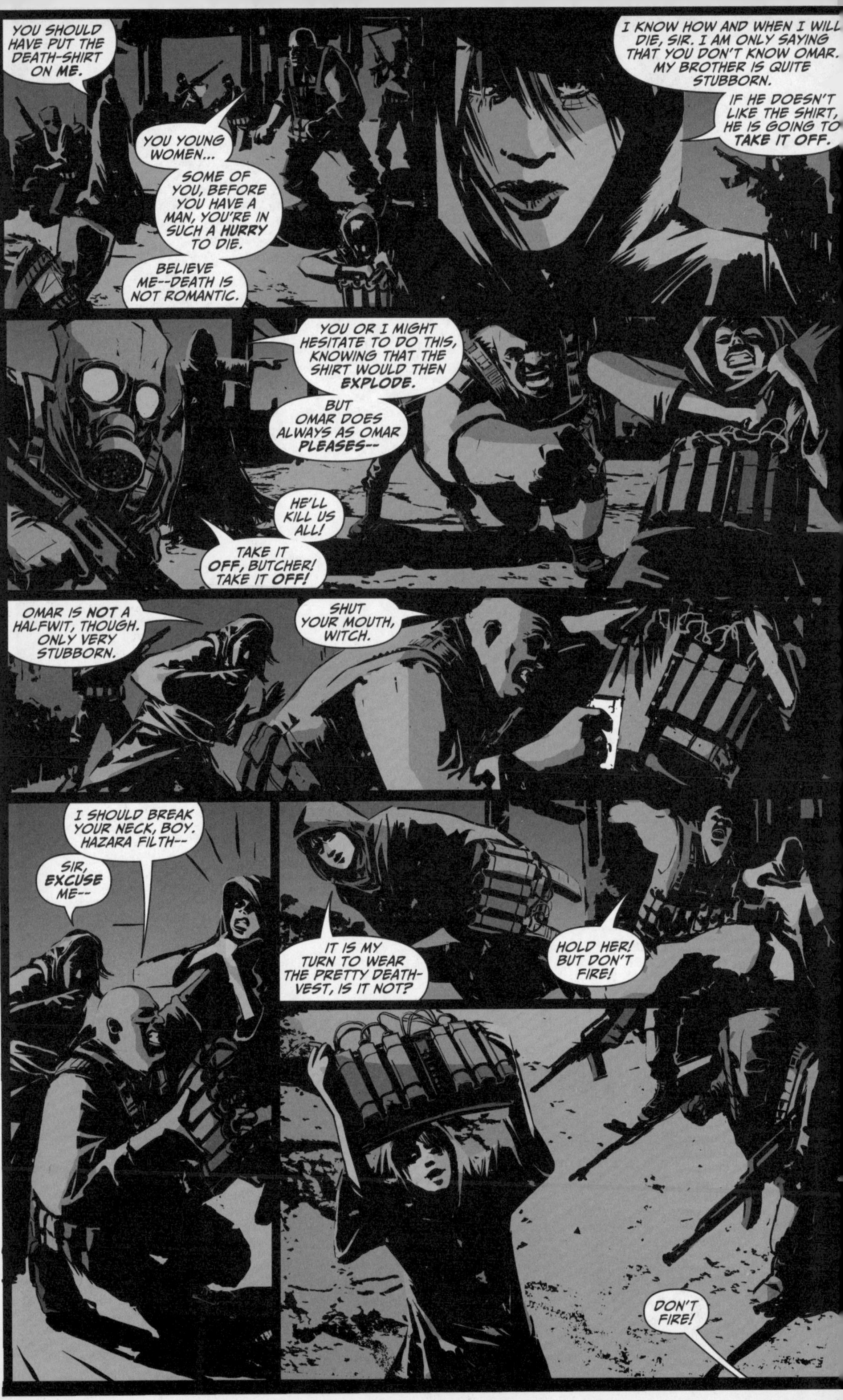
YOU SHOULD HAVE PUT THE DEATH-SHIRT ON ME.
YOU YOUNG WOMEN...
SOME OF YOU, BEFORE YOU HAVE A MAN, YOU'RE IN SUCH A HURRY TO DIE.
BELIEVE ME--DEATH IS NOT ROMANTIC.
I KNOW HOW AND WHEN I WILL DIE, SIR. I AM ONLY SAYING THAT YOU DON'T KNOW OMAR. MY BROTHER IS QUITE STUBBORN.
IF HE DOESN'T LIKE THE SHIRT, HE IS GOING TO TAKE IT OFF.
YOU OR I MIGHT HESITATE TO DO THIS, KNOWING THAT THE SHIRT WOULD THEN EXPLODE.
BUT OMAR DOES ALWAYS AS OMAR PLEASES--
HE'LL KILL US ALL!
TAKE IT OFF, BUTCHER! TAKE IT OFF!
OMAR IS NOT A HALFWIT, THOUGH. ONLY VERY STUBBORN.
SHUT YOUR MOUTH, WITCH.
I SHOULD BREAK YOUR NECK, BOY. HAZARA FILTH--
SIR, EXCUSE ME--
IT IS MY TURN TO WEAR THE PRETTY DEATH-VEST, IS IT NOT?
HOLD HER! BUT DON'T FIRE!
DON'T FIRE!

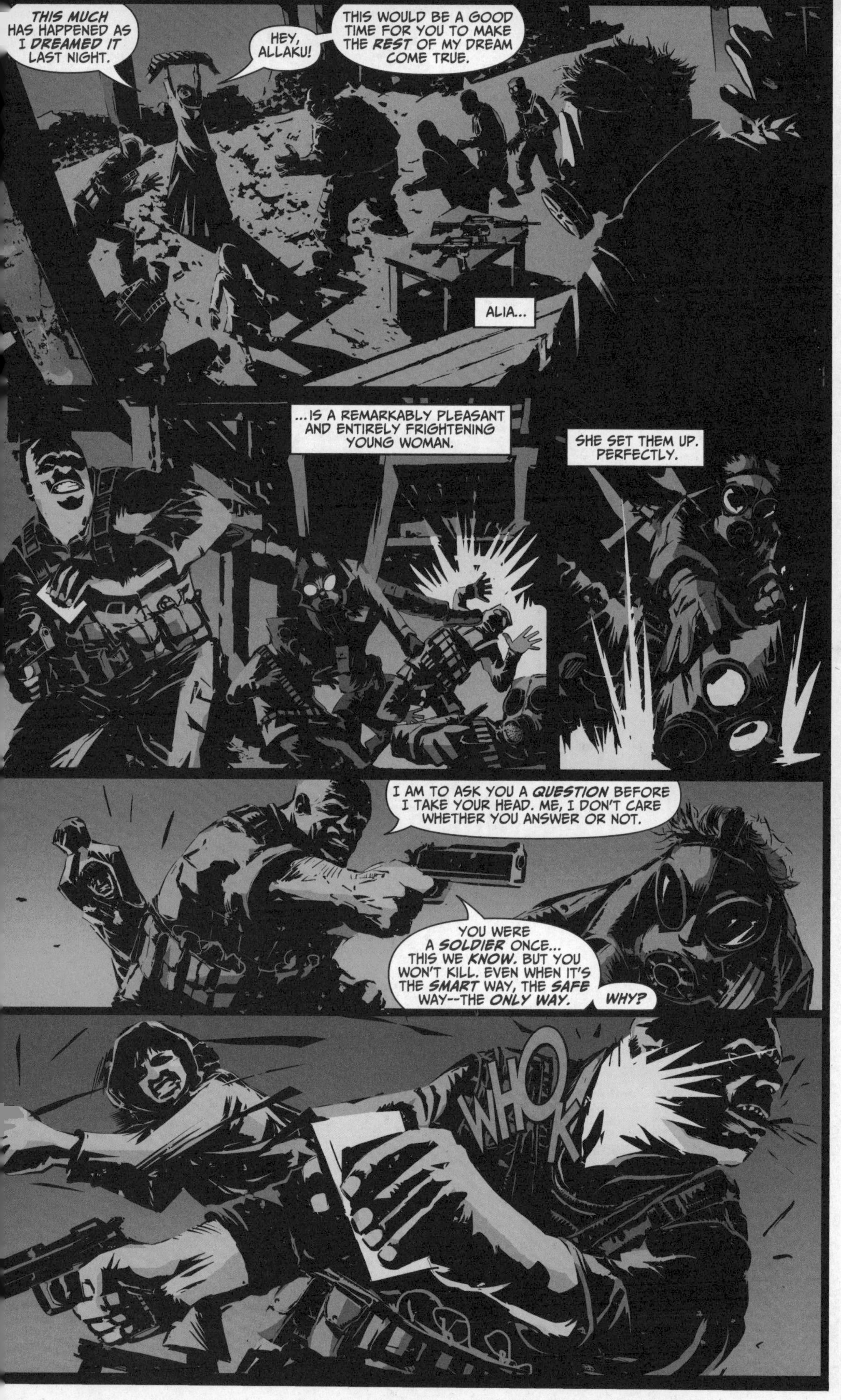
THIS MUCH HAS HAPPENED AS I DREAMED IT LAST NIGHT.
HEY, ALLAKU!
THIS WOULD BE A GOOD TIME FOR YOU TO MAKE THE REST OF MY DREAM COME TRUE.
ALIA...
...IS A REMARKABLY PLEASANT AND ENTIRELY FRIGHTENING YOUNG WOMAN.
SHE SET THEM UP. PERFECTLY.
I AM TO ASK YOU A QUESTION BEFORE I TAKE YOUR HEAD. ME, I DON'T CARE WHETHER YOU ANSWER OR NOT.
YOU WERE A SOLDIER ONCE... THIS WE KNOW. BUT YOU WON'T KILL. EVEN WHEN IT'S THE SMART WAY, THE SAFE WAY--THE ONLY WAY.
WHY?
WHOK

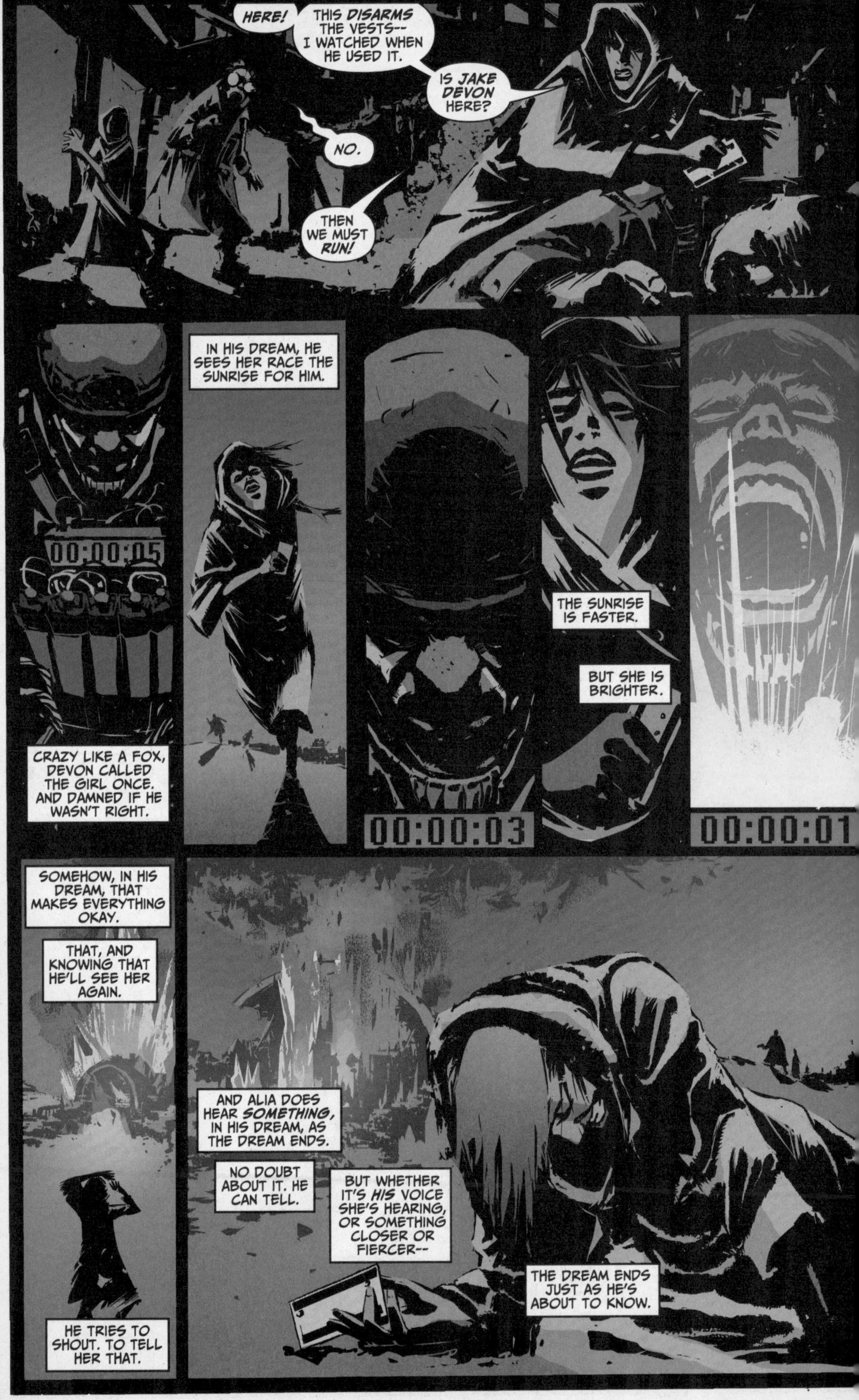
HERE!
THIS DISARMS THE VESTS-- I WATCHED WHEN HE USED IT.
IS JAKE DEVON HERE?
NO.
THEN WE MUST RUN!
00:00:05
CRAZY LIKE A FOX, DEVON CALLED THE GIRL ONCE. AND DAMNED IF HE WASN'T RIGHT.
IN HIS DREAM, HE SEES HER RACE THE SUNRISE FOR HIM.
00:00:03
THE SUNRISE IS FASTER.
BUT SHE IS BRIGHTER.
00:00:01
SOMEHOW, IN HIS DREAM, THAT MAKES EVERYTHING OKAY.
THAT, AND KNOWING THAT HE'LL SEE HER AGAIN.
HE TRIES TO SHOUT. TO TELL HER THAT.
AND ALIA DOES HEAR SOMETHING, IN HIS DREAM, AS THE DREAM ENDS.
NO DOUBT ABOUT IT. HE CAN TELL.
BUT WHETHER IT'S HIS VOICE SHE'S HEARING, OR SOMETHING CLOSER OR FIERCER--
THE DREAM ENDS JUST AS HE'S ABOUT TO KNOW.

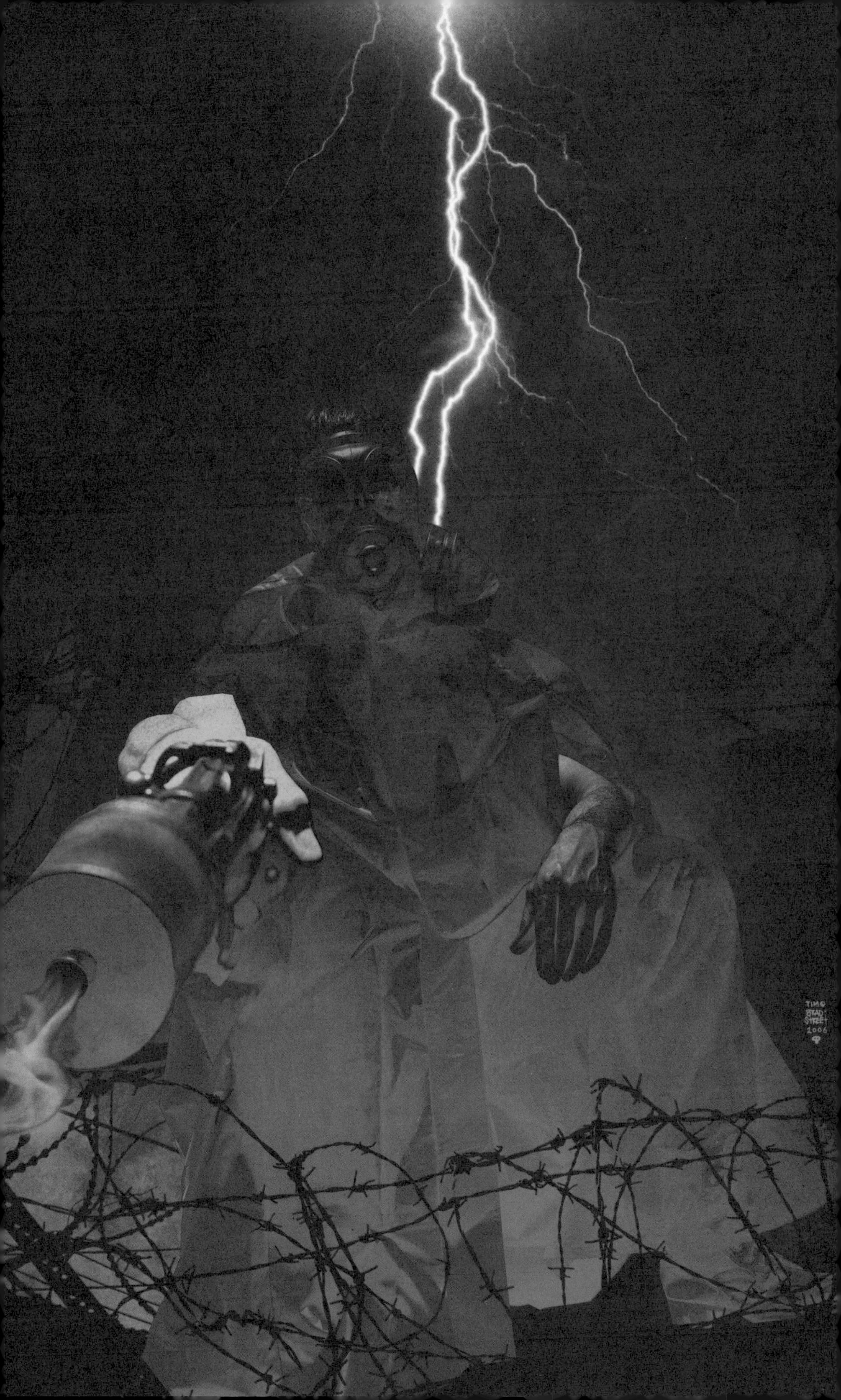
TIMO
BRAD-
STREET
2006

CHAPTER FIVE

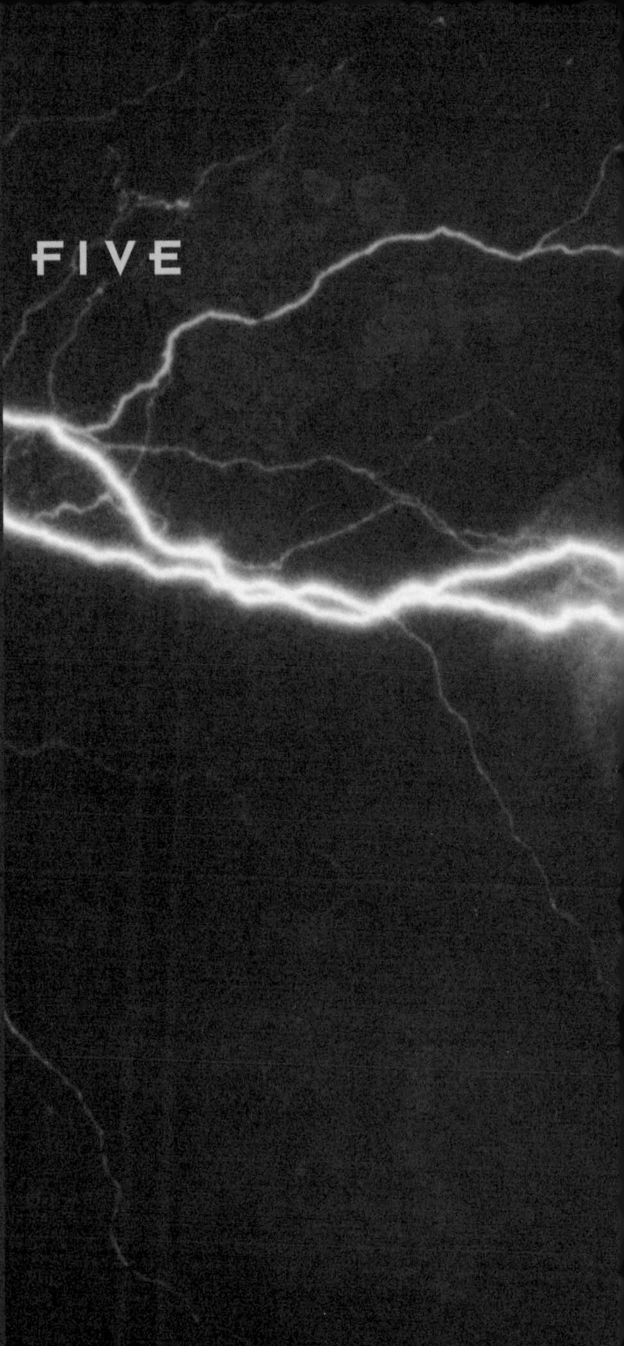

"I know I never chose my path.

The dreams chose for me."

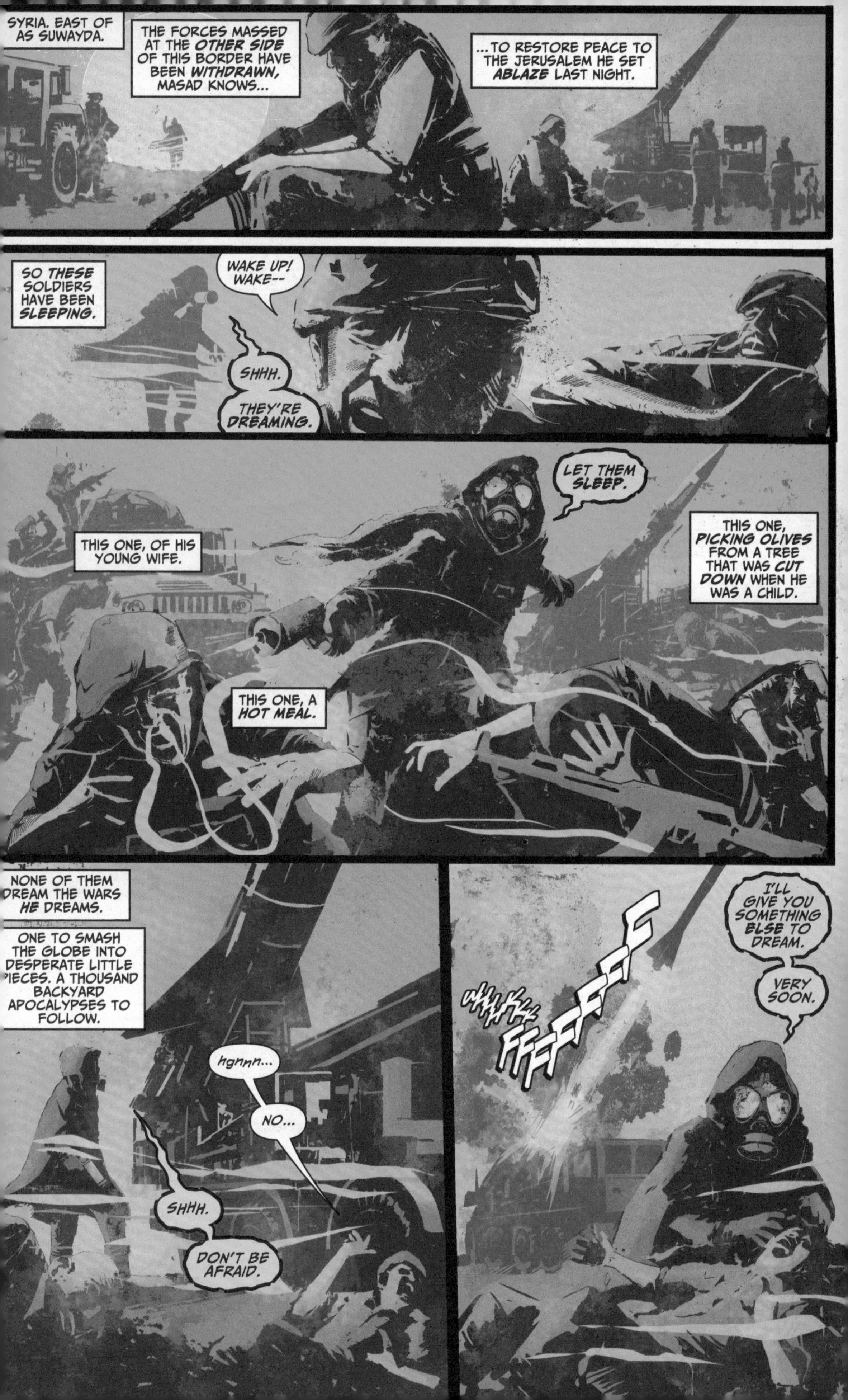
SYRIA. EAST OF AS SUWAYDA.
THE FORCES MASSED AT THE OTHER SIDE OF THIS BORDER HAVE BEEN WITHDRAWN, MASAD KNOWS...
...TO RESTORE PEACE TO THE JERUSALEM HE SET ABLAZE LAST NIGHT.
SO THESE SOLDIERS HAVE BEEN SLEEPING.
WAKE UP! WAKE--
SHHH.
THEY'RE DREAMING.
LET THEM SLEEP.
THIS ONE, OF HIS YOUNG WIFE.
THIS ONE, PICKING OLIVES FROM A TREE THAT WAS CUT DOWN WHEN HE WAS A CHILD.
THIS ONE, A HOT MEAL.
NONE OF THEM DREAM THE WARS HE DREAMS.
ONE TO SMASH THE GLOBE INTO DESPERATE LITTLE PIECES. A THOUSAND BACKYARD APOCALYPSES TO FOLLOW.
hgnnn...
NO...
SHHH.
DON'T BE AFRAID.
I'LL GIVE YOU SOMETHING ELSE TO DREAM.
VERY SOON.

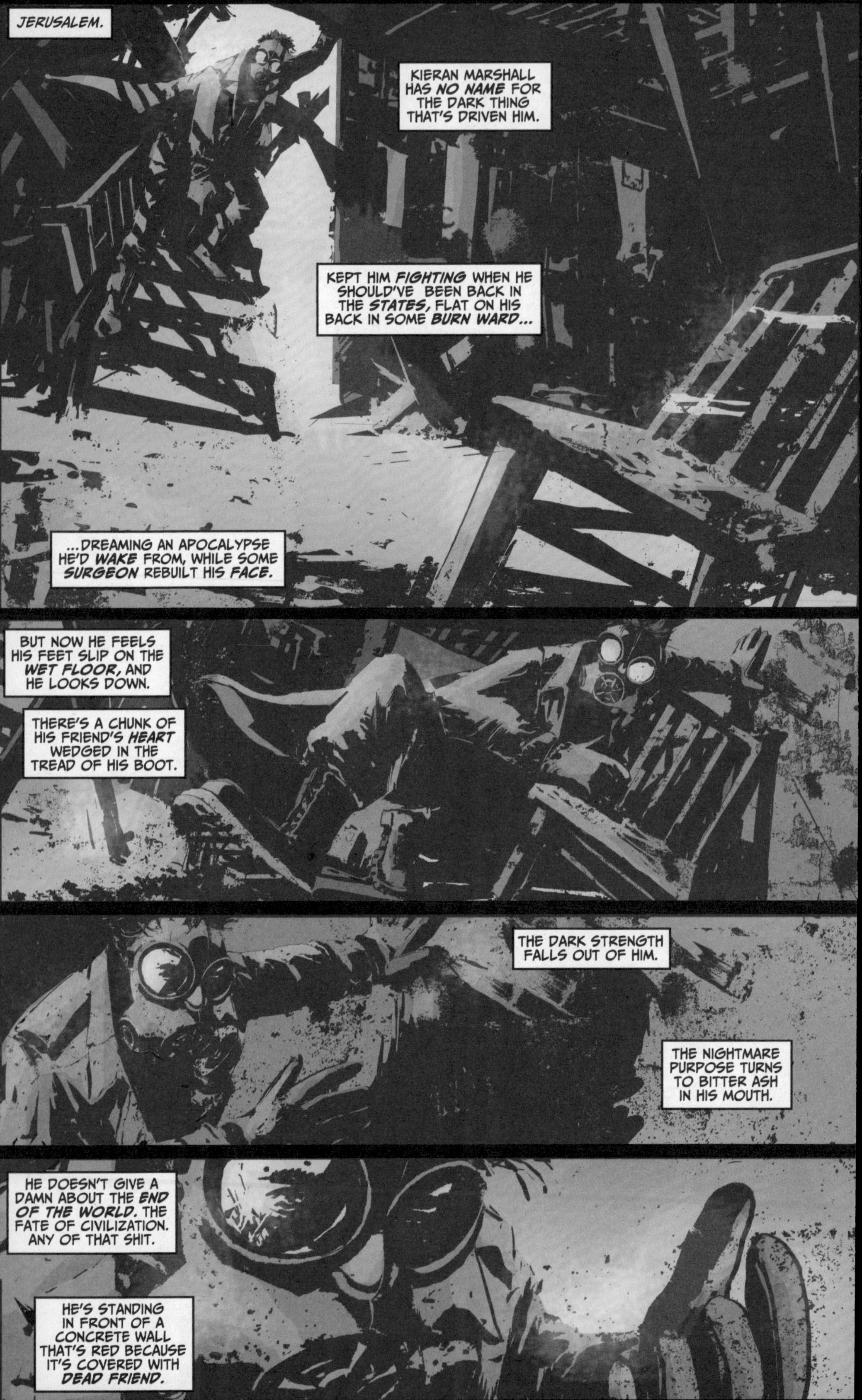
JERUSALEM.
KIERAN MARSHALL HAS NO NAME FOR THE DARK THING THAT'S DRIVEN HIM.
KEPT HIM FIGHTING WHEN HE SHOULD'VE BEEN BACK IN THE STATES, FLAT ON HIS BACK IN SOME BURN WARD...
...DREAMING AN APOCALYPSE HE'D WAKE FROM, WHILE SOME SURGEON REBUILT HIS FACE.
BUT NOW HE FEELS HIS FEET SLIP ON THE WET FLOOR, AND HE LOOKS DOWN.
THERE'S A CHUNK OF HIS FRIEND'S HEART WEDGED IN THE TREAD OF HIS BOOT.
THE DARK STRENGTH FALLS OUT OF HIM.
THE NIGHTMARE PURPOSE TURNS TO BITTER ASH IN HIS MOUTH.
HE DOESN'T GIVE A DAMN ABOUT THE END OF THE WORLD. THE FATE OF CIVILIZATION. ANY OF THAT SHIT.
HE'S STANDING IN FRONT OF A CONCRETE WALL THAT'S RED BECAUSE IT'S COVERED WITH DEAD FRIEND.

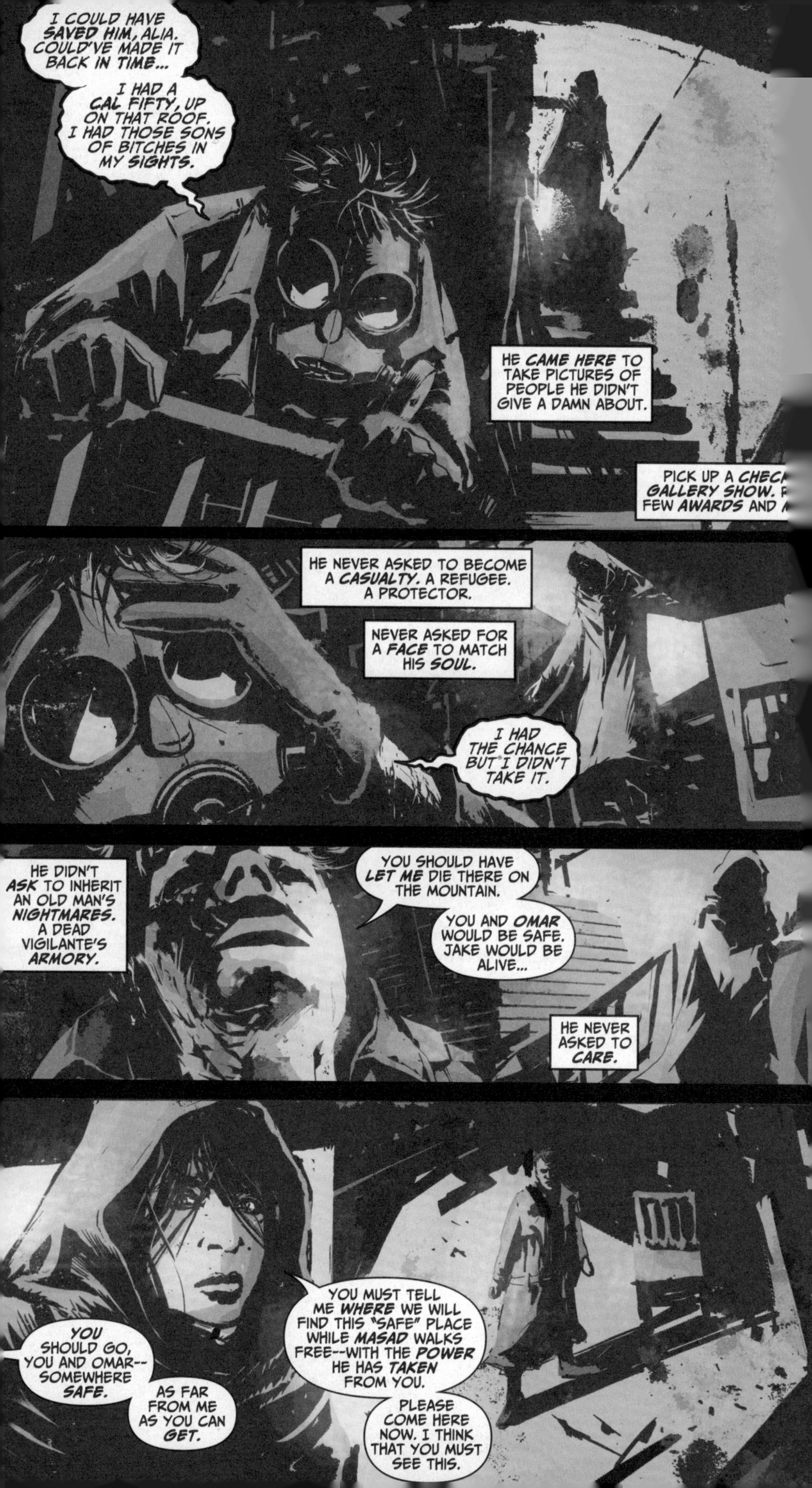
I COULD HAVE SAVED HIM, ALIA. COULD'VE MADE IT BACK IN TIME...
I HAD A CAL FIFTY, UP ON THAT ROOF. I HAD THOSE SONS OF BITCHES IN MY SIGHTS.
HE CAME HERE TO TAKE PICTURES OF PEOPLE HE DIDN'T GIVE A DAMN ABOUT.
PICK UP A
GALLERY SHOW.
FEW AWARDS AND
HE NEVER ASKED TO BECOME A CASUALTY. A REFUGEE. A PROTECTOR.
NEVER ASKED FOR A FACE TO MATCH HIS SOUL.
I HAD THE CHANCE BUT I DIDN'T TAKE IT.
HE DIDN'T ASK TO INHERIT AN OLD MAN'S NIGHTMARES. A DEAD VIGILANTE'S ARMORY.
YOU SHOULD HAVE LET ME DIE THERE ON THE MOUNTAIN.
YOU AND OMAR WOULD BE SAFE. JAKE WOULD BE ALIVE...
HE NEVER ASKED TO CARE.
YOU SHOULD GO, YOU AND OMAR--SOMEWHERE SAFE.
AS FAR FROM ME AS YOU CAN GET.
YOU MUST TELL ME WHERE WE WILL FIND THIS "SAFE" PLACE WHILE MASAD WALKS FREE--WITH THE POWER HE HAS TAKEN FROM YOU.
PLEASE COME HERE NOW. I THINK THAT YOU MUST SEE THIS.

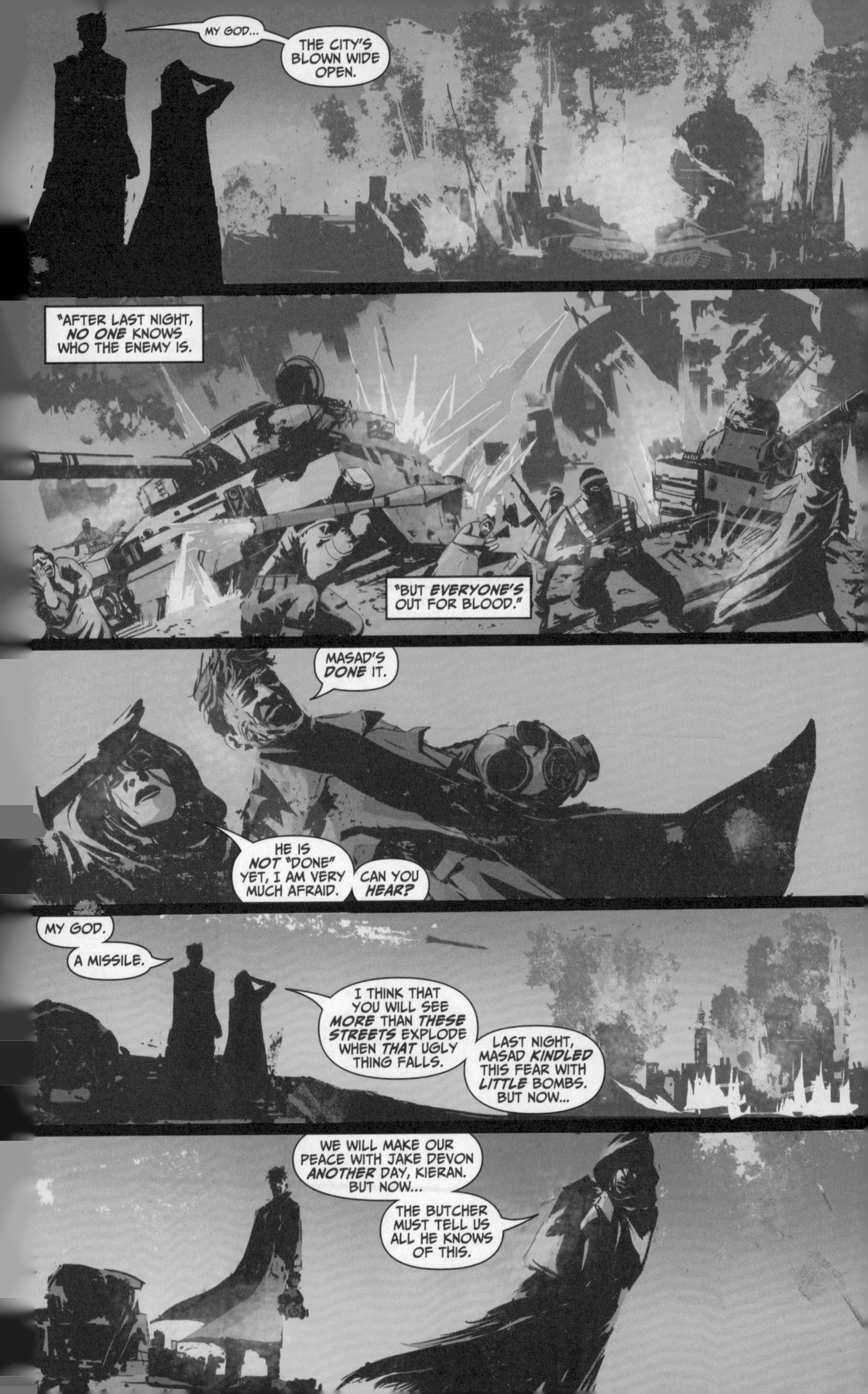
MY GOD...
THE CITY'S BLOWN WIDE OPEN.
"AFTER LAST NIGHT, NO ONE KNOWS WHO THE ENEMY IS.
"BUT EVERYONE'S OUT FOR BLOOD."
MASAD'S DONE IT.
HE IS NOT "DONE" YET, I AM VERY MUCH AFRAID.
CAN YOU HEAR?
MY GOD.
A MISSILE.
I THINK THAT YOU WILL SEE MORE THAN THESE STREETS EXPLODE WHEN THAT UGLY THING FALLS.
LAST NIGHT, MASAD KINDLED THIS FEAR WITH LITTLE BOMBS. BUT NOW...
WE WILL MAKE OUR PEACE WITH JAKE DEVON ANOTHER DAY, KIERAN. BUT NOW...
THE BUTCHER MUST TELL US ALL HE KNOWS OF THIS.

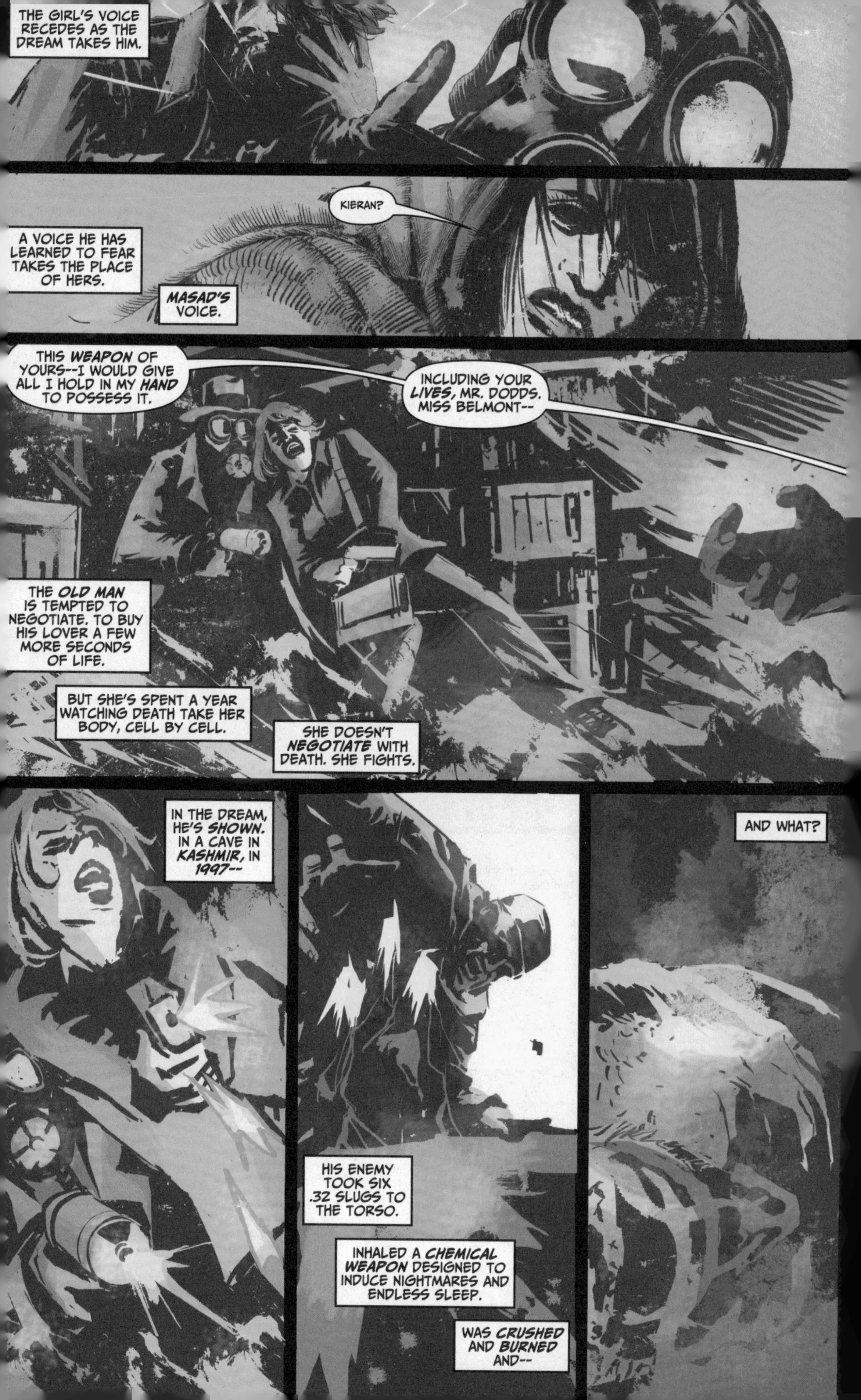
THE GIRL'S VOICE RECEDES AS THE DREAM TAKES HIM.
KIERAN?
A VOICE HE HAS LEARNED TO FEAR TAKES THE PLACE OF HERS.
MASAD'S VOICE.
THIS WEAPON OF YOURS--I WOULD GIVE ALL I HOLD IN MY HAND TO POSSESS IT.
INCLUDING YOUR LIVES, MR. DODDS. MISS BELMONT--
THE OLD MAN IS TEMPTED TO NEGOTIATE. TO BUY HIS LOVER A FEW MORE SECONDS OF LIFE.
BUT SHE'S SPENT A YEAR WATCHING DEATH TAKE HER BODY, CELL BY CELL.
SHE DOESN'T NEGOTIATE WITH DEATH. SHE FIGHTS.
IN THE DREAM, HE'S SHOWN. IN A CAVE IN KASHMIR, IN 1997--
HIS ENEMY TOOK SIX .32 SLUGS TO THE TORSO.
INHALED A CHEMICAL WEAPON DESIGNED TO INDUCE NIGHTMARES AND ENDLESS SLEEP.
WAS CRUSHED AND BURNED AND--
AND WHAT?

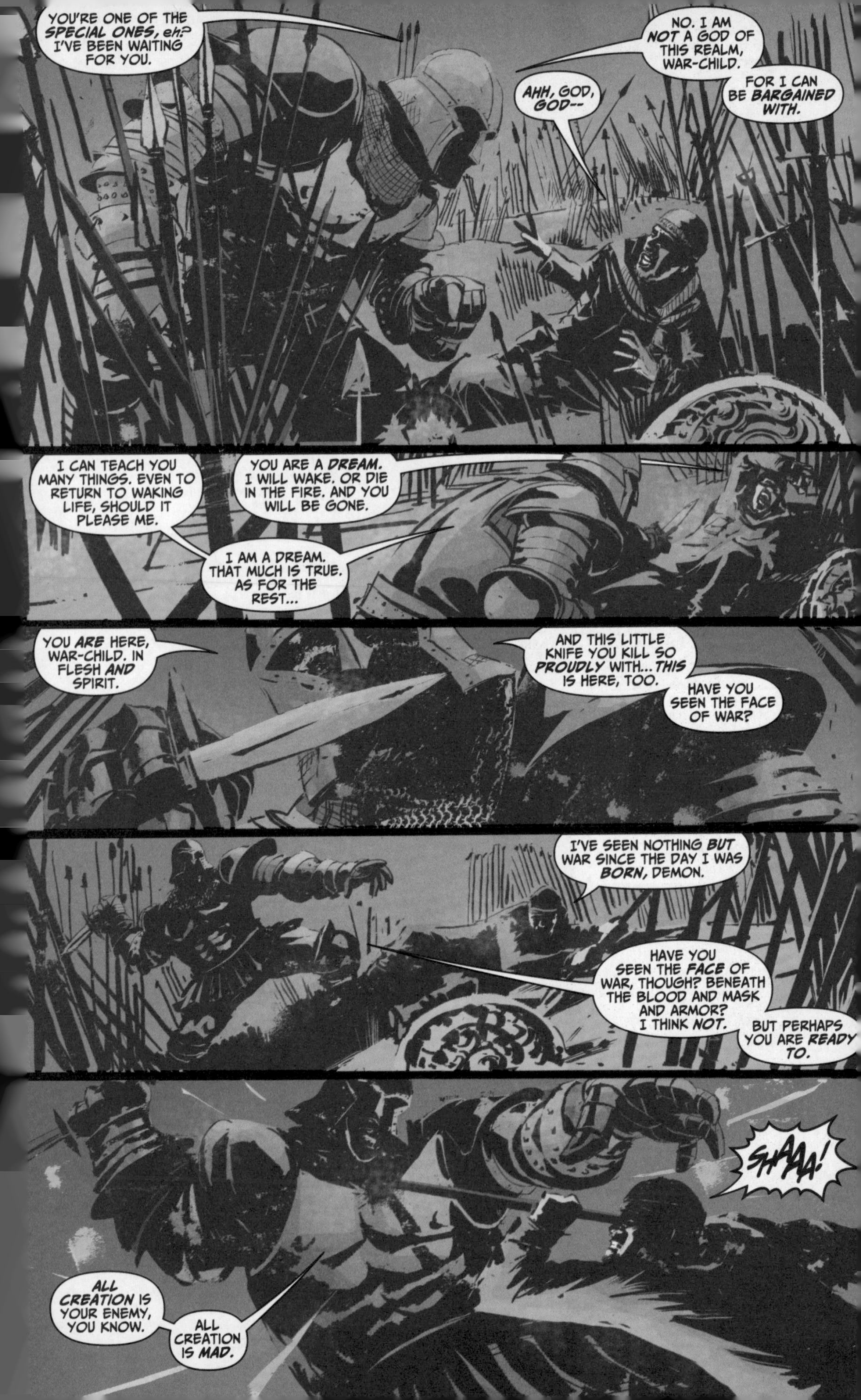
YOU'RE ONE OF THE SPECIAL ONES, eh? I'VE BEEN WAITING FOR YOU.
AHH, GOD, GOD--
NO. I AM NOT A GOD OF THIS REALM, WAR-CHILD.
FOR I CAN BE BARGAINED WITH.
I CAN TEACH YOU MANY THINGS. EVEN TO RETURN TO WAKING LIFE, SHOULD IT PLEASE ME.
YOU ARE A DREAM. I WILL WAKE. OR DIE IN THE FIRE. AND YOU WILL BE GONE.
I AM A DREAM. THAT MUCH IS TRUE. AS FOR THE REST...
YOU ARE HERE, WAR-CHILD. IN FLESH AND SPIRIT.
AND THIS LITTLE KNIFE YOU KILL SO PROUDLY WITH... THIS IS HERE, TOO.
HAVE YOU SEEN THE FACE OF WAR?
I'VE SEEN NOTHING BUT WAR SINCE THE DAY I WAS BORN, DEMON.
HAVE YOU SEEN THE FACE OF WAR, THOUGH? BENEATH THE BLOOD AND MASK AND ARMOR? I THINK NOT.
BUT PERHAPS YOU ARE READY TO.
SHAAAA!
ALL CREATION IS YOUR ENEMY, YOU KNOW.
ALL CREATION IS MAD.

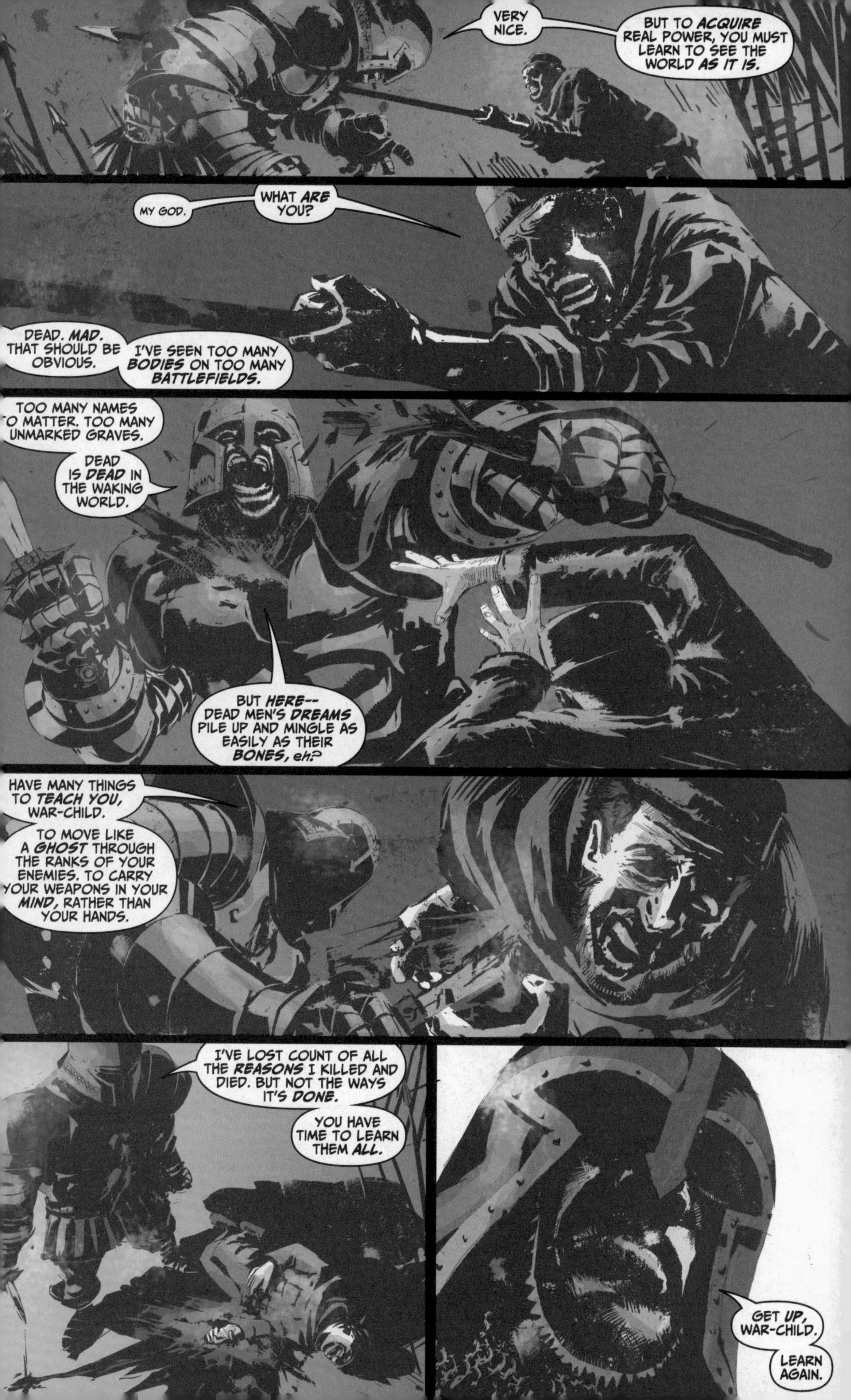
VERY NICE.
BUT TO ACQUIRE REAL POWER, YOU MUST LEARN TO SEE THE WORLD AS IT IS.
MY GOD.
WHAT ARE YOU?
DEAD. MAD. THAT SHOULD BE OBVIOUS.
I'VE SEEN TOO MANY BODIES ON TOO MANY BATTLEFIELDS.
TOO MANY NAMES TO MATTER. TOO MANY UNMARKED GRAVES.
DEAD IS DEAD IN THE WAKING WORLD.
BUT HERE-- DEAD MEN'S DREAMS PILE UP AND MINGLE AS EASILY AS THEIR BONES, eh?
HAVE MANY THINGS TO TEACH YOU, WAR-CHILD.
TO MOVE LIKE A GHOST THROUGH THE RANKS OF YOUR ENEMIES. TO CARRY YOUR WEAPONS IN YOUR MIND, RATHER THAN YOUR HANDS.
I'VE LOST COUNT OF ALL THE REASONS I KILLED AND DIED. BUT NOT THE WAYS IT'S DONE.
YOU HAVE TIME TO LEARN THEM ALL.
GET UP, WAR-CHILD.
LEARN AGAIN.

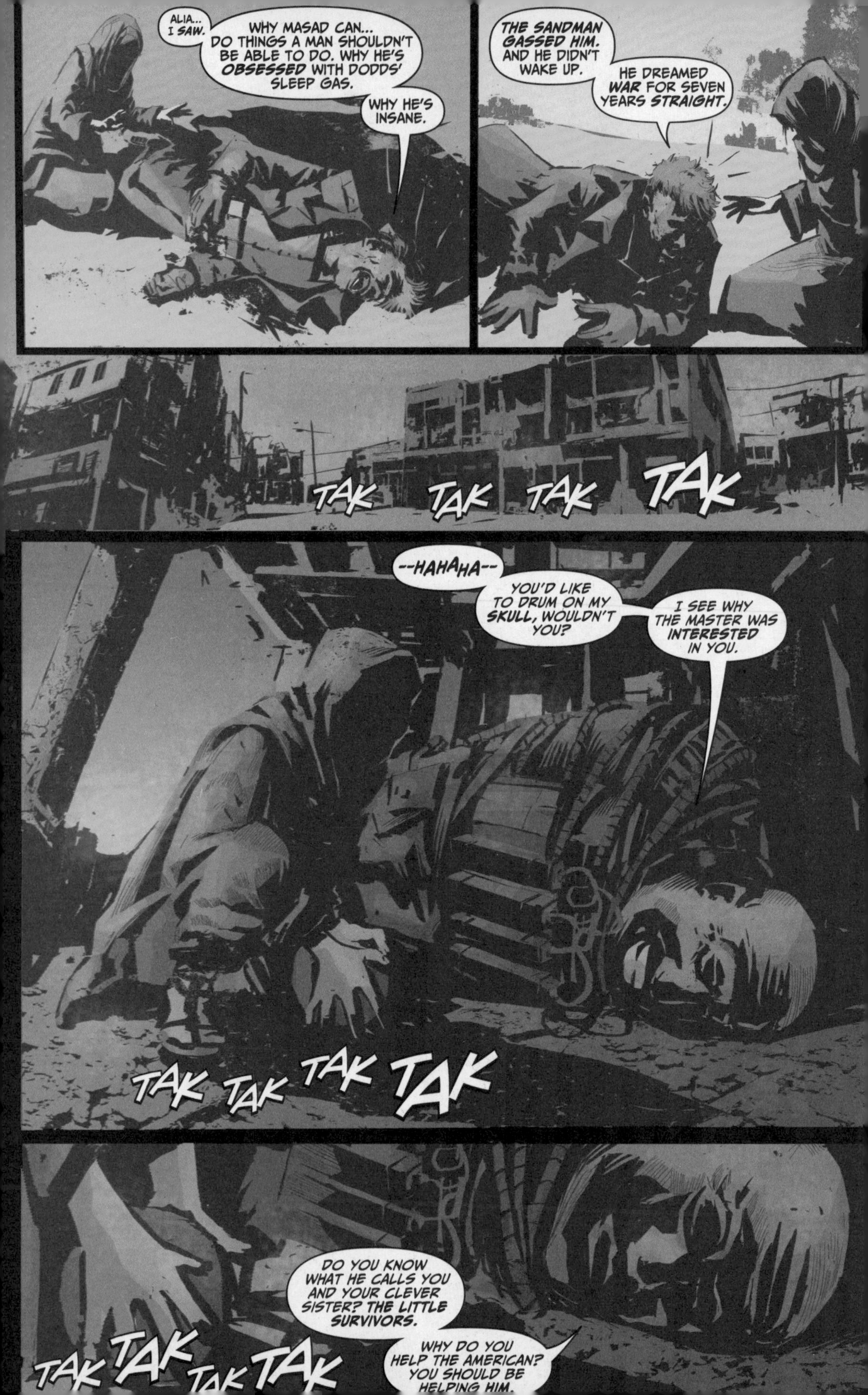
ALIA... I SAW.
WHY MASAD CAN... DO THINGS A MAN SHOULDN'T BE ABLE TO DO. WHY HE'S OBSESSED WITH DODDS' SLEEP GAS.
WHY HE'S INSANE.
THE SANDMAN GASSED HIM. AND HE DIDN'T WAKE UP.
HE DREAMED WAR FOR SEVEN YEARS STRAIGHT.
TAK TAK TAK TAK
--HAHAHA--
YOU'D LIKE TO DRUM ON MY SKULL, WOULDN'T YOU?
I SEE WHY THE MASTER WAS INTERESTED IN YOU.
TAK TAK TAK TAK
DO YOU KNOW WHAT HE CALLS YOU AND YOUR CLEVER SISTER? THE LITTLE SURVIVORS.
TAK TAK TAK TAK
WHY DO YOU HELP THE AMERICAN? YOU SHOULD BE HELPING HIM.

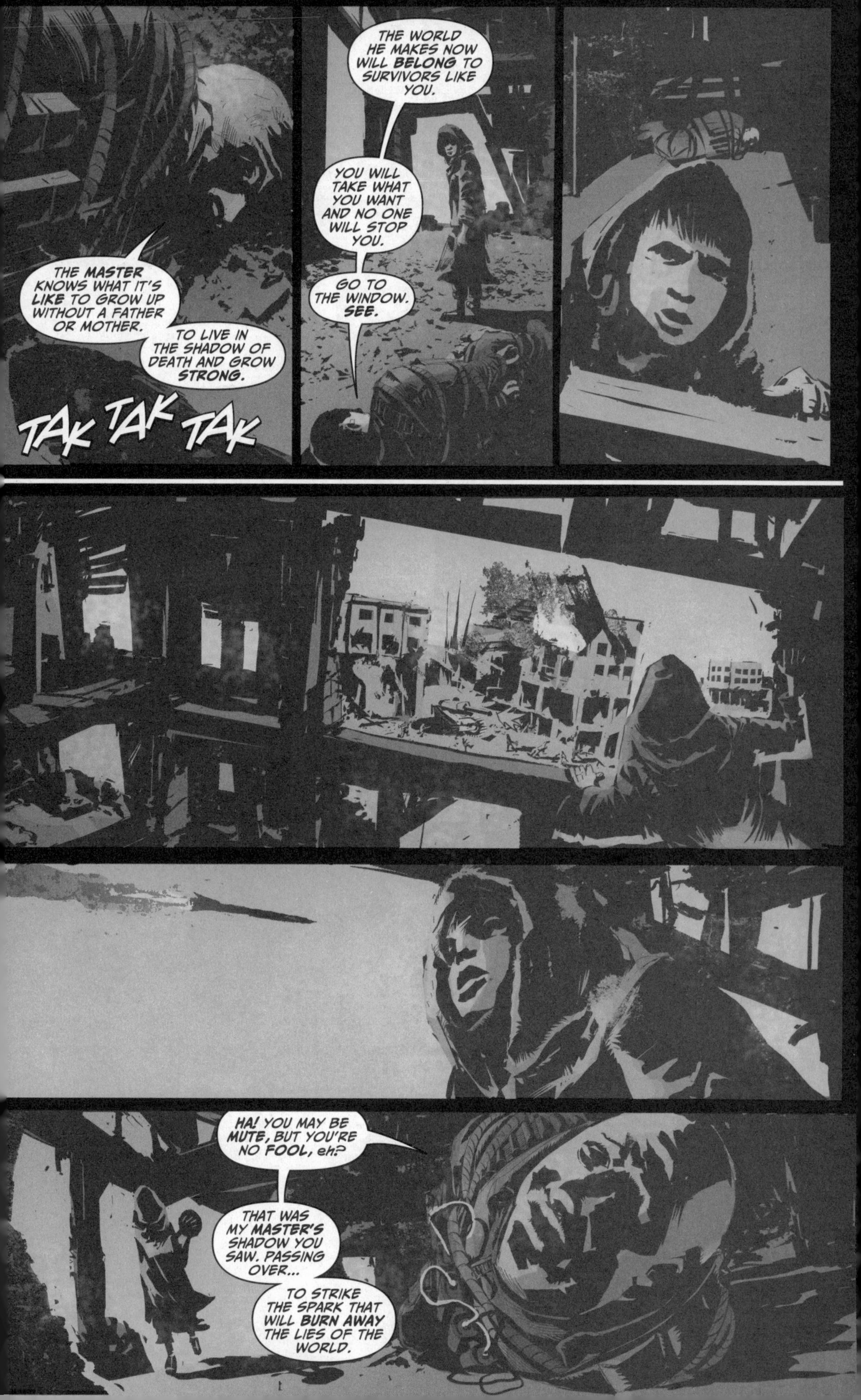
THE MASTER KNOWS WHAT IT'S LIKE TO GROW UP WITHOUT A FATHER OR MOTHER.
TO LIVE IN THE SHADOW OF DEATH AND GROW STRONG.
TAK TAK TAK
THE WORLD HE MAKES NOW WILL BELONG TO SURVIVORS LIKE YOU.
YOU WILL TAKE WHAT YOU WANT AND NO ONE WILL STOP YOU.
GO TO THE WINDOW. SEE.
HA! YOU MAY BE MUTE, BUT YOU'RE NO FOOL, eh?
THAT WAS MY MASTER'S SHADOW YOU SAW. PASSING OVER...
TO STRIKE THE SPARK THAT WILL BURN AWAY THE LIES OF THE WORLD.

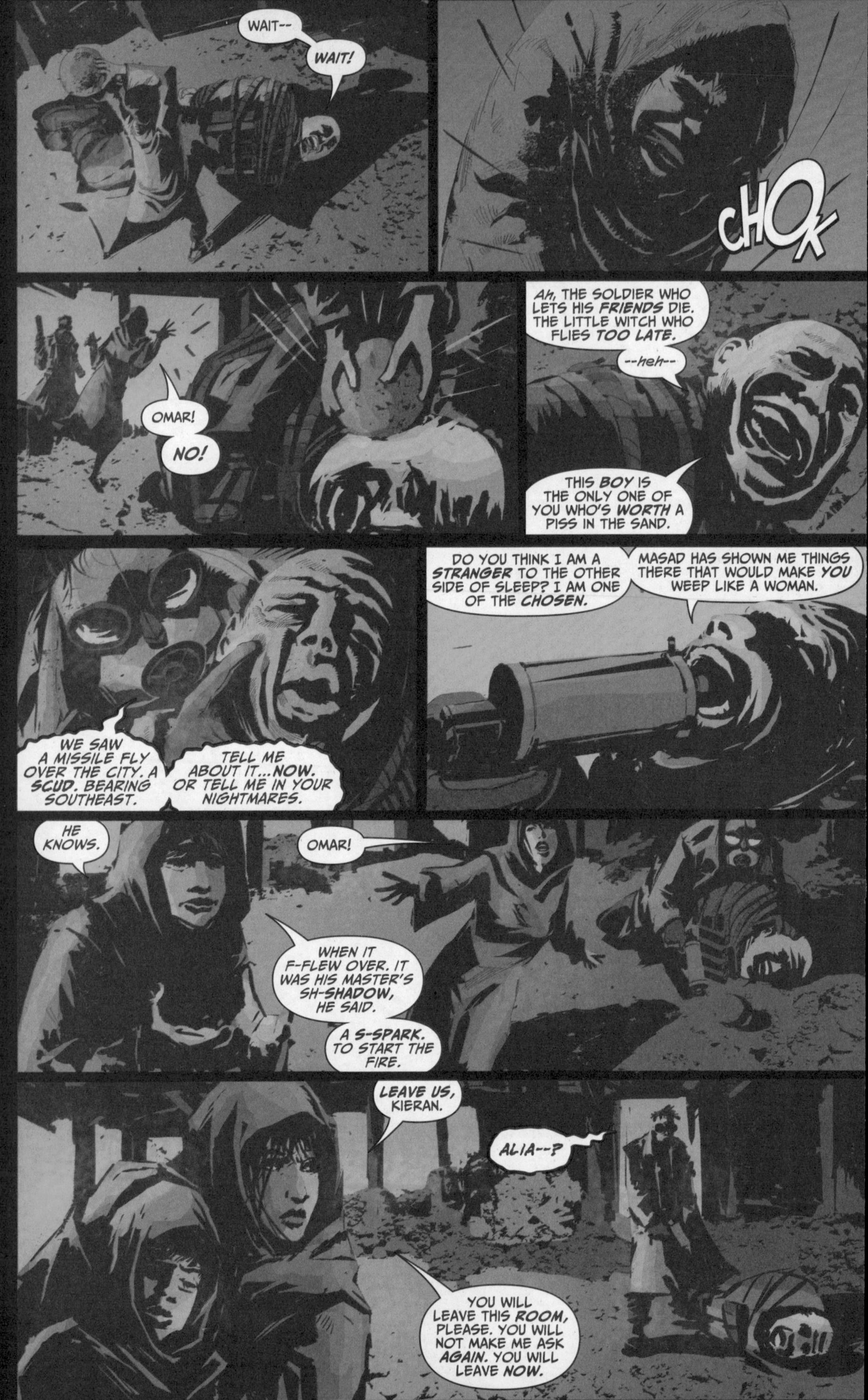
WAIT--
WAIT!
CHOK
OMAR!
NO!
Ah, THE SOLDIER WHO LETS HIS FRIENDS DIE. THE LITTLE WITCH WHO FLIES TOO LATE.
--heh--
THIS BOY IS THE ONLY ONE OF YOU WHO'S WORTH A PISS IN THE SAND.
WE SAW A MISSILE FLY OVER THE CITY. A SCUD. BEARING SOUTHEAST.
TELL ME ABOUT IT...NOW. OR TELL ME IN YOUR NIGHTMARES.
DO YOU THINK I AM A STRANGER TO THE OTHER SIDE OF SLEEP? I AM ONE OF THE CHOSEN.
MASAD HAS SHOWN ME THINGS THERE THAT WOULD MAKE YOU WEEP LIKE A WOMAN.
HE KNOWS.
OMAR!
WHEN IT F-FLEW OVER. IT WAS HIS MASTER'S SH-SHADOW, HE SAID.
A S-SPARK. TO START THE FIRE.
LEAVE US, KIERAN.
ALIA--?
YOU WILL LEAVE THIS ROOM, PLEASE. YOU WILL NOT MAKE ME ASK AGAIN. YOU WILL LEAVE NOW.

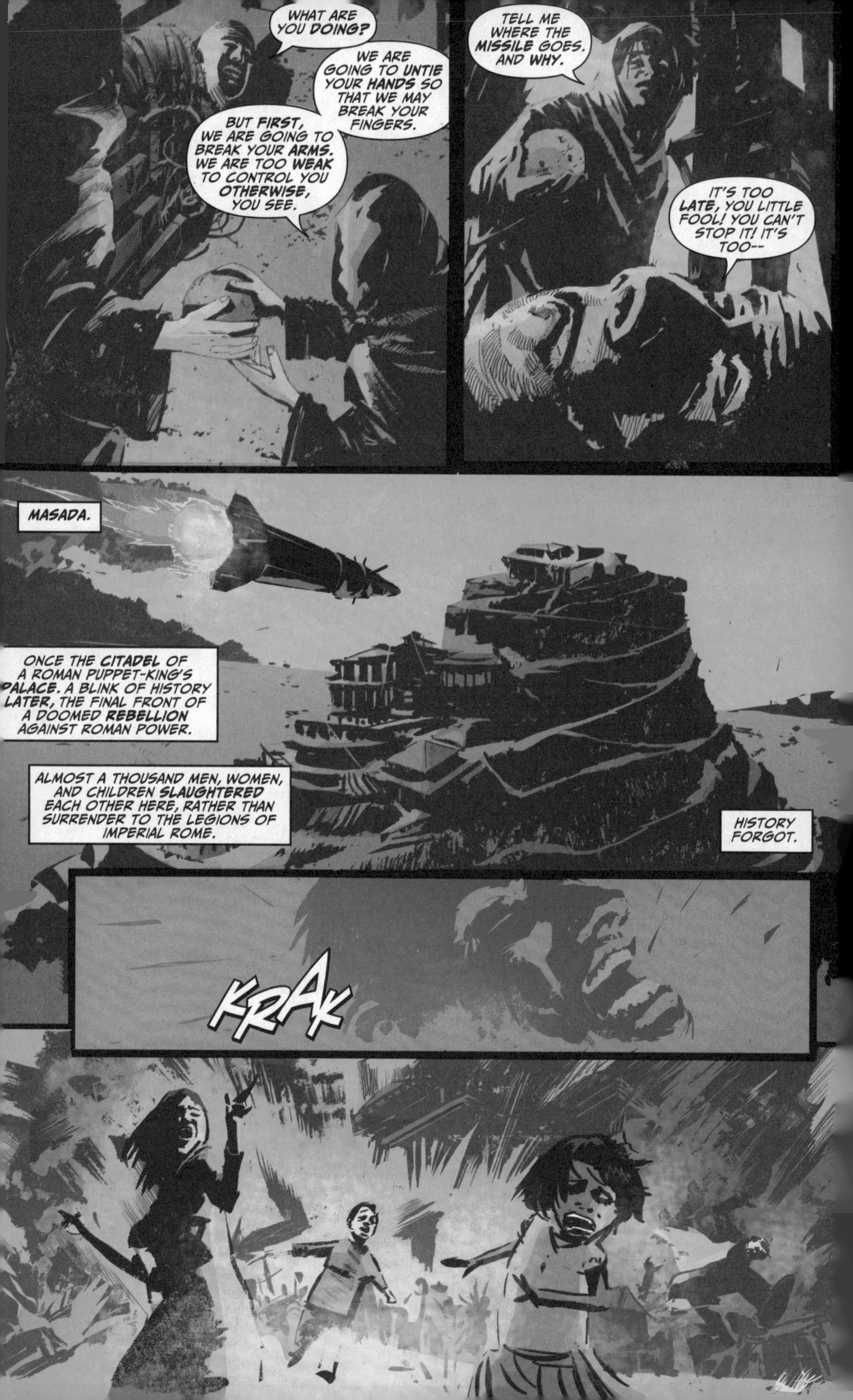
WHAT ARE YOU DOING?
WE ARE GOING TO UNTIE YOUR HANDS SO THAT WE MAY BREAK YOUR FINGERS.
BUT FIRST, WE ARE GOING TO BREAK YOUR ARMS. WE ARE TOO WEAK TO CONTROL YOU OTHERWISE, YOU SEE.
TELL ME WHERE THE MISSILE GOES. AND WHY.
IT'S TOO LATE, YOU LITTLE FOOL! YOU CAN'T STOP IT! IT'S TOO--
MASADA.
ONCE THE CITADEL OF A ROMAN PUPPET-KING'S PALACE. A BLINK OF HISTORY LATER, THE FINAL FRONT OF A DOOMED REBELLION AGAINST ROMAN POWER.
ALMOST A THOUSAND MEN, WOMEN, AND CHILDREN SLAUGHTERED EACH OTHER HERE, RATHER THAN SURRENDER TO THE LEGIONS OF IMPERIAL ROME.
HISTORY FORGOT.
KRAK

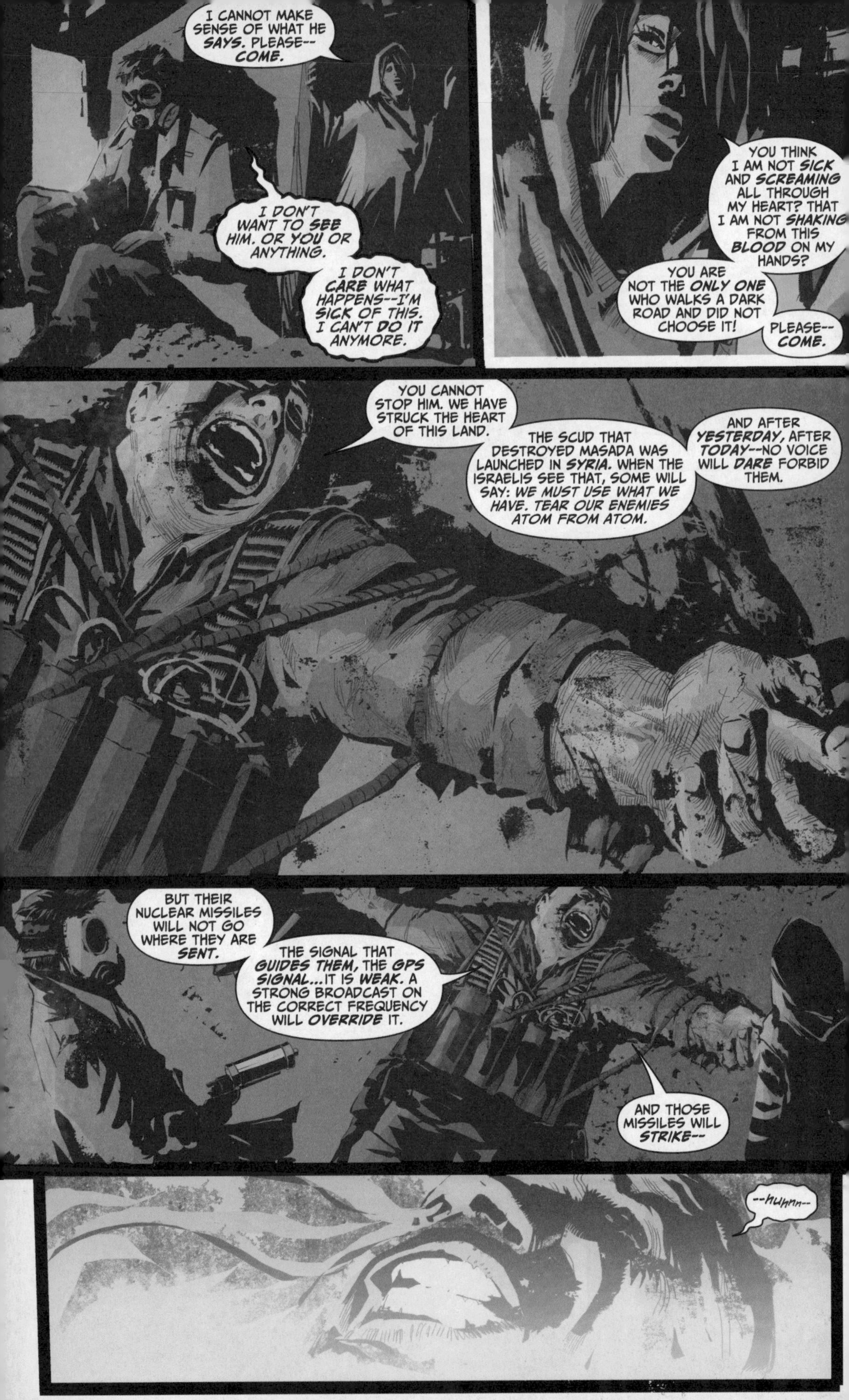
I CANNOT MAKE SENSE OF WHAT HE SAYS. PLEASE-- COME.
I DON'T WANT TO SEE HIM. OR YOU OR ANYTHING.
I DON'T CARE WHAT HAPPENS--I'M SICK OF THIS. I CAN'T DO IT ANYMORE.
YOU THINK I AM NOT SICK AND SCREAMING ALL THROUGH MY HEART? THAT I AM NOT SHAKING FROM THIS BLOOD ON MY HANDS?
YOU ARE NOT THE ONLY ONE WHO WALKS A DARK ROAD AND DID NOT CHOOSE IT!
PLEASE-- COME.
YOU CANNOT STOP HIM. WE HAVE STRUCK THE HEART OF THIS LAND.
THE SCUD THAT DESTROYED MASADA WAS LAUNCHED IN SYRIA. WHEN THE ISRAELIS SEE THAT, SOME WILL SAY: WE MUST USE WHAT WE HAVE. TEAR OUR ENEMIES ATOM FROM ATOM.
AND AFTER YESTERDAY, AFTER TODAY--NO VOICE WILL DARE FORBID THEM.
BUT THEIR NUCLEAR MISSILES WILL NOT GO WHERE THEY ARE SENT.
THE SIGNAL THAT GUIDES THEM, THE GPS SIGNAL... IT IS WEAK. A STRONG BROADCAST ON THE CORRECT FREQUENCY WILL OVERRIDE IT.
AND THOSE MISSILES WILL STRIKE--
--huhnn--

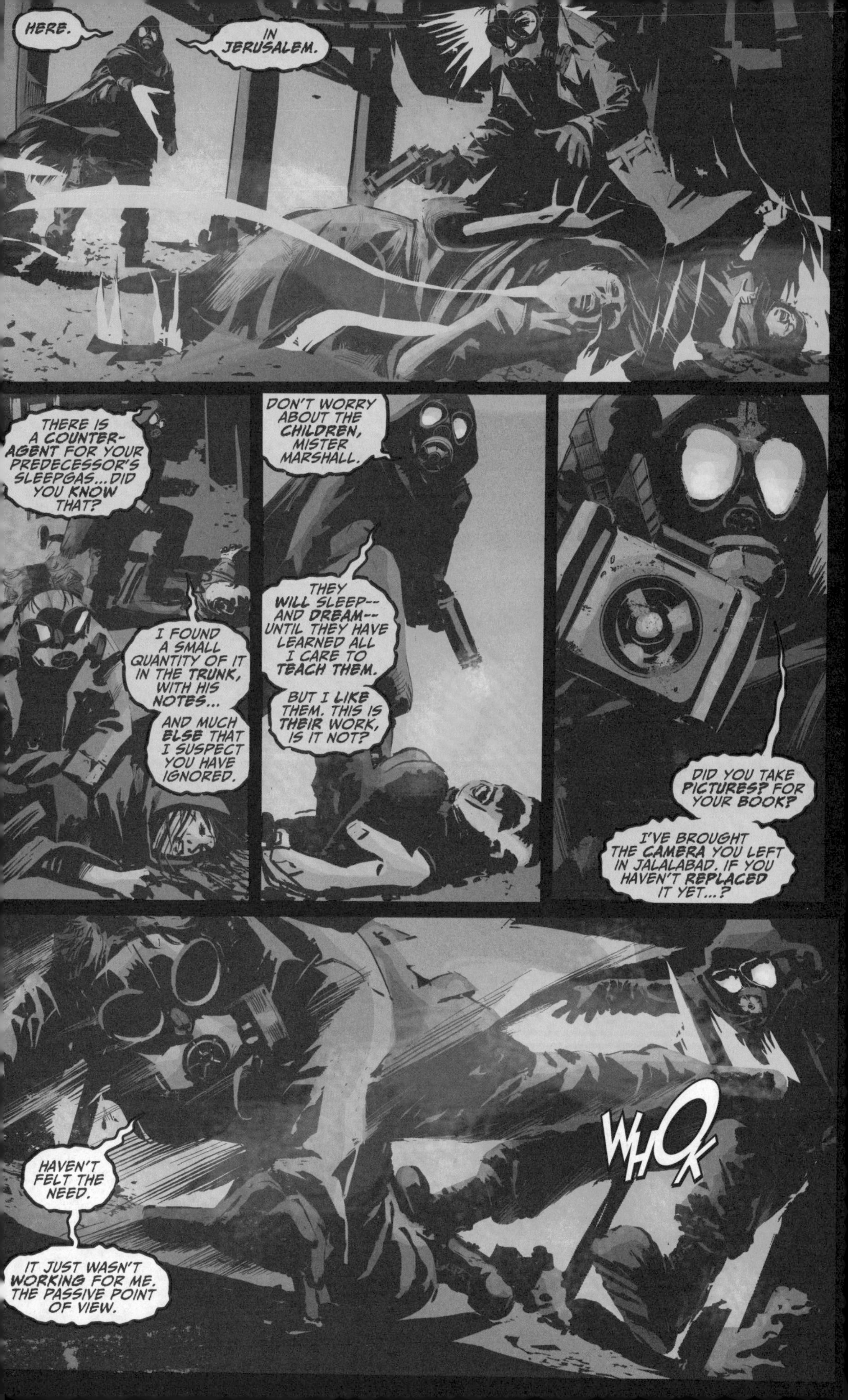
HERE.
IN JERUSALEM.
THERE IS A COUNTER-AGENT FOR YOUR PREDECESSOR'S SLEEPGAS...DID YOU KNOW THAT?
I FOUND A SMALL QUANTITY OF IT IN THE TRUNK, WITH HIS NOTES...
AND MUCH ELSE THAT I SUSPECT YOU HAVE IGNORED.
DON'T WORRY ABOUT THE CHILDREN, MISTER MARSHALL.
THEY WILL SLEEP-- AND DREAM-- UNTIL THEY HAVE LEARNED ALL I CARE TO TEACH THEM.
BUT I LIKE THEM. THIS IS THEIR WORK, IS IT NOT?
DID YOU TAKE PICTURES? FOR YOUR BOOK?
I'VE BROUGHT THE CAMERA YOU LEFT IN JALALABAD. IF YOU HAVEN'T REPLACED IT YET...?
HAVEN'T FELT THE NEED.
IT JUST WASN'T WORKING FOR ME. THE PASSIVE POINT OF VIEW.
WHOK

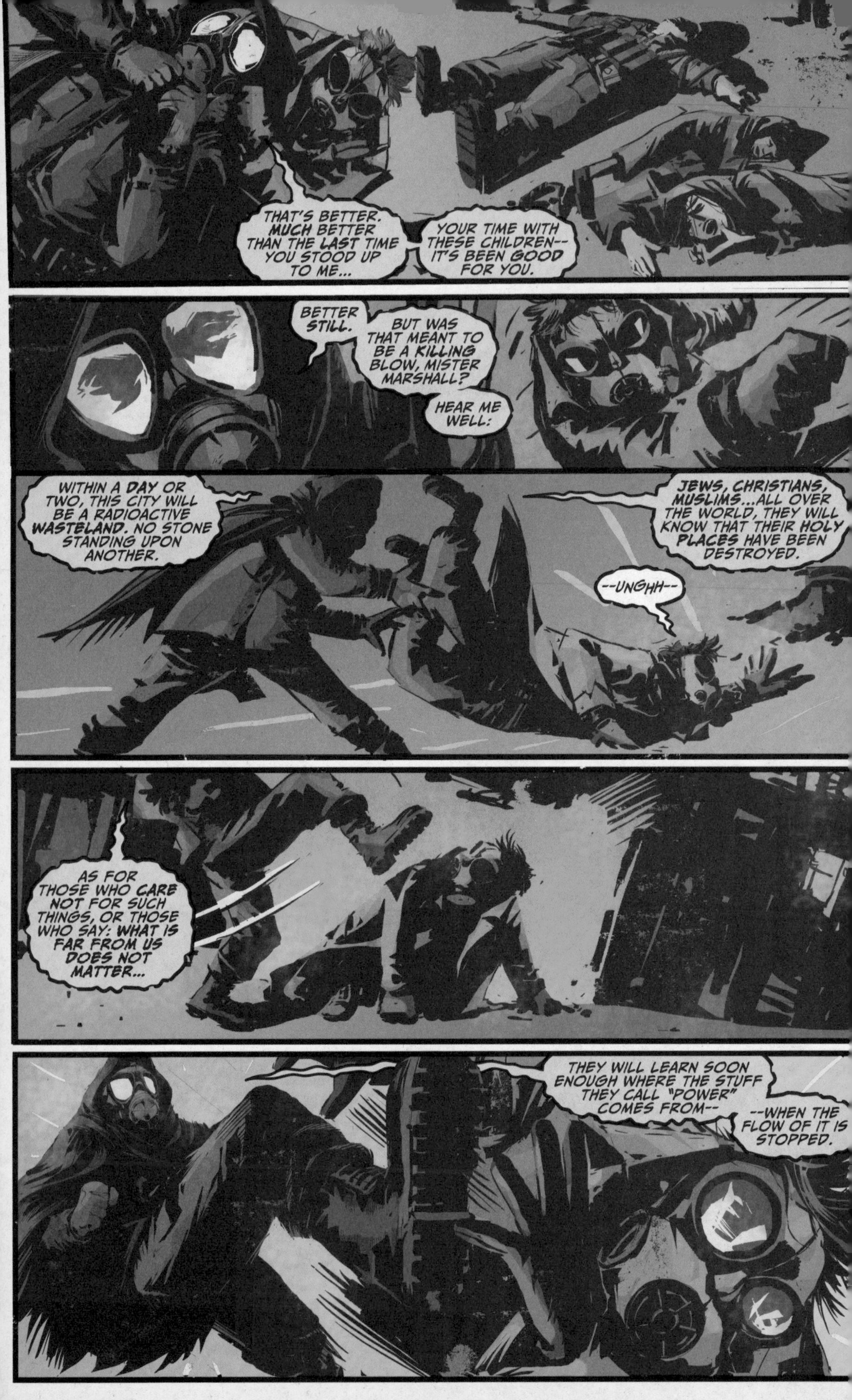
THAT'S BETTER. MUCH BETTER THAN THE LAST TIME YOU STOOD UP TO ME...
YOUR TIME WITH THESE CHILDREN-- IT'S BEEN GOOD FOR YOU.
BETTER STILL.
BUT WAS THAT MEANT TO BE A KILLING BLOW, MISTER MARSHALL?
HEAR ME WELL:
WITHIN A DAY OR TWO, THIS CITY WILL BE A RADIOACTIVE WASTELAND. NO STONE STANDING UPON ANOTHER.
JEWS, CHRISTIANS, MUSLIMS...ALL OVER THE WORLD, THEY WILL KNOW THAT THEIR HOLY PLACES HAVE BEEN DESTROYED.
--UNGHH--
AS FOR THOSE WHO CARE NOT FOR SUCH THINGS, OR THOSE WHO SAY: WHAT IS FAR FROM US DOES NOT MATTER...
THEY WILL LEARN SOON ENOUGH WHERE THE STUFF THEY CALL "POWER" COMES FROM--
--WHEN THE FLOW OF IT IS STOPPED.

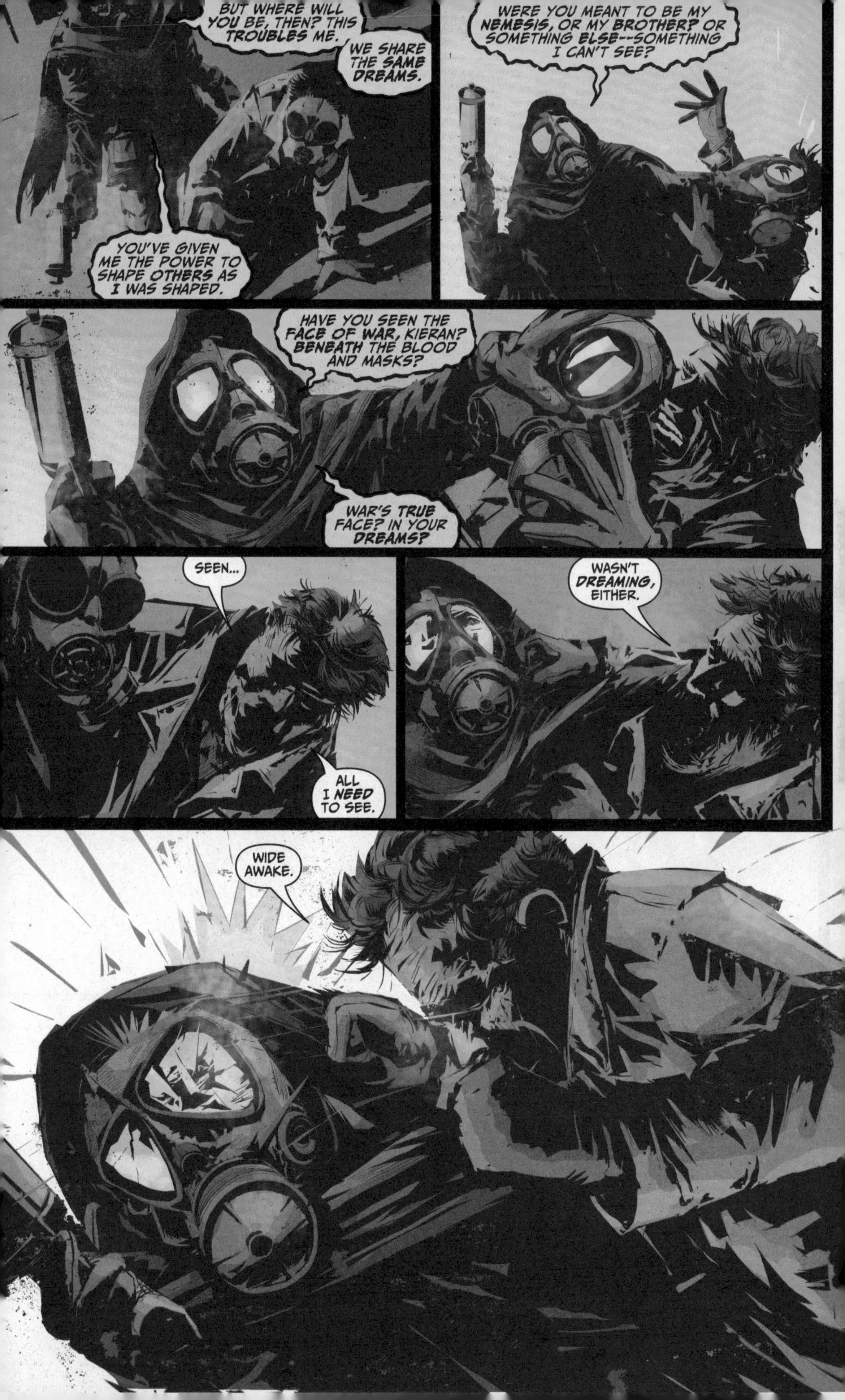

BUT WHERE WILL YOU BE, THEN? THIS TROUBLES ME.
WE SHARE THE SAME DREAMS.
YOU'VE GIVEN ME THE POWER TO SHAPE OTHERS AS I WAS SHAPED.
WERE YOU MEANT TO BE MY NEMESIS, OR MY BROTHER? OR SOMETHING ELSE--SOMETHING I CAN'T SEE?
HAVE YOU SEEN THE FACE OF WAR, KIERAN? BENEATH THE BLOOD AND MASKS?
WAR'S TRUE FACE? IN YOUR DREAMS?
SEEN...
ALL I NEED TO SEE.
WASN'T DREAMING, EITHER.
WIDE AWAKE.

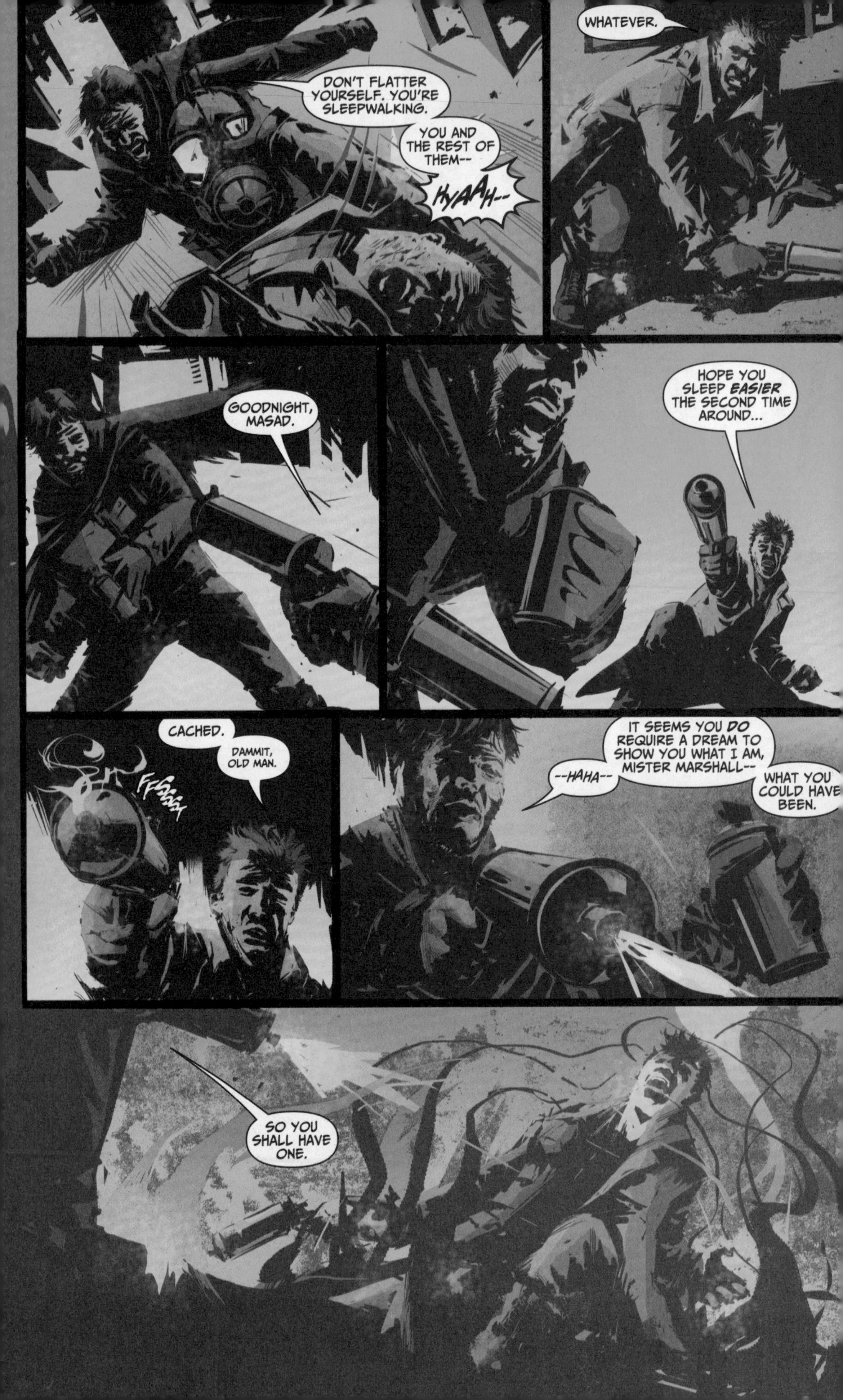
DON'T FLATTER YOURSELF. YOU'RE SLEEPWALKING.
YOU AND THE REST OF THEM--
KYAAH--
WHATEVER.
GOODNIGHT, MASAD.
HOPE YOU SLEEP EASIER THE SECOND TIME AROUND...
CACHED.
DAMMIT, OLD MAN.
FFSSSSK
IT SEEMS YOU DO REQUIRE A DREAM TO SHOW YOU WHAT I AM, MISTER MARSHALL--
--HAHA--
WHAT YOU COULD HAVE BEEN.
SO YOU SHALL HAVE ONE.

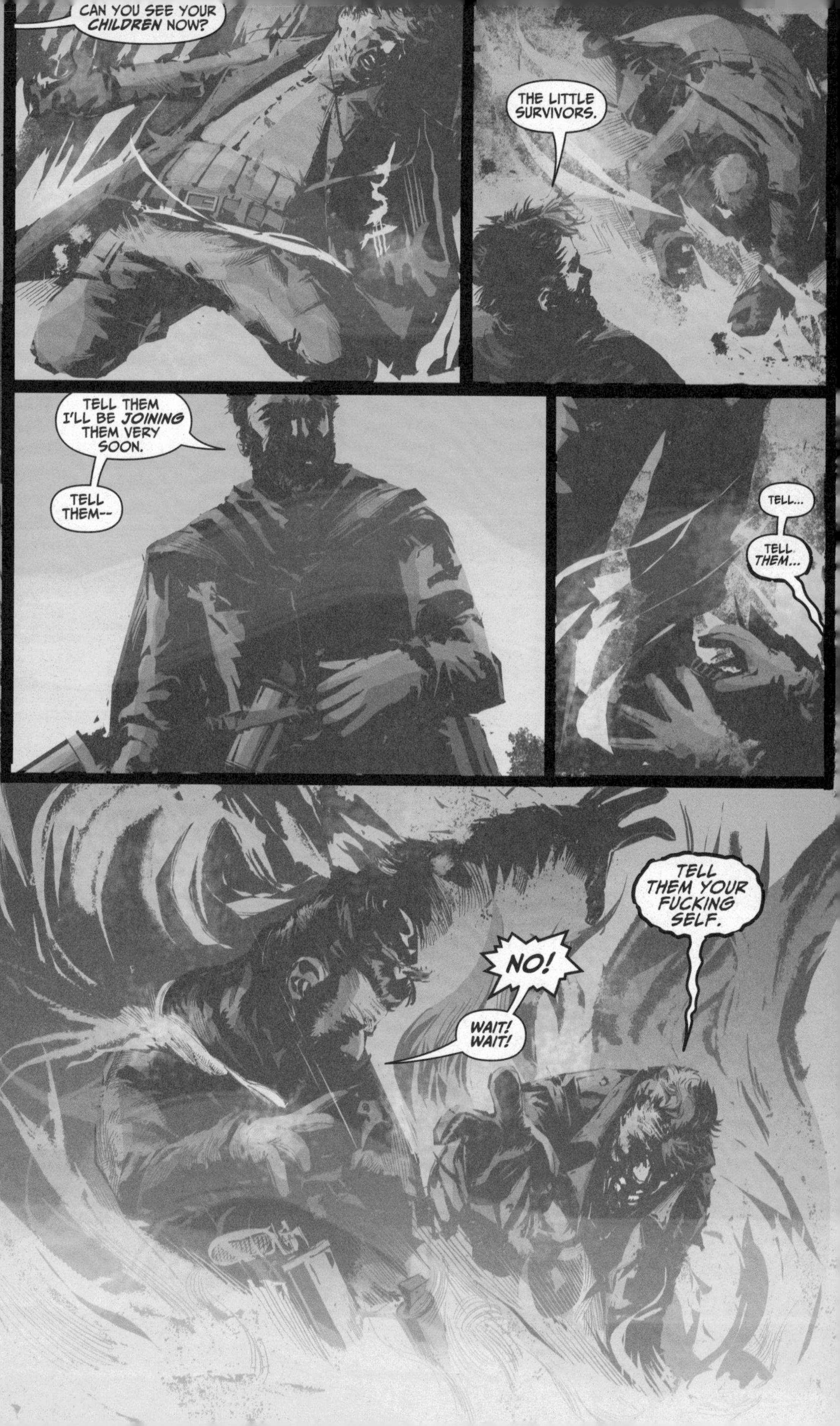
CAN YOU SEE YOUR CHILDREN NOW?
THE LITTLE SURVIVORS.
TELL THEM I'LL BE JOINING THEM VERY SOON.
TELL THEM--
TELL...
TELL THEM...
TELL THEM YOUR FUCKING SELF.
NO!
WAIT! WAIT!

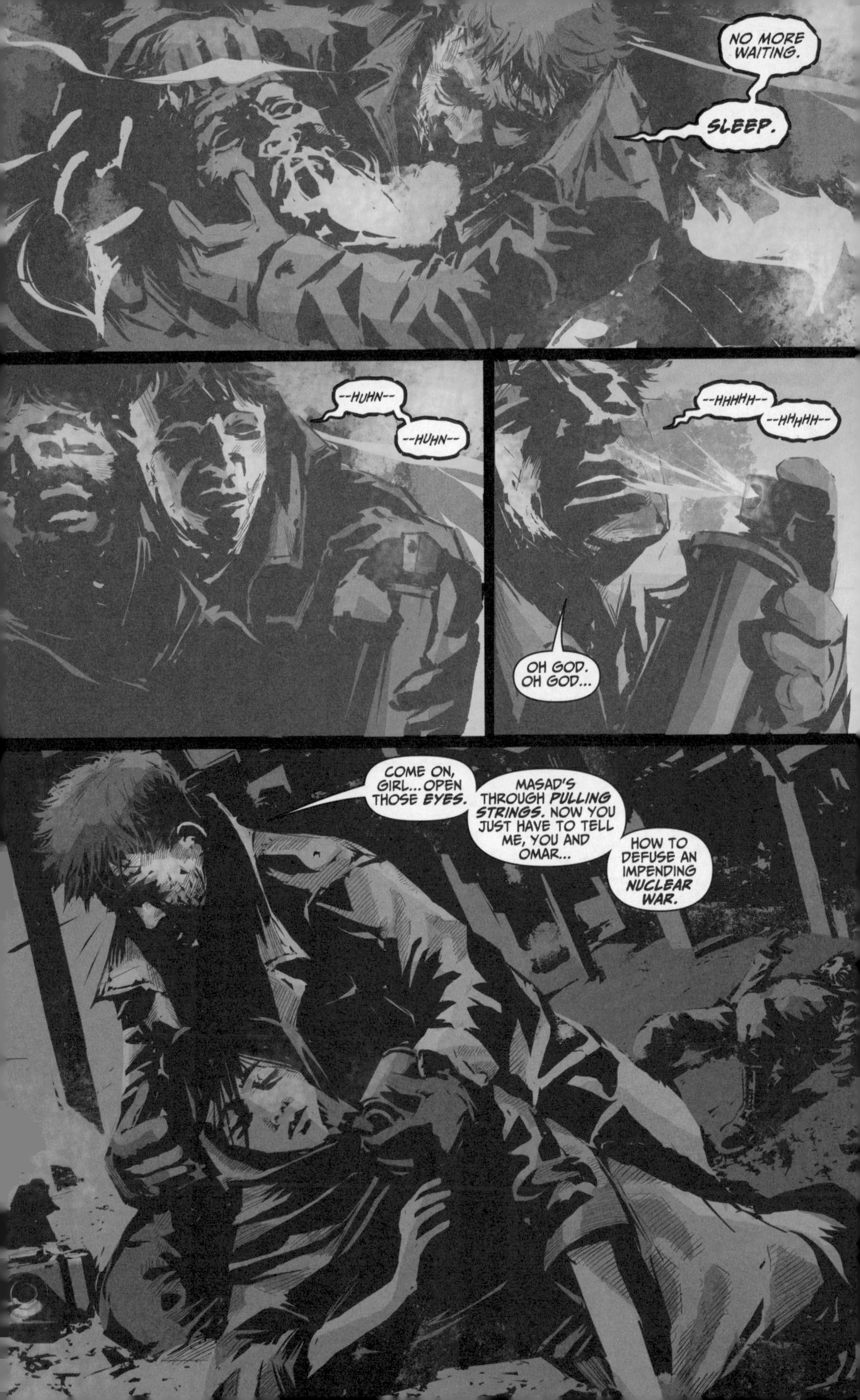
NO MORE WAITING.
SLEEP.
--HUHN--
--HUHN--
--HHHHH--
--HHHHH--
OH GOD. OH GOD...
COME ON, GIRL...OPEN THOSE EYES.
MASAD'S THROUGH PULLING STRINGS. NOW YOU JUST HAVE TO TELL ME, YOU AND OMAR...
HOW TO DEFUSE AN IMPENDING NUCLEAR WAR.

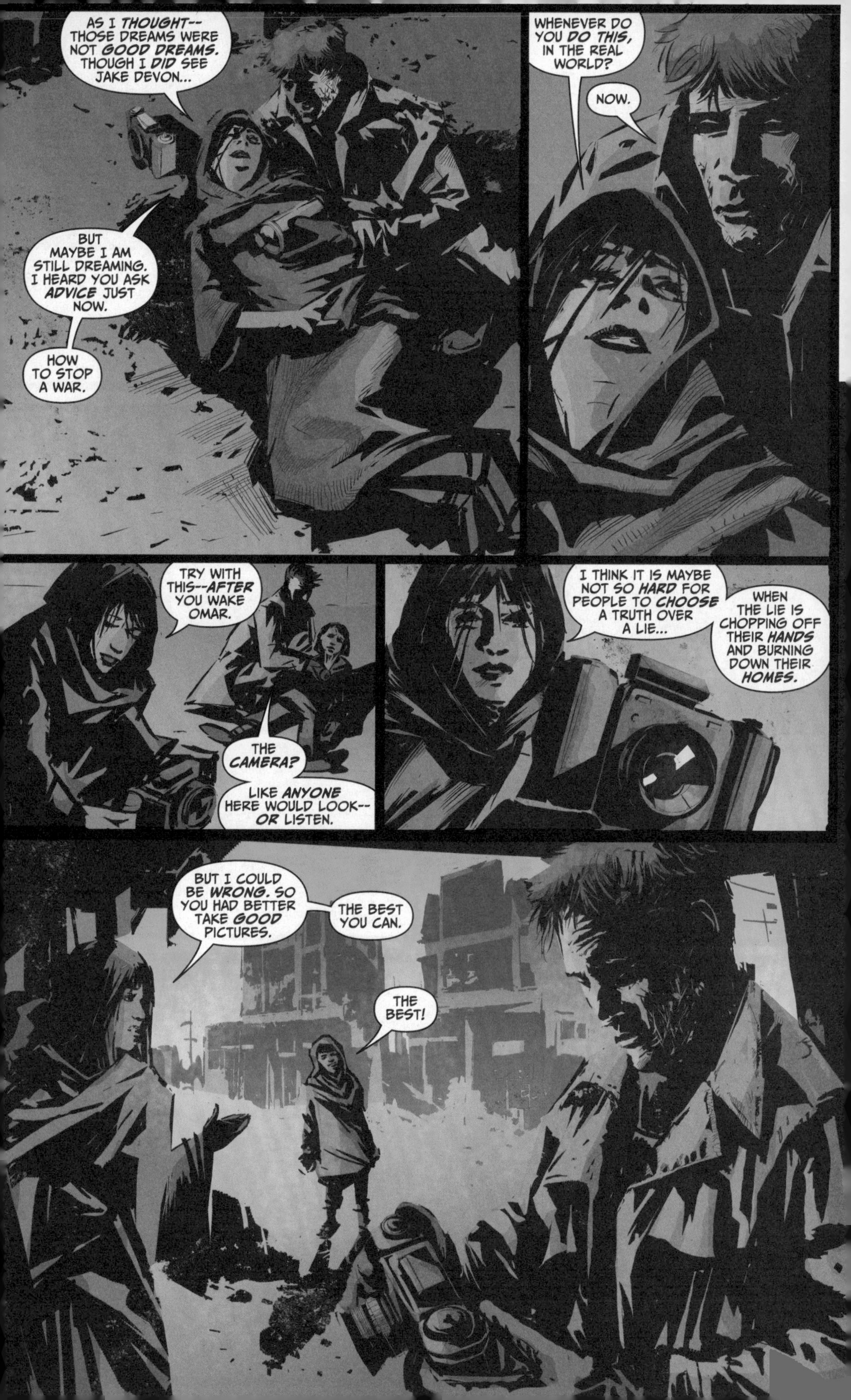
AS I *THOUGHT*-- THOSE DREAMS WERE NOT *GOOD DREAMS.* THOUGH I *DID* SEE JAKE DEVON...
BUT MAYBE I AM STILL DREAMING. I HEARD YOU ASK *ADVICE* JUST NOW.
HOW TO STOP A WAR.
WHENEVER DO YOU *DO THIS,* IN THE REAL WORLD?
NOW.
TRY WITH THIS--*AFTER* YOU WAKE OMAR.
THE *CAMERA?*
LIKE *ANYONE* HERE WOULD LOOK-- *OR* LISTEN.
I THINK IT IS MAYBE NOT SO *HARD* FOR PEOPLE TO *CHOOSE* A TRUTH OVER A LIE...
WHEN THE LIE IS CHOPPING OFF THEIR *HANDS* AND BURNING DOWN THEIR *HOMES.*
BUT I COULD BE *WRONG.* SO YOU HAD BETTER TAKE *GOOD* PICTURES.
THE BEST YOU CAN.
THE BEST!

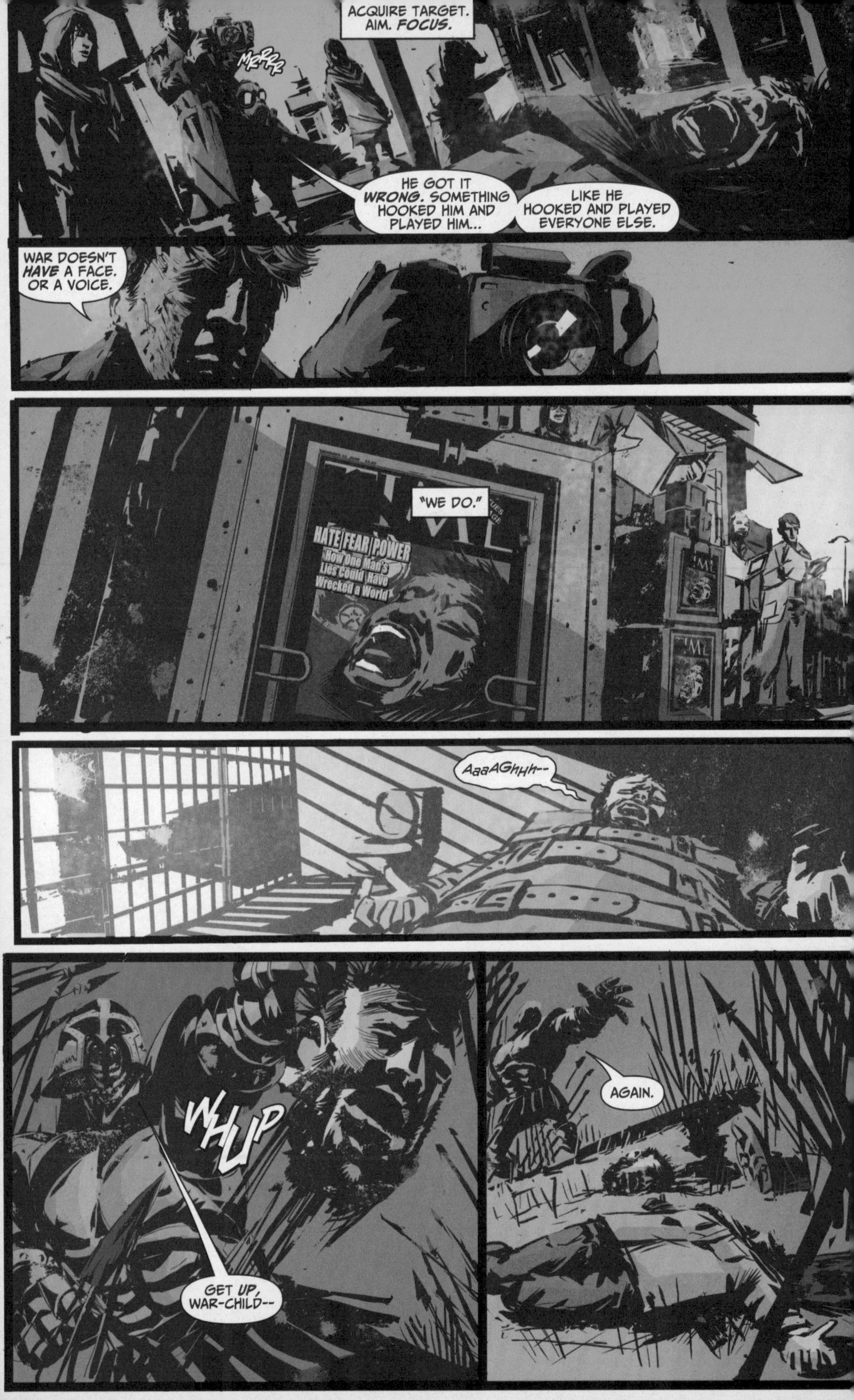
ACQUIRE TARGET. AIM. FOCUS.
MRRRR
HE GOT IT WRONG. SOMETHING HOOKED HIM AND PLAYED HIM...
LIKE HE HOOKED AND PLAYED EVERYONE ELSE.
WAR DOESN'T HAVE A FACE. OR A VOICE.
"WE DO."
HATE|FEAR|POWER
How One Man's Lies Could Have Wrecked a World
AaaAGHHH--
WHUP
GET UP, WAR-CHILD--
AGAIN.

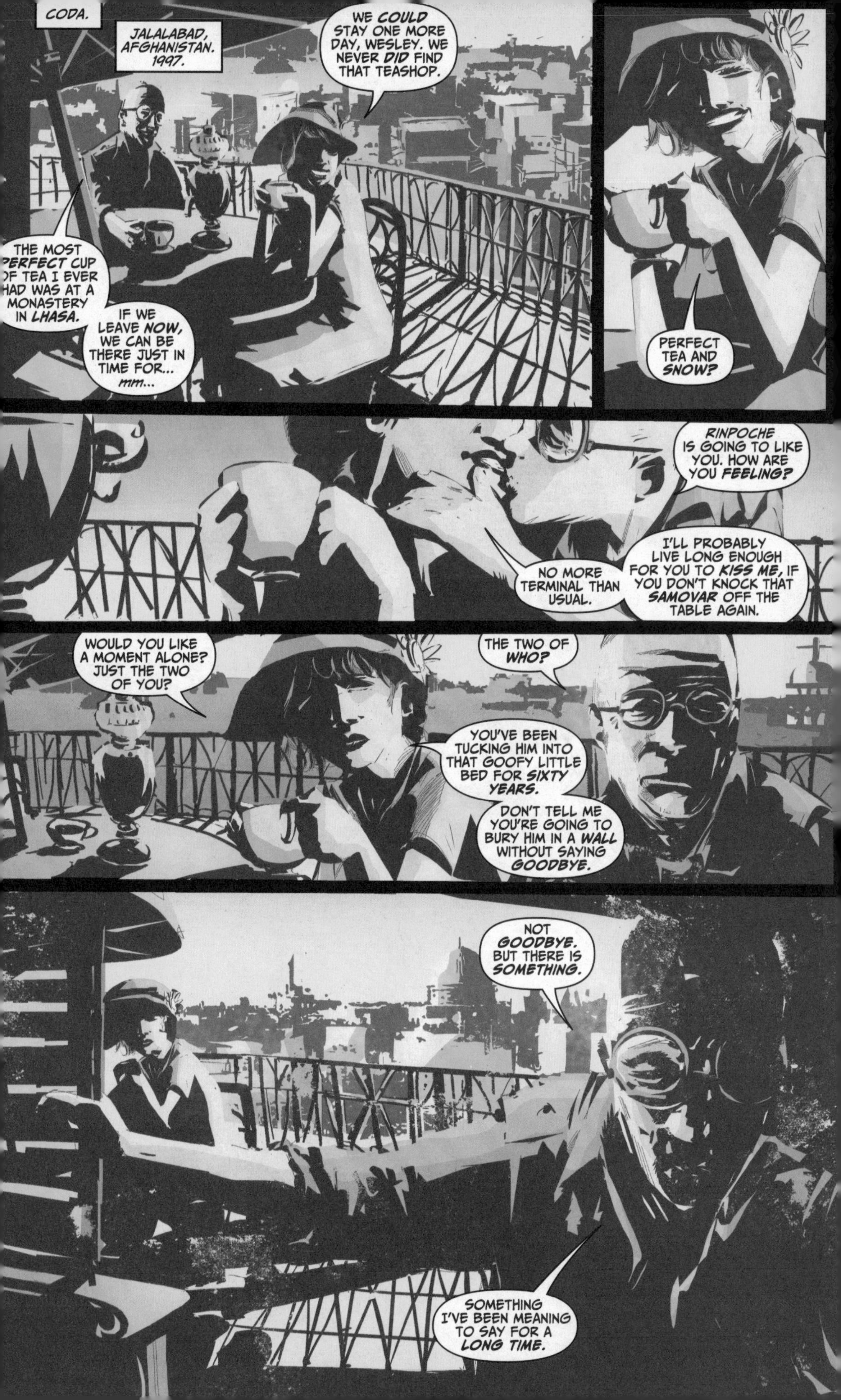

CODA.
JALALABAD, AFGHANISTAN. 1997.
WE COULD STAY ONE MORE DAY, WESLEY. WE NEVER DID FIND THAT TEASHOP.
THE MOST PERFECT CUP OF TEA I EVER HAD WAS AT A MONASTERY IN LHASA.
IF WE LEAVE NOW, WE CAN BE THERE JUST IN TIME FOR... mm...
PERFECT TEA AND SNOW?
RINPOCHE IS GOING TO LIKE YOU. HOW ARE YOU FEELING?
NO MORE TERMINAL THAN USUAL.
I'LL PROBABLY LIVE LONG ENOUGH FOR YOU TO KISS ME, IF YOU DON'T KNOCK THAT SAMOVAR OFF THE TABLE AGAIN.
WOULD YOU LIKE A MOMENT ALONE? JUST THE TWO OF YOU?
THE TWO OF WHO?
YOU'VE BEEN TUCKING HIM INTO THAT GOOFY LITTLE BED FOR SIXTY YEARS.
DON'T TELL ME YOU'RE GOING TO BURY HIM IN A WALL WITHOUT SAYING GOODBYE.
NOT GOODBYE. BUT THERE IS SOMETHING.
SOMETHING I'VE BEEN MEANING TO SAY FOR A LONG TIME.

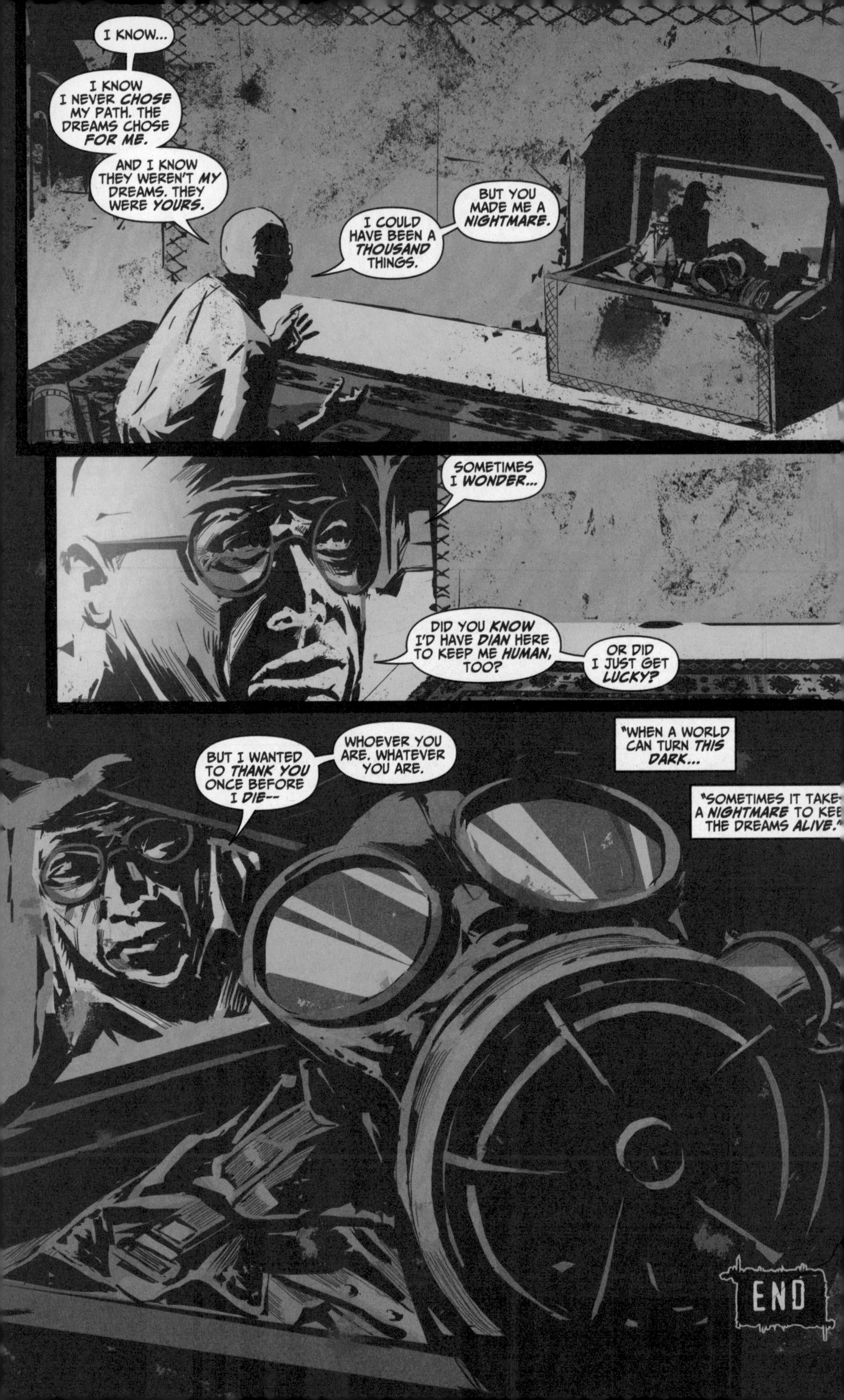
I KNOW...
I KNOW I NEVER CHOSE MY PATH. THE DREAMS CHOSE FOR ME.
AND I KNOW THEY WEREN'T MY DREAMS. THEY WERE YOURS.
I COULD HAVE BEEN A THOUSAND THINGS.
BUT YOU MADE ME A NIGHTMARE.
SOMETIMES I WONDER...
DID YOU KNOW I'D HAVE DIAN HERE TO KEEP ME HUMAN, TOO?
OR DID I JUST GET LUCKY?
BUT I WANTED TO THANK YOU ONCE BEFORE I DIE--
WHOEVER YOU ARE. WHATEVER YOU ARE.
"WHEN A WORLD CAN TURN THIS DARK...
"SOMETIMES IT TAKE A NIGHTMARE TO KEE THE DREAMS ALIVE."
END

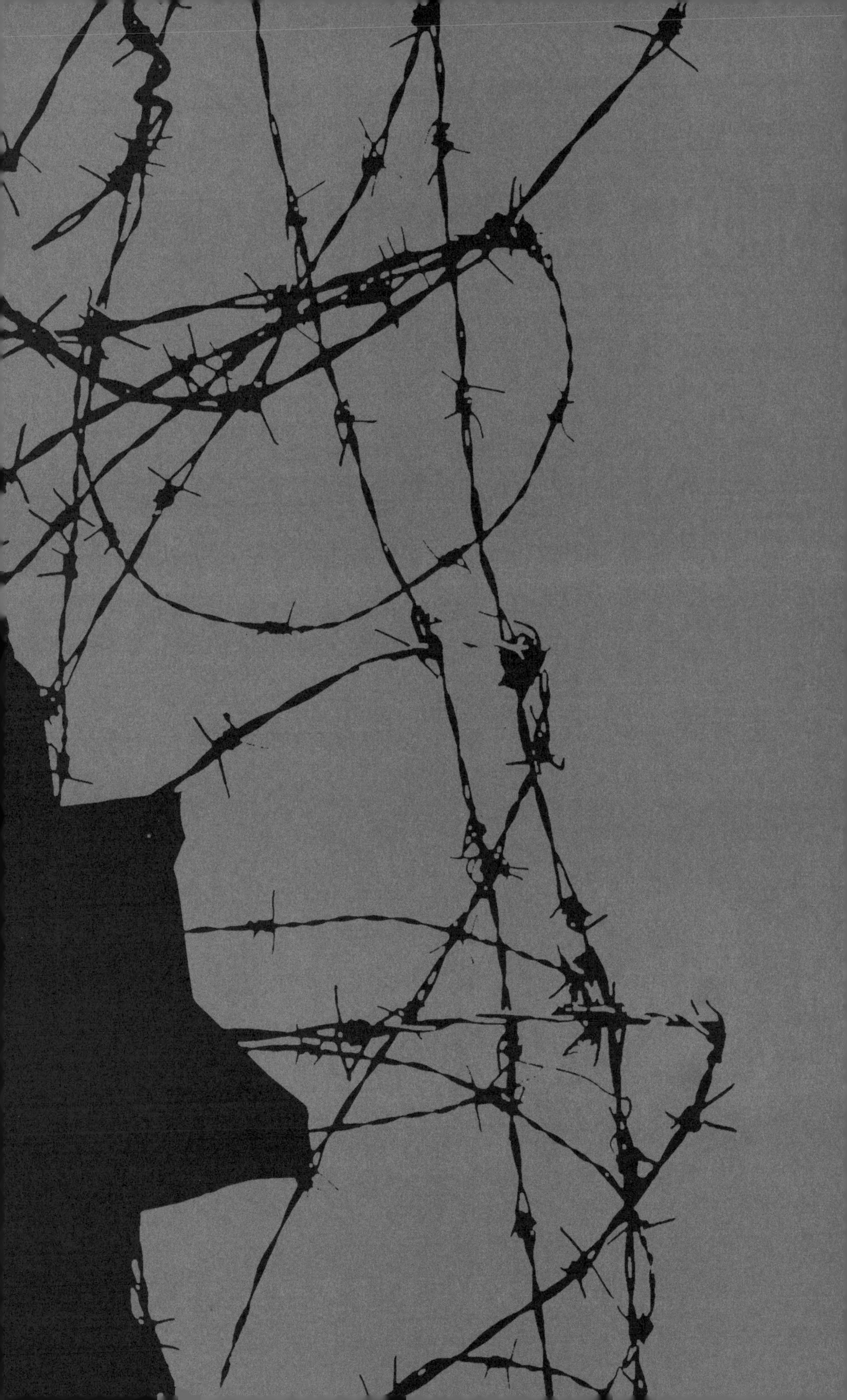

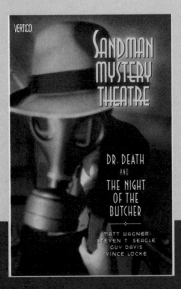

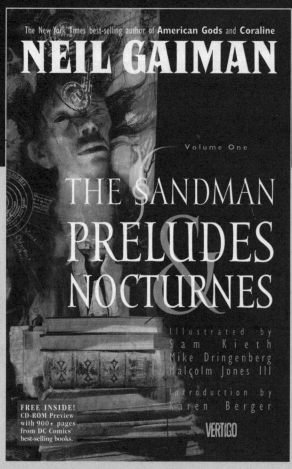
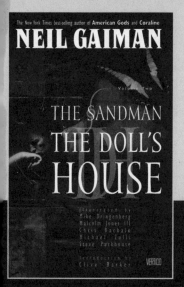
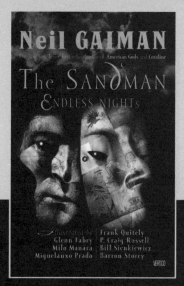

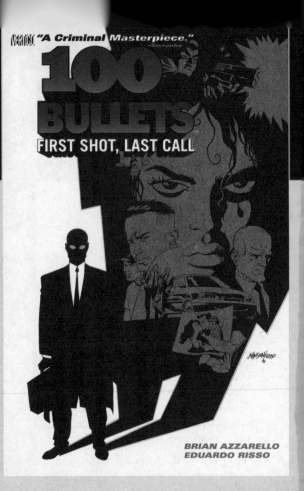